D is for Dog

Frank Manolson DVM was a member of the Royal College of
Veterinary Surgeons. He practised in the United States,
Canada, Italy, England and Central America.

Frank Manolson

D is for Dog

the care of your dog from a-z

foreword by Brian Vesey-Fitzgerald

PAN BOOKS London and Sydney

First published in Great Britain 1967 by
Universal-Tandem Publishing Co Ltd
This edition published 1978 by Pan Books Ltd,
Cavaye Place. London SW10 9PG
© Frank Manolson 1964, 1979
ISBN 0 330 25642 4
Made and printed in Great Britain by
Cox & Wyman Ltd, London, Reading and Fakenham

Foreword

Frank Manolson was a veterinary surgeon, Canadian by birth and trained on both sides of the Atlantic. He practised in New York, in Central America and in Southern Europe. For many years he worked in a large London animal welfare clinic.

He had, therefore, a very wide experience, a much wider experience than can possibly be acquired in the course of an average private practice, of dogs (especially sick dogs) and – and this is every whit as important – an equally wide experience of dog-owners.

His book is primarily intended for the would-be dog-owner. Ideally, it should be bought and read (and then re-read) by everyone who is thinking of acquiring a dog. All the breeds are dealt with, briefly and pithily: and not from the point of view of 'show standards', but from that of characteristics, temperament, suitability, and so forth. All that the would-be dog-owner can possibly want to know about the characteristics of the various breeds, the essential things which should enable him or her to make a suitable choice are here: the good points and the bad.

Dr Manolson had the courage of his convictions. He did not attempt to dodge the unpleasant. He had some blunt things to say about dog-breeders, particularly about those whom he describes as 'dealer-breeders': things which have needed saying in a book of this sort, written by an experienced and practical authority, for a long while. Much of the nervousness, ill-temper, ill-health, physical deformity, which is to be found increasingly in certain breeds today has been produced by the ill-directed efforts of ignorant or downright avaricious breeders. Dr Manolson did not beat about this bush. He had the courage to speak frankly where so many have hedged or turned a blind eye. Certainly the would-be dog-owner, turning to this book for guidance, will only have himself to blame if he buys a breed in which hereditary defects may be present or one unsuitable for his particular needs.

Having made his choice, here also is everything that the novice dog-owner can possibly want to know. Dr Manolson knew, and it is here that his wide experience of dog-owners is apparent, all the pitfalls that beset the path of the novice. His book is packed with sound advice. It will save the novice many a blunder. And it will save many a dog from leading an unsuitable, and possibly unhappy, life.

What about the experts? I would not claim to be one: but I have been owning and training dogs for a good deal longer than Dr Manolson lived. I have derived great benefit from his experience, his common sense, and his pleasantly quirky sense of humour. And I am sure that those more expert than I will do so too.

Brian Vesey-Fitzgerald

Frank Manolson died shortly before publication of this book.

A as in apology

One third of the world's population doesn't eat enough. Surely it would be better if none of us kept dogs and we sent the food to undernourished people? The obvious answer is that most of us in the industrialized countries eat too much. We could easily spare our own extra calories. The fact that we don't just indicates what an irrational lot we are. However, we can comfort ourselves with the thought that many of the world's hungry are no less rational. I have spent about half my professional life as a veterinarian, working in underdeveloped countries trying to raise standards of animal husbandry. Almost always, even in the poorest rural families that I visited, there was a dog. There aren't many scraps from the table in those places, so the poor beast usually was a little more rickety and a little more pot-bellied than the children, but he was a member of the household all the same. I don't think you'd get much of a hearing if you tried to tell them they couldn't afford to keep a dog.

What am I trying to say? First, that you can't change people's lives or raise their standards by just dumping your surplus on their doorstep. It just ends up in the wrong mouths. One can only raise standards by education and by instruction and demonstration. Secondly (and I know it's not part of the same problem), people have kept dogs for thousands of years, and whether it makes sense or not they're going to continue keeping them.

Why do any of us keep pets? There are dozens of reasons each more irrational than the preceding one. Some of us have found human company too disturbing so we make do with animals, and some actually prefer them. Some want to play God even if it's only to a dog. Most of us, however, like and get on with people but like animals as well.

Katharine Whitehorn says we keep animals because they're half-way between people and things.

We may feel that in our urban society animals are our last contact with nature, or we may feel that when everything else is changed beyond recognition animals will still be real.

I have no quarrel with anyone who doesn't keep or like animals. That is their business. I'm sure they can give me better reasons for not keeping animals than I can for keeping them. But I feel, and strongly, that if you do have an animal then you must look after it

7

properly. Most cases of neglect are due to ignorance. Obviously the people who really need to know more about their dogs aren't the ones likely to read this or any other book. But knowledge does have a way of filtering down, and if you are a little better informed you can better instruct those who aren't informed at all.

I hope this book is read by some people *before* they buy their first dog. Many families get their first dog when the wife becomes pregnant. They feel that they are going to be tied down anyway, and as they'd always vaguely wanted a dog they think they'll give it a chance to settle in before baby comes. They go out and buy some animal that is completely unsuitable or they buy a diseased pup from an unscrupulous dealer. A month or two later they are so overwhelmed with problems that they 'forget' the puppy somewhere or take it to the vet's for euthanasia. A little knowledge would have avoided the whole mess.

A subtler form of cruelty is being increasingly promulgated by the selection of characteristics within some breeds that must lead to crippled lives. Some of the gruesome details are provided under the entries for the breeds concerned. Doubtless readers can provide other examples. I know many breeders won't like what I've got to say. However, I want to make it perfectly clear that I am not condemning all breeders – not even the majority of breeders – but just that minority who have become dealers in dog fashions and will go to any lengths to breed a pup that will win the shows, even if it means producing litter mates who are semi-cripples.

For example, the breed that must top any list for sensitivity, intelligence and responsiveness is the Poodle. If you have chosen the right breeder you will get a dog that will repay your effort and love a hundredfold. It will live a joyful healthy life. Many Miniature Poodles, though, are produced by ignorant, avaricious or unlucky breeders, and if you get one of their dogs its chances of living a trouble-free life are slim.

To produce the ideal Miniature Poodle, which you may have, possibly many others, full of faults, have been produced and sold to luckless people. Conscientious breeders will destroy those 'cull' puppies but a breeder who is out for the money won't.

Why is the Poodle bred by so many unscrupulous dealers? Simply because it is popular and they can sell every one they produce. If it goes out of fashion they'll switch to the next popular breed and wreck that.

Similarly I should be a fool if I were to condemn the German

Shepherd. Anyone who has worked with a good Alsatian knows they are the absolute tops as a working dog. Get a good breeder and you'll get a wonderful dog. Go to a dealer or a pet shop and you may end up with a nervous killer.

The Chihuahua for years has been carefully chosen and bred by enthusiasts. Lately it has become more popular and some people are raising them like battery hens – each bitch in a small cage raising two litters a year. You'll get a small one easily enough, but your chances of getting a healthy one are slim.

In other words I have no quarrel with breeders who know and love a particular breed and have spent their lives improving it, but the general public ought to beware of popular breeds which are being pushed by dealer-breeders. Unless you know what you are about you may be buying trouble.

May I ask everyone who ever takes an animal to a veterinarian to refrain from saying, 'It must be harder than being a doctor because they can't tell you what's wrong?' We hear it daily. The reply is that neither can babies and neither can many insane people and neither can any of us if we've been knocked down by a car. The doctors muddle through and so do we.

May I apologize to my professional colleagues? This book wasn't meant for a professional or expert audience but for those people who have not learned what you have absorbed and forgotten. If you do take the time to glance through it you'll see that I've carefully avoided leading people into the pitfalls that often accompany a little knowledge. Every layman referring to this book will know when he's on safe ground and when he should see his veterinarian.

Finally, apologies to three veterinary colleagues whose ideas I have stolen under the guise of friendly talks. I'll spare them professional embarrassment by using initials. To John K. of New York City for those endless talks back in 1948 and 1949. We must have been the only people in Greenwich Village who discussed the deformities of *dogs*. To classmate Bob W. of Brampton, Ontario, who introduced me, a cowman, to the weird world of professional breeders and judges, and to John H., now in Coogee, Australia, who with his endless patience introduced me to London dogs and their owners. The colleagues who presently have to put up with my theories and practices I'll spare altogether.

To the memory of Betty Tay of the *Daily Mirror*. She taught millions of kids and quite a few adults (myself included) what responsible pet ownership is all about. I hear that Betty and her Yorkies have found a lovely park in heaven within strolling distance of a pub that encourages wet dogs to sit on the sofa beside the fire. If the Governor reads this could he kindly send her a double. And don't forget a saucer of mild for Toby and Daisy Belle. Put it on my account.

A few general hints

If attacked by a dog (and you have no adequate defence) stand stock still. Many dogs will only attack a moving object. Most police dogs are trained to attack until the person stops moving.

When introducing yourself to a dog, present the back of your hand to its muzzle. A dog will usually snap at fingers, but will only sniff at the back of the hand. Once he accepts that first introduction he will usually allow the friendship to develop to the stroking stage.

A dog should be stroked, not patted. Stroking is soothing. Patting is nervous.

Inconsiderate or untrained dogs who jump and place their muddy paws on your clean clothes can be curbed by gently stepping on their hind feet at the moment they leap.

All dogs should be made to sit for a moment when they enter a new place. They can then survey the situation calmly instead of tearing around nervously. After a moment they can be allowed a tranquil voyage of discovery.

A doped or semi-anaesthetized animal may not recognize you and may bite.

If you own a large dog that you can't control, stay on good terms with your lawyer.

If you think you can raise money by raising puppies from your pet bitch, don't tell your banker about it.

Teach pups to lap by pushing their heads in the food for a second. Don't hold them there. They will usually lick the food off their muzzles and then look for more.

Bathe from the tail forward. As soon as you wet the head the beast will shake.

Don't stare at dogs. They hate it.

Let puppies come to you. If you creep up on them they think it's a game and will back away.

Howling puppies should be soothed briefly and left with a hot water bottle and then ignored. If you continually answer the howls you'll never unspoil them.

When housebreaking puppies, allow a walk in the yard after every feeding. Don't feed heavily last thing at night.

Take two or three little biscuit treats when you go to the vet's. Give one before and one after. The dog may then associate the place with treats rather than nasty needles.

When powdering a dog for fleas put newspapers down first. You then have a fair chance of burning the fleas rather than just driving them into the corners.

Apply lotions and ointments before going for a walk. The stuff can then do its work. If you put it on and leave the dog alone he'll just lick it off.

Leave a favourite pillow or blanket or toy when you drop a pet off at the boarding kennel or hospital.

Take every precaution in handling an injured or ill animal. Pain will make him forget his man-taught manners and he may even bite his master.

Don't encourage snapping or leaping in a puppy. A cute trick in a puppy may become a vicious habit of adulthood.

Puppies who soil their bedding may sometimes be broken of the habit by feeding them in their bed.

If you don't agree with anything in this book write to me (care of the publishers). I'm only too happy to learn from your experience. If you're polite I might reply.

Abortion (*natural*)

The common causes of miscarriage or abortion are rough handling or shipping in advanced pregnancy, accidents, infection and malnutrition. Once it begins there is no way of stopping it, so don't get in a panic and start shoving brandy down your unfortunate animal's throat. Allow her privacy and quiet. Phone your veterinary surgeon (if it is not after midnight because eight hours makes no difference, and better a fresh vet in the morning than a dead one at midnight). If she is still straining an hour later with no results phone your vet no matter what time it is. From your description he will decide how pressing it is. Normally an abortion or miscarriage is over in a couple of hours. Later that day or the next it is important to have the vet

11

check her to see that no pups are left. He will probably advise a couple of return visits to see that there is no infection. He may be able to ascertain the cause and advise how to avoid it next time.

If an animal aborts twice running you must seriously consider an operation to have her uterus removed.

Abortion (*induced or artificial*)

Hormone injections *within twenty-four hours* of breeding are usually successful in terminating an unwanted pregnancy. After that results are indifferent. A word of warning: hormones are tricky things and can cause undesired side effects.

The hormone that is used to cause an abortion may start cysts forming in the ovary or it may start an infection .in the womb. We often see a bitch that has been aborted return in a few months with a serious uterine infection for which the only cure is the removal of the womb and ovaries. Why not take the obvious precaution of keeping her locked up, or on the lead, during the heat period and for a few days afterwards?

Abscess (*boil*)

A collection of pus which is really the body's attempt to wall off infection. That is why an abscess should never be squeezed. You may be just shoving the poison into the body. An abscess should be gently poulticed or bathed with warm salt water or epsom-salt water (three or four teaspoonfuls to a pint) until the abscess breaks and drains. Then wash with warm water to which hydrogen peroxide has been added. Bathe frequently for three or four days with warm salt water to keep the abscess open and draining. If the abscess is above the eye or in the ear or over a joint consult a veterinary surgeon, who will usually use antibiotic injections. If an abscess keeps recurring below the eye or along the line of the mouth a veterinary examination may find that a decayed tooth is the cause. If your dog develops an abscess near his anus you had better seek veterinary advice (see *Anal Glands*). *To summarize*: bathe, don't squeeze; if it's complicated or doesn't come to a head in twenty-four hours consult your vet.

Accidents

If you don't know exactly what to do, do nothing except keep the animal still and warm. Move on an improvised stretcher like a wooden box, a drawer or a stiff cushion. If there is a great deal of bleeding try to stop it (see *Haemorrhage*). If the animal is hysterical and biting, tape it (see *Tape*). Do not administer whisky, brandy or milk. The police will help you get to the closest *open* veterinary surgery or welfare clinic.

Adoption

Chances of a successful adoption are better if the foster mother has a litter about the same age as the orphaned puppies. Smear the orphans with excreta (droppings) from the nurslings, or milk from the mother. Introduce the orphans into the nursing box while the mother is out. Introduce all the orphans at once. Try to keep the mother away for a couple of hours so she will be less discriminating when she gets back. If she rejects the orphans remove them and try again at the next nursing period (usually about four hours). Few foster mothers refuse the third trial. (See *Orphans*.)

Warning: Some foster mothers will detect and kill the orphans, so keep a vigilant eye for the first half-hour.

Affenpinscher (*monkey terrier*)

A coarse-haired derivative of the Miniature Pinscher and Griffon Bruxellois. The breed has the brains and the slightly mad look of its Belgian ancestors, and the ambition and activity of the German breed. A toy weighing a maximum 3·6kg (8 lb), the smaller ones – down to 1·4kg (3 lb) – win the shows and have more physical problems.

Afghan Hound

There is evidence that the modern breed looks somewhat as it did 4,000 years ago when it was a hunting dog in its native Afghanistan. They are a powerful and extremely fast hound, and one of the most beautiful of breeds. It is very tempting to own one of this glorious breed, but do remember they are large and require space, expensive feeding and loads of exercise. Unfortunately we are beginning to see many Afghans that are flighty and nervous, and this isn't all the fault of those few people who buy them solely as personal adornment. Breeders would be well advised to put the hound back into the show-dog. With that one reservation, and a reminder that those silky locks require a fair bit of grooming, do go out and indulge your fancy.

PS: The breed has bounded up the popularity charts. Today they're seen as commonly as mongrels. Many are as unpredictable. It's not the fault of the breed. How can you expect an exuberant athlete to be happy cooped up in a prison-like flat for five days a week? Saturdays they get dragged into the fashionable pubs where the poor creatures try to avoid the burning butts of cigarettes. (Try it yourself in bare feet.) Owners' reactions vary to the fact that on Sundays pent-up energy is expended either killing deer in Richmond Park or sheep at Uncle Sam's place in Sussex. Some owners find it slightly embarrassing but amusing. Others boast about these destructive exploits. Few blame their own ignorance. One thing is certain: neither the police nor Uncle Sam's last testament will convey glad tidings. Sadder still is the fact that many a good dog has been killed in order to try and teach some people the facts of responsible dog keeping.

Age

After the permanent teeth are up it's impossible to more than guess at age. The degree of wear of teeth are but one indication, and it takes a great deal of experience to arrive at even an informed guess. Advanced middle age (seven to nine) is often shown by a few grey hairs around the mouth or eyes, but as in people some dogs or cats are young at ten while others are old at seven. An average advanced old age is twelve, and fifteen is old indeed, although some individuals do live to twenty. (See also *Geriatrics*.)

Airedale Terrier

Developed about a hundred years ago in Yorkshire by judicious breeding of hounds and terriers. Fortunately he's not popular any more because he was fast becoming an elongated, snippy, nervous animal instead of the calm but eager Terrier we value. With his decline in popularity his quality has risen, and he combines admirably the virtues of the guard and the companion. The good breeders aim at a physically and aesthetically balanced animal – the head and tail more or less of equal length – and when they succeed the result is very beautiful indeed. Middle sized, about 22·5kg (50 lb), he can be happy in a flat if he has two long walks a day and one twenty-minute stroll. His coat should be groomed weekly. Heartily recommended.

Akita (*shika inu*)

Looks like the Spitz and is used in its native Japan as an all-round hunter, i.e., for pointing, setting and retrieving.

Allergy

Usually shows in the dog as irregular swellings around the eyes and face and occasionally over the whole body. They respond within an hour to antihistamine injections. If the condition recurs your veterinary surgeon will probably dispense a supply of tablets to be used as necessary, but of course it is more satisfactory to determine the cause and eliminate it. Easier said than done.

Alsatian

Also referred to by their original name – German Shepherd. I don't suppose there is a breed more widely known, and few people can remain neutral when discussing it. Some say that like the Germans the Alsatian is either at your feet or at your throat, and I must admit that one sees many that are too ready to bite at anything. The fault doesn't lie with the breed alone. Many people buy an Alsatian or other large guard dog hoping the dog will endow them with characteristics they don't possess themselves. Don't buy an Alsatian unless you are prepared to spend the time training it properly. An untrained Alsatian is like a loaded gun. It only requires the situation to set it off. You, the owner of such a dog, are legally liable for the damage or hurt it may cause. However, if you are prepared to teach yourself and then the dog proper control, there is no breed that will repay your efforts better than will the Alsatian.

Now for more words of caution. The breed is regaining its former popularity. Soon you will see as many Alsatians in the parks as you now see Poodles.

With popularity standards decline. First because breeders don't cull as rigidly (they can sell all their pups) and secondly because the unscrupulous breeders who care only for money and not at all for the breed, jump on the bandwagon. So be careful from whom you buy. Someone who has loved and bred the breed for many years is more likely to be reliable than an anonymous commercial shop. Once you've chosen the breeder you must not then be overwhelmed by a long pedigree and a recitation of names. Long pedigrees cost little, and names mean nothing except to the professional breeder. Even a list of champions means nothing – and sometimes worse than nothing when it comes to choosing a companion dog. The characteristics that win in the show ring can be a disadvantage when you take your dog for a walk. Every veterinary surgeon can tell you about hip dysplasia (page 114) and the increasing numbers we are seeing in Alsatians. That low crouching walk so loved by the judges has resulted in a hip joint that often does not work as a joint. The socket part of the joint has become flattened so that the long thigh bone rides on the edge of the socket. Often the poor dog who has the illustrious champions for ancestors is lame for life. So please before buying an Alsatian puppy insist on a veterinary certificate. If you own an Alsatian pay particular attention to his training, his grooming (especially in the summer), and do check his anal glands monthly. If he's not absolutely reliable keep him on the lead while on the street, and be considerate to others by keeping him on the lead when you go into a shop or pub. Many people (including myself) would rather not have an unleashed Alsatian sniffing about their legs.

Amputation

Necessary where the limb cannot be repaired or where gangrene has set in. Some dogs can do quite nicely on three legs. Whenever possible the veterinary surgeon will phone an owner before proceeding with the operation, but in some emergencies this is impossible. If the dog is old or if it is overweight, it may be better to have it put to sleep. Young agile animals, or small breeds like Yorkies, Pekes and Chihuahuas, scarcely seem to notice the missing limb. I knew a black Lab called Joe who remained the town wanderer despite the loss of a limb. His owners were sensible enough to keep him on a strict diet. Extra weight on the remaining limbs can turn an amputee into a cripple.

Anaemia

The gums are pale or white in anaemia, signifying either that blood has been lost or that one of the constituents of blood (usually the red blood cells) are not being made fast enough. If the cause is bleeding we often use blood transfusions. If it's a red blood cell deficiency we attempt to determine the cause and treat accordingly. Those old-fashioned 'blood tonics' enrich the manufacturers but have little effect on the patient's blood.

Anaesthetics

We can and do use local anaesthetics (as your dentist uses to block a nerve), but because our patients can't be told to sit still and open wide we usually prefer general anaesthesia. The routine generally followed is:
1 an injection into the muscle to make the animal a bit sleepy, followed by
2 a very carefully gauged injection into the vein which puts him to sleep, and then
3 a tube is put down his trachea and hooked up to a supply of ether, oxygen and nitrous oxide, which can be used to maintain anaesthesia for the length of the operation.

The use of the three different systems allows us to use smaller doses than if we were to use just one drug, and this, of course, makes it much safer, but even so we still have unfortunate deaths in elderly or heart patients during anaesthesia. Pugs, Bulldogs, Pekinese and White Poodles are all risky patients for anaesthesia, and no matter what care we take the percentage of those who die during surgery is still too high.

If you take your pet home while he's still coming round don't be alarmed if he starts having 'running' dreams or starts snapping. Be careful you don't get bitten, and keep him in a darkened place for some hours. Don't feed for at least twelve hours, and don't worry if he's still groggy next day.

PS: Today ether has been largely supplanted by halothane. It is much more expensive but many consider it a better anaesthetic. Another advantage is that it doesn't blow up. In the parlance it's non-volatile.

For about ten years the closest veterinary 'competitor' was a dear man, the late Mr O'Mahoney. His operating theatre was the ill-converted lounge of his home. On the mantelpiece reposed an assortment of sherrys and a few of the stronger. The anaesthetic machine was simply an open mask in which he placed cotton wool impregnated with ether. It was his invariably practice to operate with a lit cigarette in his mouth. The recipe obviously worked. He never had an explosion nor lost a patient on the operating table. He died peacefully in his bed. As a Cambridge professor once told me, 'The best anaesthetic is the one you know best.'

By contrast a very bright Australian graduate I knew killed his canine dental patient, severely injured the nurse and himself and blew up the modern operating theatre because he plugged in the electro-cautery while he was using ether.

PPS: There are now also a range of knock-out injections that are so potent that by law we must keep them under lock and key. Nevertheless some vets – and in one tragic case the girlfriend of a vet – have managed to kill themselves with the stuff.

Conclusion: If drug stealing is your game you'll live longer if you stick to the human sort.

Anal glands

Two marble-sized glands which excrete a thick ill-smelling material. These glands situated, as you might have guessed, on either side of the anus, were probably used in the dim evolutionary past as a protective mechanism. The skunk, being a backward kind of a beast,

17

has simply forgotten to evolve. The domesticated dog hasn't really learnt how to live with his anal glands, and they are too often prone to fill up and become infected. The theory is that the glands are emptied naturally with defecation but, with the soft civilized diets we feed our dogs, the faeces are usually not hard enough to massage the glands gently as they pass by. The solution is quite simple. We carefully express the glands by either pressing on them from the outside or encircling them with one finger (well lubricated) in the anus. Your veterinary surgeon will show you how, but in many dogs it requires more skill than the owner can, or cares to, command. If done without care it can cause no end of harm. How can you tell if the glands need attention? Your dog will tell you by rubbing his bottom along the floor or licking it. If you delay the glands may abscess and then the proper treatment – and it's long and tedious – is applying warm salt water compresses to the area three or four times daily for twenty minutes at a time until the abscesses burst. Then take the animal along to the vet, who will probably start a course of antibiotic injections. If the abscessing recurs he may advise an operation to excise them. Many owners of long-haired dogs, particularly Alsatians or Collies, don't notice the trouble until it's well advanced, so if you own a shaggy beast get him used to a bi-monthly inspection.

Anthrax

All countries with an efficient veterinary organization are virtually free of Anthrax, but if you are living somewhere where they are still trying to learn the lessons that Pasteur taught you had better keep your pet away from the livestock – especially dead cattle or sheep. If you find your dog clawing at an 'anthrax' carcass you can attempt treatment by massive daily doses of penicillin. Be careful of your own personal sanitation while doing so, i.e. wear rubber gloves if possible, and wash them thoroughly afterwards. If your closest veterinary officer isn't on leave drop him a note. He'll be more than interested.

Antibiotics

The family of drugs that includes penicillin, aureomycin, streptomycin, chloromycetin, terramycin, etc. Unfortunately the cheaper ones should be given by injection for best effect. The important thing to remember about antibiotics is that once you begin you must keep up the level by regular doses until the infection is licked. Otherwise the bacteria become resistant to the particular antibiotic. Remember too that there is still no antibiotic effective against viruses (the family

18

of germs that cause distemper in dogs). We use antibiotics in virus diseases to stop the body from succumbing to other bacteria while it is fighting the virus.

PS: Ampicillin, one of the later cousins of the family, is often effective against a wider range of infections than those mentioned. When first introduced it was quite expensive but now it's reasonably priced. In small dogs and cats it has one other distinct virtue. If the patient is eating, the powder within the capsule may be mixed with food. This is particularly valuable when dosing short-headed breeds like Pekes or Pugs or unapproachable site guard dogs. Three strong men and a lady can struggle for an hour shoving a capsule down a Peke's throat; then, with a defiant tail wag it coughs it up! But most of them readily accept the stuff in food.

Warning: Many patients get diarrhoea after a few days on antibiotics. That's because they knock out the beneficial bacteria as well as the harmful ones. Natural yoghurt and yeast often help cure or alleviate this unpleasant side effect.

Antiseptic

Any antiseptic or disinfectant can be dangerous if not used as the manufacturer intended. Kindly read the directions before using. Dilute accordingly. Remember there's no point in pouring an antiseptic on dirt, so wash the area first with soap and water. Bathing afterwards with salt and water is often as effective as anything. Gentian Violet has the virtue of drying in and will sometimes stop the animal from licking the affected area.

Some bad infections become filthy and painful. You could hardly wash a wounded penis or ear with soap and water without the aid of a general anaesthetic. Good old-fashioned Hydrogen Peroxide – about 10 or 20 volume strength – poured over the area often helps till you can get the suffering creature to a vet.

Appenzal Mountian Dog

A 16kg (35 lb) dog from Switzerland who, like all working breeds, adapts well as a companion or guard dog. He's tricolour (black, brown and white), compact in body, shiny and alert, with a tight tail he curls over his back.

Appetite

If your pet skips food for a day don't worry about it, but two days without eating and your vet should be consulted. If he goes to eat and obviously wants to but does not eat, the chances are he has a rotten tooth or something lodged in his mouth.

If an animal has been missing for some days and comes back with a ravenous appetite, don't feed him all he wants but rather give him three small meals throughout the first day. If your adult pet has been spayed she may develop a gluttonous appetite. Keep the intake within bounds or you will have a balloon on your hands. A retired working or hunting dog will usually keep the same appetite as he had in his active days. His intake must be gradually cut down. Castrated or spayed animals will become enormous if allowed to follow their natural inclinations.

Animals with head colds or catarrh will often not eat because they can't smell the food properly. Very strong-smelling food (like ripe cheese or hare or bull meat) may tempt them.

Pregnant bitches will often have abnormal appetites. Often they will have no appetite, and I have known members of the smaller breeds to go days without eating. At about the thirty-fifth day of pregnancy the uterine horn may fold on itself, causing pain and discomfort and lack of appetite for two or three days. During late pregnancy you must give smaller meals four, five or even six times daily, as there isn't room for a single large meal.

Arthritis

The veterinary profession knows as much and as little about these painful joint conditions as our colleagues who practise human medicine. That is – we can diagnose the condition and tell what stage it's in (with the aid of X-rays and a great deal of clinical experience), but we can seldom cure, and if we do we're not sure it's been effected more by our drugs than by nature. One thing, though, we can do fairly effectively, and that is alleviate the pain, and we owe it to our helpless pets to do all we can in that direction. If the drug your vet prescribes doesn't seem to be helping, don't change vets. It's unfair to your pet. The new vet will often start with the same drug that your original vet used. The poor dog is right back where he started.

A few years ago we thought cortisone would be the answer but, although it does have some dramatic results, too many relapses still occur. Arthritis is still in the research realm, and let's hope our veterinary and medical researchers will come up with an answer.

PS: I had always assumed that most people have had enough experience of the condition with their human relatives to realize how much arthritic patients appreciate heat. Yet it's surprising how many expect faithful old creaky Jock to rest on the cold tiles by the back door. A measure of comfort can be provided by one of several simple, economic methods. Possibly the cheapest and best is an appropriately sized pillow or mattress filled with expanded polystyrene pellets. No artificial heat is provided. The animal snuggles into the material, which retains the body heat. Another sort is a properly insulated heat unit in a blanket. They use surprisingly little energy. We've used both sorts of comfort for our patients and nursing litters for ten years without problem. Some people prefer old fashioned infra-red heat lamps like we used to see so commonly in pig houses. I think they interfere with proper sleep, but are certainly preferable to nothing.

Remember too that arthritic patients are particularly stiff after long periods of rest. So let them out only briefly to do their business and then welcome them back to share the wealth of heat in front of the hearth. If they don't deserve that measure of comfort, you don't deserve a dog.

Artificial eyes

Quite obviously the dog couldn't care less, but some people insist, and where there's a demand you know the rest.

Artificial insemination

Semen is collected from the male, who is made to ejaculate into a rubber tube called an artificial vagina at the end of which is a test tube. The semen is then diluted, and may be refrigerated for some weeks or deep frozen for long spells. In cattle and horse breeding the advantages are many, and many countries have improved their cattle standards very quickly by the use of the system. The danger, of course, so far as dogs are concerned, is that one male can fertilize hundreds of females. In inseminating cattle, hard-headed experienced men choose males for well-proven reasons. They are wary of spreading undesirable characteristics through hundreds of cows, and one can only too well imagine the situation in the dog world if artificial insemination was common. One finely-boned, hair-eared, neurotic show winner could father hundreds like himself (many, of course, would be both his daughters and grand-daughters after a couple of years). The destruction of many fine breeds would be speeded up.

Artificial respiration

With the *newborn* remove all mucousy stuff from the mouth. Quickly dry with a cloth. Slap vigorously, then swing slowly back and forth ten times. Wait a second or two for a gasp. If there isn't one, swing again. If no results try mouth to mouth breathing – into the new-born's lungs, then suck and expel your breath. Inhale and repeat.

With the *drowned adult* hold up by the hind feet and swing slowly to the full extent of your arms both ways. This helps to expel any water or debris. The weight of the abdominal contents will contract and expand the lungs. Examine to make sure the mouth is clear. Swing again. This method works well with small dogs. With larger dogs clear the mouth. Drain by holding the dog upside down. Then, with the animal lying on its side, try to artificially contract and expand the lungs by slowly (twenty times to the minute) pressing down and releasing, pressing down and releasing, as you would with a human. Try for up to half an hour.

With the *electrocuted animal* shut off the current first. Try the swinging method in small animals, the press for larger. Try for up to half an hour.

Ascarids (*roundworms*)

Roundworms are so called because they are round in cross-section as opposed to the tapeworms which are flat in cross-section. The commonest intestinal worm of the dog. One form is transmissible to humans (see *Worms*).
PS: Many leading authorities suggest that all puppies should be wormed from three weeks of age. That is not a misprint: Three weeks. I'm inclined to agree regarding large breeds but I'd dose very carefully with the toys. As usual you must be guided by your own vet but you may remind him that he, like me, may be a bit too traditional. The problem, of course, is that three weeks is the weaning stage. Have they gone off because of the worm dose or because the bitch is being gradually withdrawn? That's what the art of canine husbandry is all about.

Ascites (*dropsy of the abdomen*)

Collection of fluids in the abdomen. May be caused in the younger animals by worms, but in the older animal it's invariably a serious and usually a fatal condition, because it's secondary to a serious growth or heart, liver or kidney malfunction. The only effective first aid till you get to the vet is rest and quiet.

Asphyxiation

The animal breathes in short painful gasps. The lining of his mouth and eyes turn blue. Move him to an open window and open his mouth to see if there are any obstructions. If you are quite sure it's not pneumonia, but that something like gas poisoning is causing the condition, apply artificial respiration. If you are not sure, then lay the animal in a comfortable position and leave him alone while you get on the phone to your veterinary surgeon or, better yet, find the nearest open clinic and rush him there.

Asthma

They tell me that true asthma (whatever that may be) does not occur in animals, but certainly we see a lot of wheezy old individuals who draw a lot of painful breaths. Some of the smaller toys seem particularly prone to it, and I have seen them go on for two or three years having more or less painful attacks, but recovering to enjoy yet another meal. The first principle of treatment is, of course, rest, and this is far more important than panicking into midnight phone calls. Further treatment depends on the reason for difficult breathing. It is usually the heart of the older dog that is the root of the problem, but it may be bronchial or lung trouble. Digitalis, drugs with unpronounceable names, and a rented drum of oxygen (if you can afford it) are often effective in alleviating the condition, but usually there can be no cure – just an easing of the condition. If you happen to be a heart or chest specialist you might attempt treating your own pet with digitalis, but if you are not you had better resign yourself to frequent veterinary visits – usually weekly at first, then later just once a month.

Atavism

Where one or more pups in a litter resemble neither parent but some ancestor more or less remote.

No, it's nothing you or your dog have done wrong, but is something which any text on genetics will explain to you. Don't for goodness' sake eliminate either parent as a breeder. It may never recur.

Ataxia (*staggering walk*)

An unco-ordinated walk caused by an inability to assess correctly the movement of the limbs. In young dogs this may be the result of brain damage due to the distemper virus. In older animals it may be the result of an accident or a tumour. If caused by ear mites it's easily treated. If it's the result of an accident, only time will tell if there will be a partial or total recovery. In the case of tumours it's incurable, while in the case of virus damage, time sometimes effects a cure.

Atrophy

Wasting of a muscle or an organ which is usually seen in limbs that have been immobilized with plaster. Recovery comes with use. In aged animals atrophy is an irreversible condition.

Australia

If you think Britain has stringent import regulations for animals phone the Aussie Consulate to find out what they require in their efforts to keep their continent free of some of the animal diseases. Incidentally, some animals which may introduce certain defects of a hereditary nature are banned from Australia, and I believe this is but an indication of what official policy will be in all advanced countries in the not too distant future.

Australian Cattle Dog

A handsome derivative of imported collies, and some say the native Australian Dingo. Now breeding true to type and becoming a show dog down under. It weighs about 16kg (35 lb), is about a foot and a half high and looks like a scaled down version of the Alsatian. It has black patches on the face, and the body colour is speckled.

Australian Terrier

The only Australian breed at all well known in Britain. He's 4·5kg (10 lb), plus or minus a bit, but all of that is typical game terrier, and I know of nothing against choosing him as a lively intelligent flat-mate.

Avitaminosis

Lack of one or more vitamins. Rarely seen today with the general improvement in feeding. A dog fed a varied diet doesn't need those ubiquitously advertised pills. If he's not feeling well don't feel virtuous because you give him a half dozen assorted vitamins. You're just postponing proper treatment.

Awns

Those sharp pointed seeds of barley, wild oats and grasses that dogs love to chew and that often get stuck in their mouth or throat, causing inflammation and abscesses. Prevention is, of course, better than cure, so avoid romps in ripening fields – but if you and your dog simply must go into the awns, then please check him carefully when you get home. The real danger points are the feet. The hair between the pads should be separated and looked at in a strong light. If he's shaking his head examine his ears particularly well, and if you see an awn and can't get it out, or if he's still shaking after you've removed all you see, get him to the vet's straight away. Awns will work their way down the ears to the drum and beyond. They can be removed intact within twenty-four hours of entry, but after that they disintegrate partially, and it's a long painful process of antibiotic treatment. The removal of the awns from an ear canal usually requires a general anaesthetic, and a special pair of angle forceps. I go on about it because in July many veterinary surgeons average one of these cases daily, and we'd sooner you helped to prevent it. Incidentally, if your dog has a wee abscess that seems to be travelling up his leg at the rate of a couple of inches a week, there's a chance it may be an awn that is working its way right up from the foot. It takes a skilled surgeon indeed to assess just where to cut to find the awn, because it has usually moved on by the time the abscess has formed.

Bad breath

One of the common reasons people take a pet to a veterinary surgeon. Unfortunately you can perfume Champion Jane of Bloomsbury East with Chanel, and because of her primarily carnivorous diet her breath is likely to be strong to bad. Foul breath is another thing, and this may be an indication of bad teeth (see also *Teeth*), gastritis or, much more commonly, kidney dysfunction. If the mal-odour is due to teeth or a bowel disorder we can usually set it right, but nephritis is still a touch and go proposition. If the primary cause of bad breath cannot be cured charcoal tablets may mask it.

Bandaging

Much more difficult in animals than in people. Most animals have an insatiable desire to lick their wounds, and will claw, lick, bite or rub off a bandage unless they realize it's hopeless. We therefore bandage right around the body or limb or head, even if it's only a very small area that needs attention. A good bandage is firm but not so tight that it cuts off circulation, and it must always be wide and laid flat. Do not use cord or string anywhere. Cover the entire bandage with elastoplast or adhesive tape to prevent him biting it off. Sometimes plastic will do the job when adhesive tape won't. Socks or booties on his feet (covered with elastoplast) will stop him clawing at a bandage. You may have to make an Elizabethan collar if the bandage is around the head.

Ears Put layer of cotton-wool flat on top of head. Lay the injured ear

25

over it. Put another layer of cotton-wool over injured ear. Then tape with alternating rows in front of and behind the opposite ear. Not too tight or you may cut off breathing. Use several layers. Cover with elastoplast.

Eyes Almost impossible to bandage properly (see *Elizabethan collar*).

Tail Wrap very tightly with tight layers of gauze going well behind the wound both sides. Use sticky elastoplast or tape to anchor the bandage to the hair at the base of the tail.

Limbs Place cotton wadding between toes, and a large wad under the pad. Use four or five strips of bandage running down under and up the limb. Then wind another couple of layers around the limb. Cover with elastoplast and anchor to hair above wound.

Chest or abdomen Cut holes in a large rectangular-shaped bandage for limbs. Insert limbs and by cutting strips in the free sides and tying them you have an effective 'many-tailed' bandage.

Barking

Right from the beginning allow your dog to bark at strangers. It's his normal reaction. But right from the beginning teach him the moment *you* recognize the stranger he must stop barking. This is best done by encouragement. Usually a pat as reward, but chastisement (gently) if he continues and he will get the idea. There is nothing more annoying to your friends (because if you're a normal pet owner you won't allow any criticism) than a dog that barks throughout the first half hour of a visit. The only civilized thing to do is pick him up and put him in a distant room or closet till he quietens down. A dog that barks the moment you're out of sight can often be cured by the dark closet treatment. However, if a few days of any one type of treatment doesn't work don't persevere until you are both nervous wrecks. If you have a placid, experienced, dog-loving friend who will take your dog for a week or two he may be able to effect a cure. Why? Because your dog often reflects your nervousness.

Basenji (*Congo Bush Dog*)

The modern breed doesn't look unlike rock carvings of his precursors in Egypt five millenia ago (you can save the fare to Egypt by going to the British Museum in Great Russell Street or the Metropolitan on Fifth Avenue). He is still used in Equatorial Africa as a hunting dog, and the British and American representatives have all the vigour and joy of their African cousins. He is not barkless as some claim, but just expresses himself more subtly than European breeds. His bark varies between a whisper and a laugh. He's way up on my list of favourites because he combines vitality, stamina, intelligence and loyalty in a compact aesthetic frame. Unfortunately some Basenjis bite without notice and without provocation, so I wouldn't recommend the breed for a child.

PS: Since I wrote that entry I have had several letters from clients and friends which state that they trust their own Basenji with their own kids, visiting children and grandchildren. They agree, however, that a pair can set each other off on the warpath. That's true of many breeds. Dogs are pack animals.

Basset Hound

An originally continental breed. He's got long velvet ears and a doleful expression, and a means of communication that will howl right through the phone while the neighbours are calling the police. He's a persistent but slow hunter. Becoming very popular in America, and they do make good house pets. Those who set the fashion seem to want crookeder and crookeder legs, and I would advise you in buying to overlook the cute low one with knobs instead of legs, and go for the straightest limbed specimen you can find. Some people who own Bassetts forget that they are largish dogs and they are outdoor dogs. They require as much exercise as a Springer Spaniel, and that is lots and lots.

PS: Kindly pay as much attention to their ears as you would to those of a cocker.

Bathing

Frequency: The less often the better. Most dogs will smell OK on two baths a year (remember a dog doesn't sweat) but if you simply can't stand your dog unless he is bathed regularly, try it only once in six weeks, or once a month as the positive maximum. *Comb* well before. Comb and brush thoroughly Poodles, wire- and long-haired breeds, before bathing.

Temperature of water should be about 30°C (86°F) and never above body heat. *Basin* may be filled up to dog's tummy, but better yet *pour* water over dog gently, starting always at the tail and working forward. The minute you wet his head he'll shake. *Rinse* thoroughly with at least two changes of water. *Soap:* you don't have to use a 'doggy' soap. Any good mild human soap is suitable, but 'soft' soaps are more convenient. More important than the kind of soap is the thorough rinsing. *Dry* with a rough towel. Then another rough towel. If you're doing it on a commercial basis use a blower-dryer in one corner of a kennel cage. Stand in a warm place without draughts while combing and brushing. When you go out for that first post-bath walk use the lead because the beast will immediately try to roll in the first bit of filth it finds.

Dry Shampooing is much simpler and often as effective as bathing. Use any inert powder or bran. Rub it in. Brush it out.

Don't bathe puppies. *Don't* bathe bitches more than four weeks pregnant. *Don't* bathe in cold water. *Don't* bathe ill animals.

Don't bathe for a month after an operation. *Don't* bathe any animal with any skin complaint without veterinary advice. *Do* bathe your dog after he's been swimming in the sea – if he scratches.

Memo: Thousands of happy healthy dogs are never bathed. Lots of civilized dogs are just combed and brushed.

Beagle

Breeders of this hound have always been as interested in the stamina, intelligence and character of their produce as in their appearance, yet the Beagle breeds wonderfully true to type, and that type has no outstanding physiological faults. Colour has never been a deciding factor, and all colours but chocolate are acceptable. There may be a moral here. If you want a small lively pet that is all dog with a wonderful bouncy disposition you can't go wrong with a Beagle. It's true some do develop a wandering bent, and I for one have never found a solution to their adventurous spirit.

PS: Don't coop one in a friend's luxurious apartment over a long weekend unless you're prepared to refurnish the place or lose a friend. The minority of beagles who are not so exuberantly athletic may merely express their discontent by giving the neighbours a valid excuse for insomnia.

Bed, bedding

The location of the bed is more important than the bed itself. A draught-free corner in a well-ventilated room should be appointed. The bed itself should be large enough to accommodate the animal comfortably (puppies can grow and GROW and GROW). The best beds are made of smoothly planed, tightly jointed wood. Three sides should be enclosed well above the height of the recumbent animal. The whole affair should be on legs 12–20cm (5–8 in) above floor level. A couple or three thicknesses of any *washable* blanket laid smooth and flat are suitable. Remember that fleas and other bugs can hide in bedding, so wash the whole affair fortnightly or at least once a month.

Some sensible people have dog sheets. A dog sheet is a sheet that you zip or button around dog blankets.

PS: Blankets filled with expanded polystyrene granules are lovely. They retain the heat generated by the dog's body – yet they are comfortable during the hottest day of summer. Ain't science wonderful?

Bedlington Terrier

Originally a true Terrier from the border counties, this poor creature has been modified for show and fashion and I'm afraid there is even more of lamb in it than its appearance would suggest. They can be so finicky and so nervous that one wonders how the breed ever hunted vermin, not to mention badgers and foxes. I wish breeders would explain to me how they're going to retain enough vitality in their chosen types so that the breed can survive if they persist in this folly of turning a Terrier into a powder puff.

Bee stings

Alkalis (like washing soda) will relieve the pain of bee stings, although your problem will be:

1 catching the animal that has been stung;
2 making sure it's bees, not wasps (use dilute acid for the latter); and
3 finding a suitable alkali in your picnic hamper.

Sometimes you can locate the bee's stinger on the apex of the swelling. Try to pull it out by pinching at the bottom with a couple of matchsticks. If you pull it out with your fingers you'll merely inject the balance of the stinger's contents into the hound, and add to the victim's pain. Then wash with diluted alkali. If the swellings become very large or the animal has difficulty in breathing, try to get it to a veterinary surgeon. If that's impossible there may be a doctor or dentist around who will inject adrenalin or better yet one of the antihistamines. Twenty-five milligrams of the common antihistamine is a safe dose for a Poodle. If there is pain but no danger, an aspirin will provide some relief.

Warning: Any dog in pain or in panic may bite. Have one person hold the animal either side of its neck while the other does the doctoring.

Bernese Mountain Dog

The industrious Swiss have also produced this 27kg (60 lb) animal-cum-guard-cum-companion. Because of his size and his long dense

coat he's not at his best in cities, but he makes a great village or country dog. He looks not unlike a big boned black and white Collie.
PS: In the last year or two we have seen quite a few more. Despite their increasing popularity, standards if anything have improved. Have a good look next time you're at a show.

Biscuits

The consumer (you the buyer, or your quite helpless pet) has little protection from the laws of this 'mother of the commonwealth' when you choose between available brands of pet foods. You must believe whatever the manufacturer chooses to put on the packet. Yes, dear reader, there are countries, like America, where the manufacturer must put on the label the ingredients and the proportion in which they are mixed. Obviously dog biscuit 'A' which contains seventy per cent meat and bonemeal is superior to dog biscuit 'B' which contains seventy per cent wheat flour. How can you tell under the present system of British anarchy? Impossible! And neither can your vet, and neither can I. Because they and I cannot afford the laboratory analyses. But the Government can and should. Biscuits and 'meal' foods for pets are the most economical way of feeding them a balanced diet, but how on earth can we advise you when it's usually impossible to ascertain the contents? In America there are several brands of dried packaged food which we can recommend as the *whole* diet of the dog (except for the addition of fat). They are labelled: so much meat meal so much blood meal, so much bonemeal, so much flour, and also the percentage of protein, carbohydrate and minerals. The amount of fat to be added is easily computed (fats don't store well except under refrigeration). Until this happy state of affairs comes about in Britain, I'm afraid biscuits must be relegated to the tit-bit class – useful for light breakfasts or rewards.

Lest the biscuit manufacturers claim I'm discriminating against them, may I add that many manufacturers of tinned dog food don't give us any information about their products.
PS: The situation doesn't seem to have changed appreciably in twenty years. I must add, however, that when we can't get stale wholemeal bread from our local friendly baker we stodge our own pet dogs with biscuit. We don't allow the standard Poodles to see the labels. The others can't read.

Bladder

If an animal shows pain or discomfort while urinating, or if it strains to pass water and cannot, or if it strains and passes only a drop or two, the cause is usually an urinary obstruction, and you simply must not neglect it. It is a very painful condition and if not treated within twenty-four hours may result in death. You can usually feel the full bladder by pressing at the back part of the abdomen. If there isn't a vet immediately available, you may be able to relieve the animal by gentle pressure on the bladder, but I would advise veterinary attention at the earliest possible moment. The veterinary surgeon may try to relieve the animal by external pressure, but this is usually not possible. Then he will administer a general anaesthetic and try to pass a catheter. In dogs, stones are a common cause and an operation to remove the stones is usually successful, but the condition may recur. Some male dogs have a urinary obstruction because of an enlarged prostate gland, and in those cases injections of female hormones sometimes help. If the trouble is caused by infection, antibiotics will often effect a rapid cure. If the cause is a tumour the results depend, of course, on the sort of tumour it is.

Summary: If your pet is straining to pass water get it to a vet straight away.

Blindness

It's surprising how many owners bring an ageing dog into the clinic for some minor attention like nail trimming and mention that 'he seems to be bumping into things'. An examination often reveals that the animal has diminished or little sight. If the case is incurable I would not suggest euthanasia because most pets get along quite well (in familiar surroundings) without sight. Much of their pleasure is in smelling and hearing, and it's amazing how little their temperament changes with diminished sight. Help him a bit by removing furniture with sharp edges, and keep him on the lead out-of-doors.

PS: The story is told of a person who bought a Shih-Tzu puppy (I suppose it could be told about any of the popular breeds) only to discover on arrival at home that it was blind. The dealer-breeder accepted the puppy back, refunded the purchase price and remarked, 'I'll try to sell it to someone else but if I can't I'll have its eyes removed and use it for breeding like I did with her mother.'

I can't vouch for the truth of that story but it was printed in the *Veterinary Record* (the journal of the British Veterinary Association). It is well known that some forms of blindness are hereditary. And some people don't mind dealing in misery for profit. In my experience the profits from such dealings are minimal or nil, but the suffering is great, not only for the poor afflicted creatures destined for a crippled life, but for the innocent, misguided purchaser as well. How do you tell a child that the puppy he's taken to his heart is going back to the kennels?

Blind teats

The breasts of nursing mothers should be examined daily. If one gland is swollen much more than the others it may be that the teat canal is blocked. Try to squeeze a bit of milk through. If it's open then milk that gland partially empty. Probably no suckling has chosen it, or the animal that was sucking it had died, and after a few days, if unmilked, it will dry off. If you can't get any milk through the opening apply a warm wet pad for a few moments and gently massage it outward with some olive oil. If that doesn't open the canal take her to your veterinary surgeon. He will examine the teat and decide whether it has ever had an orifice, and if it hasn't he'll try to open one; or whether the trouble is infectious, in which case it will usually respond to antibiotics.

Bloodhound

This hound of all hounds is a magnificent 45kg (100 lb) of well-proportioned bone and muscle behind a nose that can follow a scent better than that of any other breed. They are blessed with an equable disposition, and can be great children's dogs. They require good sized exercise areas, so if you're an indoor type with a mews flat they really wouldn't be a wise choice. If you're thinking of having your Bloodhound bitch bred, better set aside a large room for the growing puppies, because the breed is noted for having huge litters. Ten or a dozen is not at all unusual, and there's always someone around who will tell you of their efforts to raise sixteen. The breed standard keeps emphasizing the pendulous folds of skin over the face, and I would advise that breeders have gone quite far enough in this regard. You see, if the eye is buried in mounds of skin there's bound to be trouble. It's really unfair to a dog to subject him to the plastic surgery necessary to remove all that skin so that the eye can assume a more physiological relationship with the outside world.

PS: Large breeds are subject to a condition called Gastric Torsion. The stomach twists. Gases build up into a bloat which in seconds can reach an alarming size. Unless treated within minutes – not hours – the condition is almost invariably fatal. There is no effective first aid but an experienced surgeon or nurse may be able to pass a tube or punch a trocar or needle into the area to relieve the gas. Vets operate to undo the twist. Sadly I must report that over fifty per cent of all the bloodhounds I've known have suffered from this nasty syndrome. All one can suggest to the devotees of this wonderful breed is that they should be aware of the problem and its symptoms. Early recognition can save a life. Some say that heavy meals should be avoided and enthusiastic exercise restricted after all meals.

Boarding Kennels

Vary widely from well-run, roomy establishments with good outdoor runs to scruffy little corners of scruffier little shops. You pay your money and you take your choice. The least you can do for your dog is inspect the premises before you leave him. If many of the cages have two or three animals you can be sure the place is over-crowded. If you see stale food in the pens you can be sure it's badly managed. Ask the people what vet they use. If they say, 'Oh, we manage that ourselves,' better look elsewhere. Your best bet is to take your husband along. He may not know anything about animals, but he can probably recognize a well-run place when he sees it.

I mustn't forget to mention dear Miss Tootbody down the road who will take two or three 'recommended' pets for short periods. If you get the right Miss Tootbody you can be sure your dog will have the best holiday of its life.

Don't put a dog under a year of age in kennels if you can possibly avoid it. Don't put any dog in kennels unless it's been vaccinated against distemper, infectious hepatitis and leptospirosis (the triple shots).

If your dog is inclined to be 'yappy' or bark a lot, try to find an alternative to kennels, because the kennel people, in sheer self-defence, will put him in a dark secluded corner or a soundproof cellar. Yes, they will, madam. I've seen it and I know. Don't inundate the kennel people with lots of your pet's favourite foods. You're missing a glorious opportunity to unspoil your dog. They will feed a fully balanced diet even if it doesn't include breast of pheasant or salmon trout. Do please tell the kennel people if your dog is under treatment, and what sort of treatment he's having, and do ask them if they'd mind having Chippy's favourite pillow or rubber bone thrown in his cage. Don't be surprised if Chippy comes back considerably thinner. He probably didn't eat for three or four days until he got used to the place, but that won't harm him. Do check him on your doorstep, and if he's acquired fleas or lice dust him well and take him for a walk before you allow him indoors. He may have become 'unhousebroken'

33

or acquired new habits like barking in the kennels, so you'll have to be patient with him for a few days and let him gradually get back to normal. If he has runny eyes or diarrhoea a couple of days after his return have the vet check him.

PS: Commercial boarding establishments must now be inspected, approved and licensed by local authorities. The average owner may fairly assume that a 'licensed boarding kennels' indicates the place is OK. In fact, in some places the inspection consists of little more than a visit from anyone in the office who wants a trip to the countryside and a cup of tea. I know several licensed boarding establishments who were inspected by people who are as qualified for the task as I am for piloting Concorde.

Conclusion: Licensing is too often a licence to take money for nothing. If you want to be sure inspect the place yourself. Please note that any good place will be fully booked for holiday periods months ahead.

Bonemeal

A harmless natural source of calcium and phosphorus available at chemists or food stores. Make sure you get the feeding not the garden sort. Especially valuable for puppies and pregnant and lactating females. Use about a teaspoonful a day for a Yorkie, and up to three tablespoonfuls for a nursing Labrador with a half dozen pups.

PS: The feeding sort is becoming increasingly difficult to buy. Perseverance. Don't be fobbed off by substitutes. You're after natural bones which dogs naturally eat. Don't worry too much about overfeeding. The worst that can happen is a day or two of constipation. A good jog in the park will cure both of you.

Bones

Any bone can kill any animal if he chews it down to splinters and those splinters lodge in the wrong place. Only large marrow bones should be fed, and these should be taken from the animal before they're crunched down to swallowable bits. Thousands of dogs live long happy lives without ever seeing a bone, so unless you're really sold on their virtues why not buy one of those hard rubber things the pet shops sell, and let Bozo chew on that? We're always answered, 'But surely bones are a dog's natural food.' Yes, they have always been a part of dog's natural food, but, 1, that was in the days when dogs were dogs and not centrally heated and overfed like their owners, and 2, we have no way of finding out how many wild dogs or wolves crawl off into the underbrush to die of peritonitis caused by a penetrating bone splinter. My colleagues and I can tell you that every Monday and Tuesday we are presented with cases suffering from the after effects of the bones of the Sunday joint. I can't tell you why they got away with it as long as they did. Symptoms vary according to where the stoppage or penetration occurs, and I think they are too varied to attempt a description. I will say, though, that almost invariably when an owner says about his ill dog, 'He's got a bone stuck in his throat', the dog actually turns out to have tonsilitis or bronchitis. You see, the dog can't clear his throat as we do, so his spasmodic retching efforts looks to the uninitiated as if he's trying to clear a bone. Actually most undigested bones lodge in the rectum, and a careful enema will clear them. The really tricky ones are those that lodge in the oesophagus or the intestine. These require skilled surgery to remove.

If your dog has had one bowel stoppage due to bones and you persist in allowing him bones you don't deserve to own a dog.

PS: When the first version of this book went out, a vet from Northampton wrote me and said, 'Absolute nonsense. I feed my dogs and cats all sorts of bones – fish, chicken, beef, the lot – and all right off our dining-room table.' I must admit that today I do exactly the same. I must point out, however, that I now live in a rural area. Our pets have unlimited exercise. If we didn't throw them bones they'd find their own. The neighbouring farmers don't mind if those bones belong to rats or rabbits. They do however tend to shoot anything that interferes with their pheasants or their sheep. Our dogs can digest bones but not bullets. I still wouldn't advise feeding cooked bones to a dog that spends twenty-three hours a day in a flat.

PPS: We throw the bones to the standard poodles, the chows and the Yorkshire Terriers, the Siamese and Balinese, without discrimination. In this respect the Russians may be right: environment is more important than heredity. Don't expand the theory.

Border Terrier

Among the smaller of the Terriers, weighing about 7kg (15 lb). Indomitable hunters, and they haven't been wrecked by popularity or the show ring. They have loads of stamina and unlimited courage. If you're at all attracted by the breed don't hesitate. Get one. You'll have a tough but loyal pet. There is a tendency in some strains to be too straight in the hind leg, and I believe breeders shouldn't try to make the breed any 'showier' than it is, or else we'll start to get Perth's disease in this Terrier as we have in some of the others.

Bore

A person who talks about his own pet, and won't listen when you talk about yours.

Borzoi (*Russian Wolfhound*)

This magnificent product of the Czars isn't doing much wolf hunting today. Like Norwegians, of whom there are more in America than in Norway, there are more Borzois in New York and Paris than there are in Russia, and in those cities they attempt to keep the wolves out of harm's way. Unless the breeders wake up and stop narrowing his skull this breed will have followed fashion to the logical conclusion of imbecility.

Boston Terrier (*Boston Bull*)

This unique looking product of Massachusetts is a veterinary problem-and-a-half. His eyes protrude too far, and few live out their lives without corneal ulcers or worse. His head and throat have been shortened so that he can't breathe freely. His shoulders are so large in relation to his hips that often he can only be delivered by Caesarian section. It's a breed that started out well, and its characteristics weren't too abnormal forty years ago when he first started topping the popularity poll in America. Popularity and breeding to a standard that emphasized his physical eccentricities all but killed the breed. There are a few survivors in Britain and quite a few in America, but your chances of getting one that can lead a long and healthy life are small.

PS: Several breeders have approached me at shows, and turn out to be extraordinarily nice people. They've pointed out that they're well aware of the problems and are trying their best to breed for health and longevity. They also suggest that as there are no dealer-breeders involved (Boston Terriers are too difficult to breed commercially), they will probably succeed. And they rightfully add that few other breeds can convey so much sheer joy and delight. I think much of what they say can be said of most of the other relatively unpopular breeds.

Bowels

Dogs can have all the bowel ailments that we do, and a couple more besides. Ulcers are rarer than in the human, but we see more bowel tumours. The commonest complaints we treat are diarrhoea, constipation and vomiting. Haemorrhage from the bowel is a fairly frequent

36

symptom of many bowel conditions, and we see it often in distemper and the other virus conditions in the dog. Unless it's an obviously uncomplicated case of either diarrhoea or constipation you had better get veterinary diagnosis of the actual case. The only safe first aid in all cases of bowel trouble is to cut off all food and water. Any inflamed organ wants rest in order to heal. Get the animal to a vet within twenty-four hours.

Boxer

Of the three common large breeds of German working dogs, the Boxer is in my opinion best suited by temperament for a family and household dog, although proper training is, of course, necessary and shy nervous examples are to be avoided. Boxers are naturally bumptious creatures, and a bounding five months' old Boxer can do unbelievable damage quite unintentionally and almost without noticing it. A room full of Dresden China and a playful Boxer puppy is a situation I'd give a fiver to see. The following conditions are becoming so common in Boxers presented to us that I think you should be warned to watch for them in buying a puppy: undersized, narrow-chested, small-boned, malformed mouth (so that the teeth don't meet), in-turned eyelids (see *Entropion*), and undue nervousness. I can hear the howls of rage from some breeders. I am not trying to discourage anyone from getting a Boxer. I have owned one and know what delightful creatures and staunch companions they can be, but surely progress in a breed doesn't consist of shortening a head and throat that are already quite short enough, or in wrong inbreeding to the point where the strain loses the Boxer's normally equable disposition. A little more regard for the average owner who often gets the culls from the show ring. Words of advice to people who already have Boxers: please don't let them get overweight. They can be gluttons if allowed. Have his teeth checked every couple of years, especially if he has a 'bad' mouth.

PS: You will be seeing more of them with tails man hasn't chopped. I think they look terrific. And so do they. Stand back while they swish their appreciation.

PPS: One can understand why some people won't cull a white Boxer puppy, but it is astonishing that some people deliberately breed them. It's not simply a matter of aesthetics. After all, lots of dreadful-looking people find mates. The fact that most white Boxers spend a disproportionate amount of time being treated for serious complaints would indicate that nature has read the 'standards of the breed'.

Brabaçon

One of the three sorts of Griffon Bruxellois, the Brabaçon is short-haired and therefore not as quizzical looking as the other sorts. The Brabaçon is bred in two sizes, one about 3kg (6 lb) and one about twice that. In intelligence and trainability both sizes are definitely in the Alsatian class. Their outstanding fault is their protuberant eyes and many spend their last years in semi-blindness.

Brandy

Vastly overrated as a medicine for animals, and usually used at the wrong times. It must not be given as first aid after an accident, heart attack, fainting spell or fit. It may be used sparingly for your old ginger tom who creaks into his bed after a half-hearted dinner or for that old old dog who feels the cold at night. Your vet may allow it in some pneumonia cases, but even if your pet doesn't take to it regularly very few veterinary surgeons will refuse a tot on a chilly night.

Bread

Wholemeal or rye bread is nutritious and can be included as part of a dog's diet, rather than the more expensive biscuits. Most Greyhound kennels use loaves and loaves of returned baker's bread when they can get it. White bread, of course, is not only not nutritious (the richer but darker part of the grain having been removed), but may be bleached with chemicals, one of which has been known to cause a condition called canine hysteria. The amount of bread that can be fed is largely determined by the amount of activity. A racing Greyhound can take a loaf and more and utilize it properly, but half a slice is enough for an old Cocker who prefers to lie by the fire.

Briard

One evening in the swinging sixties there came into my surgery on the King's Road a distraught couple and a big shaggy black bitch showing the unmistakable signs of labour. 'She's a strong looking kind of sheep dog,' I thought to myself. 'She'll slide them out like melted butter.' Which she did. But she took the whole night to produce the dozen. The following morning I was informed that my sleepless night would go down in history. That was the first litter of Briards born in Britain. In their native France they are an ancient, respected breed used not only for sheep herding but for police and army work. They are popular in America where some people call them 'fun dogs'. Others say they are one of nature's jokes. I will admit prejudice but I find these large shaggys full of character, sensible and responsive. I would humbly suggest that if you can only spare your pet one pat a day and an occasional stroll, budgies are going cheap cheap.

Bronchitis

The owner usually complains that his pet is retching as if he has a bone in his throat. Bronchitis is usually part of a wider disease picture, and we usually treat it with antibiotics and also usually warn that it may be some days or weeks before the virus or bacterium has wreaked all its havoc. If your veterinary surgeon requests daily visits he does so to keep the antibiotics circulating in the body at a fairly constant level – and he will usually insist on two injections *after* you think the animal is better. Nursing consists of keeping the animal dry and warm (but not over-heated) and out of draughts, and nourishing it with small easily digested meals. A cough syrup may be prescribed and this is usually best given between meals and last thing at night. A codeine will often relax a feverish animal and allow it proper rest. Please don't use any pills unless you ask the attending surgeon. They may simply negate the ones he's using. Some Poodles, particularly white ones (and, of course, I'm talking about the miniatures and toys), seem to get attacks throughout their lives. If yours is one never let him get wet without drying him properly, and don't allow him to stand with his head out of the car window.

Bruises

Of course, the poor dears bruise just like you and me, even if you can't see it under all that hair. In puppies they're soon healed, but in the middle-aged, warm to hot water compress applications will relieve the pain and hasten healing.

Brush, brushing

The stiffer the tufts the better; and best of all are those plastic sorts which are cheap, washable and don't scratch. Use this for the initial clean through and then a softer brush for the final rub down. Brush gently lest you pull out too many living hairs with the dead ones. Professional groomers and breeders advise never to brush against the lie of the hair especially in wire-haired dogs, but a bit of a 'circulation raiser' doesn't hurt. Long-haired and wire-haired animals should be groomed daily. Two or three minutes is all it need take, except in really hairy beasts like Pekinese or Old English Sheepdogs. Short-haired dogs should be groomed weekly, or only fortnightly if they are clean.

PS: An extremely useful and vastly underrated grooming aid for thick-coated animals like Alsatians and Persian cats is a rake comb. It looks like a small version of an ordinary garden rake but has two parallel sets of teeth. Surprisingly difficult to find in the shops, they are well worth the search. Unlike ordinary combs they don't glide over the surface of the coat. They get right down to the dead hairs in the undercoat.

PPS: Countless thousands of dogs live happy, long lives without ever feeling a comb or a brush. Don't ask me to share a bed with one.

Bulldog

This symbol of British tenacity was used for bull baiting some five hundred years ago. Most authorities are agreed that it was developed from the Mastiff. Over the past hundred years it has developed into the type that we see today. I know that I'm calling down the ire of all lovers of the breed when I say that most of the specimens I've seen are incapable of walking or breathing without difficulty. I should think that few of today's Bulldogs could master a calf, let alone a 'game' bull. They are lovable, kindly beasts, and one cannot but help be attracted by their displays of affection. For this reason it's all the more necessary to deplore standards that almost ensure chronic respiratory trouble, lameness, eye trouble and Caesarean sections. Regretfully I would advise you not to get one unless you're absolutely obsessed with the idea. Before you breeders start complaining, may I say that if you produce a pup that can live a healthy, normal life I'll be first in line for one.

PS: All these years later I'm still standing at the front of the queue.

Bullmastiff

Developed from the Mastiff and the Bulldog. This 54kg (120 lb) rectangular block of muscle is responsive to training and can be as gentle as it is strong. If you can afford to keep one I know of nothing against the breed. Pay particular attention to training. An untrained Bullmastiff can kill you. As with all large breeds they must not be allowed free rein for their appetites, or else you will own a monster.

Bull Terrier

Developed about one hundred and fifty years ago from the Bulldog and the Terrier. They are certainly a more normal beast than the former and they have some of the speed of the latter. Bull Terriers may be either coloured or white. The white offspring of the coloured should not be mated with pure whites if you are interested in pure white offspring (pure white being double recessive for white). White Bull Terriers are often born deaf. There is no cure. One can only use superlatives to describe the musculature and strength displayed by the breed. It is combined with a wonderfully docile disposition, a fondness for children, and when aroused a real ferocity. We too often hear reports of Bull Terriers going beserk and killing four or five dogs and cats in as many minutes, but fortunately this is limited to a few strains. Any dog that displays this unpredictability should be put down, but if you can't bring yourself to the decision please don't breed from such an animal. Highly recommended.

Burns

If possible give an aspirin or a codeine as first aid. The commonest burns occur on the pads as the animal walks or is chased over hot ashes or cinders. If the surface is unbroken or blistered, cover it with a dry, clean pad and bandage the whole foot. If the surface is broken use any soothing ointment and bandage the foot. The second most common burns are scalds on the back caused by spilling hot water or food as the animal gets underfoot near the stove. Apply a many-tailed bandage – but tied underneath. Remember that symptoms usually take days to show. Use a soothing ointment if the skin is broken, but only dry gauze if it is blistered or entire. We see many burns caused by cigar ash dropped in the eye, particularly in breeds with pro-tuberant eyes like the Pekinese. If you have a soothing ophthalmic ointment or even just penicillin ointment, squeeze some over the surface of the eye.

If there is ash in the eye wash it first with cool saline (teaspoonful of salt to 6dl (1 pt) of water and boiled) then apply ointment. Then phone your veterinary surgeon and describe the mess, and he'll tell you when he wants to see it. A final word: most scalds don't blister for three to six days and don't heal for weeks.

If the burns are extensive and severe, or if there is a great deal of pain, phone the police, who will help you to the nearest veterinary surgeon on duty. Be careful. Any animal in pain will bite. Meanwhile, give aspirin or codeine (the former is still one of the effective anal-gesics), bandage loosely with dry clean strips of any available material.

How do we treat burns today? Usually by a long series of injections of penicillin and one of the steroids in carefully graduated doses. We

41

dress daily with dry sterile bandages, and later use ointment when the new skin is forming (see *Bandaging*).

PS: Minor burns may be extremely painful. During those moments of blind panic even the smallest dog will react to your well-meaning ministrations with teeth. Protect yourself by wrapping the patient in a blanket or by wearing protective gloves. Many well-meaning people get taken to the emergency ward of a hospital after they've taken their burned pet to the vet.

Bursitis

Inflammation of the lining of the joint. Fairly common, especially around the elbows and hocks. The only effective first aid is rest. Later your vet will ask you to bathe or poultice the joint and will tell you whether to use hot or cold (depending on whether it's inflamed or not). Larger dogs and stoic cats can be bathed by standing the affected limb in a pot, but usually one is best advised just to hold cloths against the joint.

PS: Massive breeds like Great Danes may develop huge swellings around the joints which have to be surgically removed. Prevention consists of providing an ample soft bed, so no matter how hard they slump into a resting posture they don't injure those ill-protected areas behind the elbows and hocks.

Caesarean Section

This operation is common today because:

1 the heavier accident rate with better animal hospital facilities means that there are more recovered pelvis-fracture bitches about, and many pelvis fractures usually make normal delivery impossible;

2 many bitches, particularly inbred toys and miniatures, simply don't have the strength for normal delivery;

3 like ourselves our dogs are exercising less, and so losing their normal muscle tone;

4 some breeds with heavy shoulders and narrow hips (like the Boston Bull, the English Bull, even the Pekinese) produce puppies whose forequarters are larger than the narrow pelvic passage of the mother;

5 with the improvement in veterinary surgical techniques many vets would rather operate early on than take the chance of a complicated forceps delivery.

What should you do to help your bitch? Inform your veterinary surgeon at least a fortnight ahead of the impending event. He may request an examination, or may merely ask you to keep in touch. In any event use your head, and if your bitch shows any signs of labour about five o'clock in the afternoon, don't wait until midnight to get into a panic. Veterinarians aren't lazy types as a rule and they'll work around the clock, but few surgeons will undertake a serious operation on their own. Two assistants are the minimum I would consider – one to watch the anaesthetic and one to look after the puppies as they are taken out of the uterus. I don't know of any veterinary establishment that keeps a full surgical team on duty around the clock. Most have teams who can be called out at an hour or two's notice. Do all you can to give them every chance of getting there in time. After the operation the bitch may be sent home in a matter of hours, but three or four days is more usual. Don't worry about the odd swelling around a stitch, but if the bitch is uncomfortable take her in for a visit. If your bitch has had two caesareans I would suggest that your veterinarian's advice regarding spaying (ovario-hysterectomy) be followed. You have travelled a long road from animal lover to businessman if you insist that your prize winner should produce yet one more litter.

Cairn Terrier

A small Terrier that originated in the west of Scotland and its islands. It was originally a ratter and has lost none of its spirit, despite the fact that it became rather fashionable in the 1930s when some of the Royal Family kept a few. It may be any colour except white. Whether colour is the reason or not I cannot say, but we see fewer neurotic Cairns than we do West Highland Whites. The latter is a derivative of the Cairn developed by selective breeding for the colour white. It's a small breed that doesn't leave hair all over the furniture, and so makes an acceptable flatmate. All the same one shouldn't forget that they've got a lot of energy to work off and that's best done out of doors.

Calcium

Along with phosphorus and vitamin D, it's necessary for proper bone formation. Growing youngsters and pregnant or nursing females need lots of it. The best natural source, of course, is milk, and after that bonemeal. Remember too that many adult animals simply will not touch milk. If your pet is living on an almost purely meat diet you must add the odd teaspoon of bonemeal.

Callus

You know. Like the things grandfather had on his hands. They are fairly common on elbows and hocks of overweight animals. Check the bed for any hard edges. If your guard dog is asked to travel constantly in the back of a lorry, provide a thick blanket. Generally we don't advise treatment of calluses unless they are painful or growing.

Cancer

The cells of a part of the body go mad and multiply without pattern. There are as many sorts of cancer as there are types of tissue in the body. One may see blood, bone, muscle, fat or lymph gland tumours, and various combinations. We try to divide tumours into benign and malignant sorts. The former are usually localized, slow growing and are either easily removed or are not likely to cause pain or death. The latter are usually more widespread, fast growing, and either inoperable or are likely to cause pain, malfunction and death. However, cancer follows no rules that we know, and a benign tumour may become malignant. I suppose the commonest cancer we see is that of the breast in the female dog. We used to consider it a benign tumour. But increasingly we see an apparently recovered bitch one or two years after the initial operation on the breast, who is having difficulty in breathing. We X-ray and listen to the chest and diagnose lung cancer, for which there is no cure. The benign breast tumour has become malignant. Similarly, we are always adding to our store of knowledge about other tumours. Both veterinarians and their colleagues who practise medicine on the human are getting better at diagnosing, classifying and operating on cancer, but the real answers still lie in the research laboratories. Maybe the anti-vivisectionists can tell us how to find a cure without research? With the present state of our knowledge I can only advise as follows.

Any growth or swelling should be seen by your veterinarian within a few days of your noticing it. Many can be easily excised in the early stages, but delay invariably complicates the picture. If the diagnosis is one of inoperable malignant cancer and you are terribly upset, ask the surgeon if he can hospitalize your pet for a day or two while you consider the best course to follow. Many people on hearing the diagnosis make a hasty decision for euthanasia (usually the wise one), but then afterwards they have regrets and feel they may have acted without due consideration. For your own peace of mind do take that extra day or two. Most early cancers are uncomfortable rather than painful, and even that discomfort can be controlled by drugs. Later on it's simply not fair to yourself or the animal to let it linger on. If you're in doubt about the diagnosis, don't hesitate to tell your veterinarian you want a second opinion. He will either recommend a colleague who has made a speciality of the condition, or he may give you a letter stating his findings and allowing a colleague to give his opinion. No veterinary surgeon will take over a case without permission of the first surgeon. The reason is a humane one – to eliminate needless repetition of what may be painful or uncomfortable examinations, but also because medicine is not an exact science like mathematics. There may be valid differences of interpretation of symptoms shown. The layman is all too likely to condemn one of the surgeons involved or, if he is distressed about the fatal prognosis, to blame the disease itself on the profession.

Canker

A common term wrongly used to describe a multitude of ear troubles. It is not, as the patent drug vendors would have you believe, a specific disease for which there is a specific cure. An ear, like any other organ, may be inflamed and infected. It may contain an abscess, an ulcer or a foreign body like an awn of grass. It may (as in the case of most Miniature Poodles) contain matted hair which traps infection in the ear. Obviously pouring 'canker' powders or pills or ointments down the ear without first finding out the cause is not only a waste of time but postpones proper treatment, so that an acute condition becomes chronic. The only home treatment for any ear condition that is not fraught with danger is as follows. Gently trim the hair off the external ear. Gently pluck the easily seen dead hairs emerging from the ear canal. Pour lots of warmed olive oil or liquid paraffin down the ear. Do not attempt any poking in the ear itself. Wipe off the surplus oil. Pour in more oil which will float the dirt out. If the animal is in pain give it an aspirin, and make an appointment with the veterinary surgeon.

Summary: Don't use powders or pills under any circumstances. Don't poke into the ear. Use oil generously. If it persists or is painful see the vet (see also *Ears*).

Cannibalism

One of the natural instincts and a real problem for the bird breeder, but seen fairly often in the canine and feline worlds. The strong members of a litter will sometimes destroy a weaker brother or sister, and if one of the litter has an open wound they will nibble at it until stopped. A wounded animal will occasionally eat its own flesh surrounding a wound. Obviously one must isolate weak or torn animals and dress the open flesh.

Castration (*neutering*)

Usually refers to the removal of the testicles of the male animal, but may be used to describe the removal of the ovaries of the female.

Castration of the tom cat is usually a simple straightforward operation and most people think that castration of the dog is equally safe. Actually castration of the dog is a difficult and dangerous business because the sac containing the testicles is absolutely lined with blood vessels that seem to bleed and bleed and bleed despite ligatures and cautery. Occasionally we are presented with a dog who as a result of a fight or an accident has a gaping bleeding hole in his scrotum. After some minutes or hours one controls the haemorrhage. When the animal wakes from the anaesthetic the first rough movement may set it off bleeding again.

I am not trying to say that castration of the dog is an impossible operation – just that it's one that requires care and skill.

When do we advise it? Seldom in the normal dog because most dogs can control their sexual drive (or have it controlled by man's training) so that they are still primarily interested in being their master's dog. But some overcharged individuals just stop at home long enough to rest and eat between sexual forays. If hormone injections don't work the only cure is castration.

A dog with a tumour on its testicle must undergo the operation. Many ageing dogs develop incurable prostate conditions. Castration often helps.

Finally, in some monorchids (where only one testicle has descended) your vet may recommend removal of both the descended one and the one that is still trapped up above.

PS: Randy dogs are often effectively curbed, without side-effects, by the same pill that is used for birth control in bitches.

Catalon Sheepdog

An all-purpose working dog, widely distributed throughout Spain. There are both long- and short-haired varieties. There is also a Catalonian Sheepdog common only in the Province of Catalonia. I have met Spanish shepherds in Utah and in Alberta, but I've never seen either a Catalon or a Catalonian Sheepdog in Britain or America.

Cheese

Strong smelling cheese will sometimes tempt ill animals and start them eating again. It should be tried in flu or catarrh cases where the sense of smell is impaired. You see dogs enjoy their food as much if not more through the sense of smell than the sense of taste.

Chesapeake Bay Retriever

An American breed, not nearly well enough known in Britain. It was developed over a century ago by crossing Newfoundlands with Otterhounds.

It stands a little over 60cm (2 ft), weighs 32kg (70 lb) or more, is a sort of dark red colour and has a short, hard but wavy coat that is almost as water-repellent as the new synthetics. The pads of the toes are joined, giving the feet a webbed effect.

If you like their appearance (some people are put off by their orangey-yellow eyes) don't hesitate. He won't miss many ducks during the season, and the rest of the year he'll look after the kids as well as any other breed.

Chewing-gum

Children will stick their gum on their pets, and in the most awkward places. Dogs will often pick the stuff up between their toes. Don't panic! Let it dry for a few hours and then it can be picked off easily. However, if it's attached to the eyelids and is driving the animal to distraction you had better phone a veterinary surgeon. Often a general anaesthetic is necessary to get it off safely.

Chihuahua

Sometimes called the Mexican Hairless, but the latter is in fact a distinct breed and weighs over 13kg (30 lb). The Chihuahua is a fine-haired breed that the fanciers have kept under 3kg (6 lb). There is also a long-haired sort. These tiny, usually over-pampered lap dogs are the descendants of a breed that still exists in the Indian villages of Central America. There they survive on a sparse diet of corn, coconut and whatever they can steal or catch. I know you don't believe it but I've seen packs of fifty to a hundred of those village Chihuahuas (skinnier, mangier, slightly taller and, of course, much tougher versions of Aunt Martha's neurotic beneficiary) hunting wild pig or peccary in the forests of British Honduras, and not one that wasn't eager to get his fang in first. I don't think civilization's version would survive a retransplantation, but it could certainly stand a lot less nervous petting and solicitous overfeeding. Of the lap breeds, this and the Pekinese are my favourite. One doesn't seem to run into many yappy Chihuahuas, but that's an opinion not a fact. But now for an unpleasant fact or two that are facts and not opinions: The kneecap or patella of about every third Chihuahua I've seen in the last few years has been one of the slipping sort. Several have had both kneecaps out. We are beginning to see many with hip joints that don't function, and too many with nervous tummies. Maybe it's time for an admixture of the real hardy Central American type. But certainly shows should eliminate all those with joint problems. How are they going to do it if they retain the present show standards? I simply don't know. The show standard actually states that, where two dogs are otherwise equal, the prize should be given to the smaller. Remember we are talking about a breed that weighs in for the championship fight of the show world at 3kg (6 lb) or under. It sounds even better in the original, and I quote:'*Weight.* 1–3kg (2–6 lb) with 1–2 (2–4) preferable. If two dogs are equally good in type, the more diminutive is preferred.'

The British, American and Continental standards all agree on this. Now, I ask you, how in the name of common sense can a creature that has been shrunk in a few short generations to a third of its forebears' size be superior to its cousin who hasn't been shrunk? Before you breeders rise up in wrath may I ask you how many of your 3kg (6 lb) bitches require Caesareans, and how many weighing 2kg (4 lb) have had normal deliveries?

How many of the teeny weeny ones have knee joints that actually work? How many have hip troubles? And do you have one dog weighing 1·5kg (3 lb) that doesn't have to have its eyes bathed every day? I'm sure that normal 1kg (2 lb) Chihuahuas exist. I just haven't seen them. But I do see people – just average people without any interest in the show world – who are terribly distressed because their pet can't live a normal healthy life.

One can't tell them to exchange their wee bundle of trouble for a slightly larger bundle of less trouble. They're already attached to the poor creature – wonky knees, painful hips and all – so we do our best to correct the faults and allow a semblance of normal life. But I do advise anyone about to buy to get the largest Chihuahua they can, and I do wish the breeders would consider saving their breed by following the same advice.

PS: In Malta I met people who swore by their ancestors' souls that the Chihuahua was well known on their island centuries before

Columbus sailed into the unknown. And sure enough there are ancient frescoes which contain remarkable likenesses to the modern breed. There are also a lot of good, living specimens of the breed. I don't know if that proves anything about its origins, but for me it certainly reinforces my ideas about their hardiness. Any creature that can survive Maltese cooking can't be bad.

Children

Puppies and young dogs are quite undependable and should never be left alone with toddlers. A child may start a game and the young animal doesn't know where to stop. Some ugly accidents can happen. Adult animals vary greatly according to breed, and even within normally dependable breeds there are individuals who never can be trusted. One of the breeds known for their gentleness with children is the St Bernard, but I knew one that had been kept chained and developed into a vicious brute. Generally speaking the larger the dog the better it is with children. Lap dogs and miniatures vary greatly. The only sure guide is the dog itself, and you can only assess its character and its love for the children after two or three months of observing its behaviour with them. Pregnant and nursing bitches should not be left to be molested by the kids. They can be erratic.

Children can learn much from animals if a common-sense approach is used. An older child should be made to feed and groom his pet. He can learn the value of regularity and training. The relationship between the dog or cat and a child is something quite special, however, and without being mundane or sentimental I believe it transcends any sort of every-day listing of practical values. Often a child will confide in a pet when he or she will talk out their problems to no one else, and the psychologists tell us this is a healthy relationship. When adults persist in this relationship we're told it's not such a healthy thing, but who the hell else can many lonely older people talk to?

A child should be expected to feed his own pet (although you should choose or buy the food), keep its water bowl changed, clean both its bowls daily, air the bedding and take it for regular exercise. He should train it to heel and come on command, and pause at crossings.

Many children grow up with a fear of animals which they get from their parents' attitude or warnings. The common-sense approach is to tell your child that animals not on a lead are not to be approached, and those on a lead may be approached and patted after getting their owners' permission.

PS: In the same way as children should be kept away from some animals, so should animals be protected from some children. Many a fracture has been caused by a drop from a child's uncertain grip. Car accidents and serious dog fights can occur when too young a child is allowed to take pets for a walk. Some children can and do tie elastic bands or cord around appendages of animals. Some children paint their pets! Some tease them unmercifully. Not unnaturally the dog reacts by becoming neurotic or nasty.

I can bear witness to the following. A chap has a compound in south London in which he stores forty taxis. It is surrounded by a twelve foot fence. Inside an Alsatian patrols at night. A twelve year old boy climbed the fence and was set upon by the dog. Despite the owner's early intervention the lad was badly mauled and had to spend six weeks in hospital. On his release he obtained an iron bar and climbed the fence. The dog set upon him but the owner was quickly there and no serious damage was done. Nevertheless, as it was the second attack, the magistrates ordered the dog's destruction.

Chow Chow

This black-tongued Chinese edible dog is a rugged individual who will give all his devotion to one owner and be disdainful or downright dangerous to anyone else. In addition to the long-haired sort that we usually see, there is a smooth-coated variety. The former require proper grooming if skin conditions are to be avoided. We see the odd Chow whose owners have never bothered looking beneath the coat, and who have the most dreadfully inflamed anal glands. Train your Chow from a puppy to allow regular inspections. The face that Chow fanciers like is almost designed to produce entropion (inturned eye lids), but fortunately in Britain many breeders are aware of the problem. If you are a strong dominant personality you would enjoy owning a Chow.

PS: I took my own advice and got one. Like our cats she obeys us – when she feels like it. Unlike our cats she sleeps outside beside the bedroom window no matter what the weather. On occasion she has to dig herself out of the snow in the morning. She never barks by day but guards well at night. Many visitors are terrified by her. They claim, 'Their bites are fatal. That's why they have black tongues.'

We took our two children and two neighbour's kids to a chow show. We told them to look but not touch. A while later and each kid had chosen a favourite to cuddle up with in the show pen. The kids survived. The dogs caught fleas.

PPS: One of the reasons Chow breeders are so aware of congenital deformities is that a formidable veterinary surgeon who engenders not only the respect but the awe of her fellow vets breeds these oriental enigmas. Every vet and every Chow breeder will know who I mean. Long may her enthusiasm and intellect reign.

Christmas

Give it a little thought and you'll realize spring is a better time to introduce a new puppy to your home. Nature thinks so too.

Claws

Nursing puppies should have the points of the claws trimmed off if they are scratching the mother. Puppies' dew-claws should be removed (by a veterinarian, please, if you don't want a mess) when they are but a few days old.

Dogs who get a lot of exercise may never need their claws trimmed. However, it's best to check periodically and see that they're not getting too long. Sometimes they'll wear unevenly and the odd claw that is longer is liable to get cracked or broken off.

A well-trimmed claw should just touch the ground when the pads of the toes are flat. It's difficult to tell exactly where to cut, but practice soon makes perfect.

The one thing you must never do, because it's painful and cruel, is cut into the quick of the claw – the upper portion which contains the blood vessels and nerves. With light-coloured claws it's easy to tell, but with dark claws, like the ones Scotties are blessed with, you must judge the position of the quick. Your veterinary surgeon will be happy to show you how.

A broken or cracked claw can be as painful as a broken fingernail. As the dog puts weight on the foot he winces with the pain. First aid consists of smearing it with a soothing jelly or paraffin, placing cotton padding between the toes and bandaging the whole foot.

Some dogs will chew at their claws as some people chew their fingernails, and for the same neurotic reasons. Boredom is a prime cause. A tired dog is more likely to sleep than one who has been alone in a flat all day. You can try breaking the habit by bandaging the foot for a day or two, but you had better consider whether the two of you wouldn't be better off with a few longer walks each day.

Cleft palate

Check the mouths of new-born puppies who by their cries indicate they are not able to nurse. The palate may not have closed, and with the aid of a light you'll be able to see the space.

They may be fed with the aid of a medicine dropper until the vet can arrange to operate and close the gap. However, there is evidence that the condition is hereditary. Usually euthanasia is advised.

Clipper rash

Usually caused by bruising or clipping too close, but some dogs with sensitive skins will redden up into sores no matter what. Usually treated with calamine lotions and one of the antihistamine-cum-sedative preparations. If it happens to your dog I'd take it along to the veterinarian, and report his findings to the clipping people. If they are having a spate of complaints they may find that one of the girls is forgetting to wash the clippers between dogs or, a more common occurrence these days, she's just lost all interest in the job and isn't taking proper care.

Clipping

Trimming, manicuring, styling, etc. Poodles, wire-hairs and others, attend the fashion parlours every month or two to get clipped and bathed. It's really quite simple, and I'm surprised more people don't do it themselves. There are only two or three companies that make the clippers, and one (American, naturally) almost has the field to itself. Any supply house will tell you its name. The clippers have interchangeable heads with fine, medium and coarse blades.

The animal is first combed out to make the hair stand out and remove any mats. Then the coarse head is run over the body to reduce the hair uniformly. Then use the medium to cut down the hair over the loins or ankles or whatever your neighbourhood thinks is in fashion. Finally, the fine head is used around the head and neck and tail and whatever other bits you and your neighbours (you should have gathered a fine crowd by now) think should come off.

Another combing, a brushing, a final combing to pat the mistakes in place, and the job is finished.

Usually the animal is bathed after the clipping, and then dried and combed.

Mistakes on white or grey dogs can and are covered with powder. On the blacks they usually don't show so badly.

If you are sending your wee precious out for his beauty treatment remember that it is beauty not treatment. It's not like a five-thousand mile check up on a car. They are giving him a hair cut – no more, no less. I say this because we are presented daily with pets with widely varying complaints – right from eczema through to dislocated hips – and the owner can't understand it because 'Mitzi was only clipped last week.' It's probably a carry-over from the days when barbers did surgery to fill in the hairless hours.

Highly nervous dogs are usually best clipped at a veterinary establishment that has a clipping service. It's not a primary source of income and they can dally longer. Too, proper sedatives can be used if necessary.

Wire-haired dogs like Airedales and its smaller cousins should be plucked not clipped. It's an art, not a science, and ten minutes of watching an expert will teach you more than any book.

Club Row and Petticoat Lane

The market in the East End of London that sells puppies and kittens and birds and other living creatures along with the rest of the merchandise. I'm sure there must be honest dealers down there, or else why would the public (and more than a few from the West End) find their way down there week after week? Unfortunately I've never seen a puppy from Club Row that wasn't suffering from malnutrition, parasites or distemper or all three. It's quite understandable when you realize that many of the puppies are taken away too early from their mothers, given indifferent food and thrown in with all sorts of other puppies. Their resistance is low and just one ill puppy can infect the lot.

Aside from the tragedy of these suffering puppies (who must undergo an average of a month's treatment with every chance of permanent damage even if they do recover) the whole operation at Club Row must be seen as a testimonial to salesmanship.

Those polyglot puppies of indeterminate ancestry emerge as champions of every breed known and unknown. I've had a great 60cm (2 ft) high ball of fluff with feet the size of saucers stuck on the table with the confident assertion that it was a Manchester Terrier. Anything with a patch over one side of its face is a 'Jack Russell'. I've been asked to examine Chinese Terriers, London Lancers and London Lungers, Ceylon Spaniels and Cornish Corgis, all of whom looked as if they had the same busy father.

One doesn't mind the gullible people and the super salesmen. No real harm is done. But I do wish the puppies could be spared that diseased beginning.

PS: Tradition dies hard in England. Several dog generations have gone by. The only difference at Club Row now is that the proprietors have moved to the salubrious suburbs.

Clumber Spaniel

He's sort of a giant Spaniel, eminently trainable, not as fawning as most Spaniels, but his size makes him cumbersome in the field and not in demand as a pet, so there are few about. If you're fond of Spaniels but can't lay your hands on a sane Cocker or a handleable Springer and find the King Charles just too precious you might try finding a Clumber breeder. They average about 27kg (60 lb), are white with citrus-coloured markings, and are inclined to run to fat when they're retired from work.

PS: One midnight a few years ago Betty Tay of the *Daily Mirror* phoned me to meet her at Euston Station. There was a shipment of dogs going to a laboratory in Scotland. Eleven were nondescript. One was a Clumber Spaniel. Portraits of each appeared on the front page of the paper that morning. No one came forward to claim the mongrels, although several anonymous callers phoned to say they had left their pet at the 'kennel' with the firm understanding that it was to be 're-homed'. Some had actually paid a fee. Such is the rarity of the Clumber that it was immediately identified by several breeders. Although the person who had decided to get rid of him never had the nerve to contact us, we had no difficulty finding an enthusiast who wanted him. May I add that he was particularly nasty (who wouldn't be in those circumstances?), but I wouldn't judge by that. It's the only one I've ever seen outside a dog show.

Cocker Spaniel

Who today is breeding those wonderful cockers we used to see? They were affectionate and cuddly in the home and absolute masters of the outdoors; they were tractable and trainable and lived long healthy lives. I wish someone would tell me because all I see today are wee neurotics with eye troubles and ear troubles and feet troubles and skin troubles. Many are snappy. Most are shy and nervous. When a friend tells me he's thinking of getting a Cocker for the family I shudder – not as violently as when they say they're getting a Miniature Poodle – but it's a good unhealthy shudder all the same. Fortunately though even the public – the long-suffering public – are waking up, and one doesn't see so many Cockers about any more. As the numbers decline the strictly commercial breeders will be culled out, and we may then begin to see the Cocker re-emerge as something approaching a physiological whole.

Codeine

$\frac{1}{4}$–$\frac{1}{2}$ a tablet for wee toys, $\frac{1}{2}$–1 tablet for miniatures, 1 for middle-sized breeds and 2 for the Alsatians and Labs will lessen pain while waiting for professional advice.

Collapse

An ill animal that is out flat and breathing in short, shallow gasps may sometimes be kept alive until the vet comes, by keeping it warm. Use hot water bottles. Don't pour brandy or anything down its throat. Make sure the hot water bottles are well insulated or you will burn the animal.

Collars

Dogs should be collared when they are still puppies. The collar stays on during training and walks. The collar shouldn't be so wide that it rubs or so narrow that it cuts. Leather properly cared for is better than plastic. Toys and neckless creatures are better with harness. All should be saddle-soaped weekly.

Choke collars are necessary training aids for some of the larger breeds. The chain should be wide and flat. A narrow choke collar is cruel because it cuts.

The clip of the collar to which you attach the chain should have its opening at the side, not at the end. In that way the strain of the lead isn't likely to weaken it.

PS: The clip should not be of the sprung-steel spring sort. They can and do get caught in noses, ears and all sorts of unlikely places. We often have to anaesthetize the animal to get the things off. Get the sort with a wee bolt that slides back and forth.

Collie

Everyone knows them, and if you know animals at all you must like them. They are an ideal size, gloriously coloured, and as intelligent, trainable and responsive as a dog can be. The *only* dogs that so far have been trained to be guide dogs for blind *children* are a variety of the smooth-haired Collie. From this exacting test of loyalty, intelligence and reliability down to the level of the everyday family pet the Collie has no peer. Naturally they vary a great deal. There are dozens of types and varieties, but your chances of getting a good, healthy, intelligent specimen are as good with the Collie as with any of the other popular breeds. I have seen a few, very long in the head, who were complete imbeciles. Lots of vets will bear me out when I say that the long narrow head has reduced the brain capacity of some fashionable varieties. If you live in town or if the dog is going to spend most of his time indoors choose the smooth-haired Collie. The long-haired sort, when confined or allowed to become overweight, gets skin complaints that can drive him, his owner and the vet to drink. The only advice I can offer you, if you are a lazy type with a long-haired Collie, is to train him from an early age to accept the brush and comb, and nag your wife or children to groom him every day.

PS: The old fashioned black and white collie variously known as the Border Collie or the Welsh Collie or just 'the farm dog' is possibly the most underrated dog anywhere. Like the Russians and Chinese, most don't bother with beauty contests. However, as one amateur enthusiast (a coal miner) told me, 'Give me ten Alsatians and I'll produce one obedience champion. Give me ten Collies and I'll guarantee nine.'

One word of warning: they can be suspicious of strangers and, being canny creatures, may bide their time until you are momentarily distracted. The worse bite I ever received was inflicted by a Border Collie. A further word of warning for those who place undue trust in appliances: he was wearing a muzzle at the time. It just made it more difficult to pry his jaws apart.

Colour

No horse is a bad colour.

You hear it at every auction, and I suppose the reason they say it is because our prejudices or preferences are so ingrained that we will pay more for a beautifully coloured and well marked horse than for a superior horse whose colour or markings don't appeal to us. Personally I believe we should be allowed our colour prejudices. There are only two dangers. The first is that if you select exclusively or primarily for a particular colour you are quite likely to be less selective about other qualities. For example, some breeders of Great Danes are so concerned about producing Harlequins that temperament and conformation are just afterthoughts. After one has seen yet another beautiful but impossible Harlequin one begins to develop colour prejudice.

The second danger is that if a new racist were to try to improve the human race by deductions based on animal breeding the Europeans would just have to go. White-headed cattle have their own funny eye diseases. White Bull Terriers are often deaf. So are many white cats. Some white Alsatians get the most incurable complaints, or so it seems to some of us who have tried to treat them. The clincher, of course, would be the white Miniature Poodle. After studying them there could be no survival for the whites.

Actually the only breed of dogs in which white is dominant genetically is the Samoyeds. In the Collie white and blue is dominant to tricolour. In all other breeds nature prefers the darker colours, but man has imposed his preference and often this hasn't done the breed any good.

Conjunctivitis

Inflammation of the membranes of the eye lids. It may be a localized condition affecting only one eye or both eyes, or it may be a symptom of a generalized illness. Home aid consists of bathing with salt water (a teaspoon of salt in 6dl (1 pt) of water, boil and allow to cool). Keep the animal in subdued light. If the condition doesn't clear up in a day consult your vet (see also *Eyes*).

Constipation

One of the virtues of advertising is that everyone everywhere knows the meaning of constipation. In the dog it may be caused by:

1 Lack of exercise
2 Bones in the diet
3 An improperly balanced diet
4 Too dry a diet or lack of water
5 Continual dosing with oil or salts or proprietary remedies all of which can destroy the tone of the gut
6 Injuries like a broken pelvis
7 Spinal disc paralysis
8 Any disease of long duration
9 Inflamed anal glands
10 Enlarged prostate gland
11 Lack of grooming of long-haired dogs
12 Neglecting to clean the behinds of recently weaned puppies or to massage the tummies of orphan pups

plus a myriad of other neglects and reasons.

Unfortunately there is no easy way of telling if an animal is

57

constipated. Most laymen seeing an animal straining assume it to be constipated, but in fact it is more likely to be bladder trouble. They pour oil down the animal's throat and wait a few hours for it to work while the animal's bladder fills to the danger point.

An animal with a bone lodged in its rectum will strain. If you can feel it, and if an enema moves it, well and good, but usually an anaesthetic is necessary to relax the animal sufficiently to get the bone out.

So if an animal is straining it is best to get it to the vet, and let him decide why it is straining and what to do about it.

Most constipated animals simply get more and more mopey, and occasionally give a half-hearted strain. An observant owner will know when it last moved its bowels and arrive at the right conclusion.

I think the safest laxative is olive oil – a teaspoonful up to three tablespoonfuls depending on the size. The advantage of olive oil is that it's a natural oil, and the animal can absorb and utilize it. It doesn't just coat the gut as does liquid paraffin, but of course the latter may be used.

The things to avoid are purgatives like castor oil. If there is an obstruction and you use castor oil the bowel may be ruptured as it violently contracts on the obstruction.

Never, never give any vomiting animal any laxative or purgative.

If you are gentle, an enema of warm water may be attempted.

An animal that lacks 'gut tone' (a phrase that makes my sister shudder but she knows what I mean) may be helped by a couple of feeds of raw liver every week.

Generally speaking you look for the cure in the cause, and to prevent the condition you must certainly look to the cause.

Grooming, no bones, lots of exercise, a proper diet, access to fresh water – in short proper husbandry, and there should be no problem. Don't for goodness' sake follow the stupid and cruel advice given out to humans to continually dose themselves with somebody's liver salts.

Nobody including the manufacturer really cares what you do to your own insides, and presumably you should be responsible for what poisons you inflict on yourself, but your dog shouldn't have his guts destroyed just because he trusts you enough to take what you give him.

Convalescence

This is the period of recovery between illness and health. It varies considerably according to the age of the patient, the length and severity of the illness and the general constitution of the patient. A six-months'-old puppy who has a simple fracture of the radius will be completely recovered in a month or less, whereas an older animal may be limping for months and an aged animal may never be completely right. A recovered distemper case may have bouts of invalidism all its life long. The common-sense rules of convalescence are too often overlooked by the general public. If your pet has undergone treatment for a general illness don't for goodness' sake start on those five-mile walks the day he's discharged as cured. The disease or the injury may be medically cured but the body has slowly to regain its strength. Gradually increase the periods of exercise. Avoid the wet and the snow. Use a plastic raincoat if it's summer and a blanket if it's winter. Dry feet immediately on going indoors. Postpone breeding for at least one heat period after a prolonged illness.

Remember too that an animal that has been ill is far more likely to pick up anything else that's going the rounds, so keep him isolated as much as possible. And one more thing. Recovered animals will often have a voracious appetite. Control his diet rigidly and don't give in to those tail wagging entreaties for just another biscuit. Those five extra pounds will be awfully difficult to get off later on.

Cord

Puppies will occasionally play with string or cord, and they'll usually end up swallowing some. When you arrive home you're met by a distressed animal with a bit of material hanging out of its mouth or even out of its anus. Try to identify the material and try to recall whether it was attached to a needle. If it was don't start tugging unless you can dislodge the needle first. Get someone to hold the slobbering beast on a table under a good light. Open its jaws and see if it's just caught around a tooth or balled up between its molars. With a bit of patience you should be able to get it out.

If an end has disappeared down the gullet, and you're quite sure there's no needle attached, then try a gentle pull, with emphasis on the gentle. If it resists then get the animal to a vet. Often an anaesthetic will relax the body enough so that the cord comes out easily, but some will require surgery.

If the cord is dangling from the anus please, please, don't pull it sharply or you may evert the bowel or worse. Cut off all but an inch of it (to prevent the animal tugging at it), pour in lots of olive oil or liquid paraffin (down the throat in case you hadn't guessed), and if it's past midnight go to sleep. If it hasn't passed next morning you had better go down and queue at the vet's.

Corgi

Originally a Welsh cattle herder, it has become a common sight in suburban gardens all over the Commonwealth. I can't remember when I first saw the photograph of the Royal Family showing George VI, the Queen Mother, the Princesses and the Corgis, but that photograph must be unique in the annals of dogdom in that it was followed by the world-wide popularity of a breed that was relatively uncommon before.

If you could get a Corgi from the Queen's kennels you'd have every chance of getting a wonderful dog.

The Corgi at its best is a vigorous, playful, tractable, trainable and affectionate dog, equally at home in a flat or in the field.

Unfortunately I see very few Corgis who even vaguely fit the classification of family pets. Many are snarling imbeciles quite incapable of restraining themselves from biting anything that moves. This is a completely prejudiced view, and I have no statistical studies to bear me out. It's an opinion arrived at after watching dozens of Corgis with average owners who blithely say, 'Watch him. He'll bite. He bit me yesterday when I tried to look at his ear.' And sure enough: you have placed him on a table; you approach him with the usual meaningless but pacifying phrases; whammo! His teeth close where a second before you were.

I had a visit a while back from a fellow veterinarian whose practice included one of the important Corgi breeders in Britain. Over our noontime pints we discussed the breed. He said that from all he could make out the so-called better Corgis were all descended from a very few top dogs, most of whom carried the recessive character for what was best called lunacy. The chances of getting a non-vicious Corgi, he felt, were slim.

I know that breeders and owners of Corgis by the score will call forth the wrath of the gods to destroy me and my opinions. But all their words can't undo the distress of the many people who have bought, in all good faith, what they hoped to be a family pet, and then after a half dozen 'incidents' bring it in to the clinic with the request that it be put to sleep.

There must be as many disillusioned ex-owners of Corgis as of Alsatians – and that's saying a lot.

If you do have a Corgi, and you love him and he loves you, be careful after middle age of letting him jump from heights. The long spine does predispose to spine trouble, and an awkward jump can result in weeks of pain.

Cortisone

A family of drugs that were brought to market with wide publicity a few short years ago. They were going to eliminate arthritis and lots of other diseases from the face of the earth. Cortisone can be a valuable treatment in certain selected cases. Like everyone else, doctors and veterinarians are susceptible to those clever advertisements thought up by those well-tailored bland young men, and as a result we tend to use the drug in cases where simpler medicines might work. For example, many skin conditions will respond to cortisone injections or pills, and often in a most dramatic manner. Why then not use it? First, because it is expensive, and secondly, because cortisone is a strong drug that may have adverse side effects. For example, the manufacturers tell us not to use cortisone in cases that have kidney trouble, but in the middle of a busy clinic, if a client insists that the old conservative treatment isn't having any effect, the temptation is very strong to switch to cortisone. Of course you can't really be sure the animal doesn't have weak kidneys. One might in fact be curing a simple condition and aggravating a very grave one.

I use cortisone as an example, although in fact many drugs are used more because of commercial pressures than scientific rationale. What one does about it I simply do not know. I can't believe the situation would improve if governments took over the drug business. I suppose one approach might be more independent money for the pharmacology departments at the colleges.

What can you do to help? Don't be pressuring your veterinarian into changing the treatment. It's amazing how many people get impatient because Lucius, who has been scratching for three months, doesn't stop twenty-four hours after the first professional visit.

A final word about cortisone used locally in the form of drops or ointments. It can be very effective and it has no side effects. In that form it is really valuable in certain eye and ear conditions. But – don't use up an old tube or bottle if Fifi gets a scratched eye. If there is an ulcer on the eye (a wee eroded spot) the cortisone can actually retard healing. In other words if it's new trouble in the same old eye the same old bottle won't necessarily work, and may actually do harm.

Coryza

One of those words that always crop up in animal and bird books. I'm not quite sure what it means except that it has something to do with runny noses. If a dog and particularly a puppy has a runny nose distemper is one of the possible causes. So if your Victorian landlady diagnoses coryza, you reply that indeed it is but that's just a symptom and the real cause of that particular symptom is probably something else. A plugged and raw nose may be gently bathed with warm water, dried and olive oil applied. It will relieve the discomfort, but if the condition persists into the next day get into the clinic queue.

Cruciate ligament rupture

The cruciate ligaments are tough bands that hold together the two long bones of the hind leg (femur and tibia). They may be ruptured during a car accident, by a bad fall (usually while jumping a fence and getting caught) or by a sharp hard blow. The animal is lame in the affected leg and usually holds it up. X-rays are taken and everything seems normal. Usually the vet will ask to see the animal in a few days, and if it's still lame he will give a general anaesthetic and confirm his suspicions by manipulating the joint. The only remedy is surgical, and it consists of the rather tricky business of getting in there and replacing the ligament that is ruptured with a strand of thick nylon. I give this long explanation of a relatively rare condition because most people are surprised that something that is not a bone fracture requires surgery and that there is no urgency to get the operation done.

Curly Coated Retriever

A beautiful working breed now almost extinct. He's about Labrador size, black or liver in colour and covered in tight taut little curls. I just don't know why the breed has gone right out of fashion because it had a reputation as a superb worker both in the field and the water.

Dachshund

How many owners of 'Daxis' do you know? I find that most of them are indifferent to cool about animals as a whole, but have been introduced to a Dachshund through some friend and have then gone off the deep end. I must admit that 'Daxis' have marvellously ingratiating ways and have no objectionable household characteristics aside from a tendency to bark too much. I would advise against overfeeding. The breed can eat itself into the ground – and I mean just that. It may look cute to see a tummy that scrapes the grass, but the heart will never last beyond eight years. Dachshunds were originally hunting dogs and they require lots of exercise. Do not allow them to jump more than four or five times their height. The outstanding fault of the breed is its long back, and too often we're rung at midnight with a description of acute pain. An X-ray reveals a spinal lesion, and the outlook is four to six weeks of nursing through partial or complete paralysis. The crooked hind legs are, of course, prone to knee displacement. Toy Dachshunds seem to get more than their fair share of tonsilitis, and I believe that we see more diabetes in the Dachshund than their numbers would warrant, but this latter is an opinion based on observation and not a confirmed fact. Oh, one more thing. American veterinarians claim that 'Daxis' are more prone to intestinal obstructions caused by their tendency to chew everything in sight. Despite all these drawbacks I wouldn't hesitate in recommending the breed. People who are interested in the future of the breed should invite (and by that euphemism I mean raise funds) the veterinary profession to set up a research project to study posterior paralysis. It's bound to be a long-term affair, but we simply must tackle the problem on a scientific level.

Dalmatian

Originated in what is now Yugoslavia. White with either liver or black spots. Gets on well with horses and familiar in sporting prints as a coaching dog. If you are house-proud but like a large dog this breed may be the answer as they have less 'doggy' odour than most breeds and are easily kept clean. Some strains are cursed with congenital deafness, and as there is no cure you must make sure your prospective puppy can in fact hear. Dalmatians form their urine differently from any other breeds, and their bladder stones (if they develop them) are unique; but it's nothing to be concerned about in purchasing a puppy, nor can you do anything about it, except rush the animal to the vet if it strains while passing urine.

Dandie Dinmont

A wee Terrier from the border counties, who looks and acts like a grizzled backwoodsman shopping in Tiffanys. He minds his own business and gets what he wants. I'm all for the breed, and I hope that that high-loined back the breeders are so fond of doesn't get pushed up further by selection, else we'll have another breed with spinal trouble. If you want a real individualist you simply must consider the Dandie Dinmont.

Dandruff (*scurf or scales*)

Formed by dead skin cells, and it is usually an indication of some other disease. Animals who live a healthy energetic outdoor life are less prone to scurfy skins. However, if a dog is always shedding those

63

unsightly flakes you can try vigorous brushing which will, of course, remove them but will also massage and so add tone to the skin. Sometimes increasing the fat in the diet will eliminate the condition. Constant bathing will do no good and may even make it worse.

Deafness

For simplicity I'll divide deafness into three sorts. The first, congenital or hereditary as in some strains of white Bull Terriers, we can do nothing about it except by selection. The second sort is the result of an infection. If your pet is persistently going at its ears or holding his head to one side a veterinary examination is certainly indicated (see *Ears*). The third sort comes on gradually in advanced middle age, and as it would be difficult to assess the effect of hearing aids the problem so far is without solution.

Death

It's difficult to tell the exact moment of death. Breathing becomes shallower and stops. The pulse becomes faint and thready and difficult to find. Touching the eye produces no reflex, and the eye itself becomes glassy. The body gradually loses its heat.

Deerhound

An ancient breed evolved from the Greyhound. It is among the most beautiful of all breeds, and lends grace to any country home. I emphasize country because he needs long romps not wee expeditions to the local tobacconist. House manners usually perfect. It stands 75cm (30 in) or more high, weighs up to 45kg (100 lb), and has a long wiry coat.

Dehydration

Loss of the tissue fluids, and the most important cause of death in many conditions. An animal, through continual vomiting or diarrhoea, will lose so much fluid that life cannot be maintained. It takes many days for an animal to starve to death, and we are never concerned in the treatment of an acute condition with food intake, but if the animal is not drinking or is bringing the water up we must replace its fluids with injections (subcutaneous or intravenous) of salt in water or sugar in water.

Demodectic mange (*also called follicular mange*)

One of the two sorts of mange, the other sort being sarcoptic. I believe there is more nonsense talked about mange at the local pet shop than about any other condition, and certainly proper treatment is far too often postponed. You see, some well-meaning chap says, 'Oh, yes, that's mange. Lard and sulphur. Works every time.' The misguided owner proceeds to apply it. Three days later the dog is a mass of sores, so the owner puts more junk on. The condition gets worse. He goes around to the local pet shop who sells him John Smith's Mange Cure, which may have been designed for sarcoptic not demodectic mange, and may in fact be composed of some popular remedy of some forty years back (you can't find out from the label). A week later the poor animal is a complete nervous wreck, because those parts of him that the mites have left alone the medicines have irritated. At this stage we are usually presented with the animal and the following story, 'He was perfectly all right yesterday. Do you think he picked something up in the park?' The only points to this long dissertation are:

1 Diagnosis is necessary before treatment.
2 Wrong treatment irritates and postpones a cure.
3 Often a skin condition will start as mange, but with constant scratching will become something else.
4 Often two or even three medicines are necessary at one and the same time, but they must be chosen for the right reasons.
5 Please don't postpone proper treatment.

Dermatitis

Literally inflammation of the skin. May be caused by fleas, lice, scratching, mange, bacterial infection, harsh soaps or medications, clipping too closely, etc. The only safe first aid is any cooling, soothing lotion like calamine and an aspirin. If you can't determine the cause maybe your veterinarian can.

Dew-claws

Those 'hanging' claws found a little way up the foot. They are vestiges of what was once a useful toe. They may be easily removed by a simple operation when the puppy is a few days old. If your adult dog has them check every two or three months to see if the claw is circling around the flesh. If it is, cut off the point. Does that sound too obvious to be mentioned? I've seen Pekinese, Cockers and Yorkshire Terriers, among others, with dew-claws that had grown around and pushed the points right into the flesh. Strangely enough the owners don't notice the condition unless the dog goes lame or bleeds. We rarely see the condition in short-haired breeds because, I suppose, even thoughtless owners can see the dew-claws without bending too far.

A torn dew-claw should be padded with ointment-soaked cotton wool and bandaged.

Diabetes

Symptoms are ravenous hunger and thirst with loss of weight. Take a fresh sample of urine along to the veterinary surgeon. He will test it for sugar. Dramatic improvement occurs after the first couple of shots of insulin. Some animals recover completely and require no more insulin, but most must have daily injections. After a week or two of adjusting the dosage your vet will show you how to test the urine, and how to gauge the dosage. He will ask you to keep a daily record, and he'll want to see that record and the patient weekly or fortnightly. The only bit of advice your vet may forget (he is a busy man) is about sharpness of needles. If your pet is getting daily injections he will soon learn to hide if those injections are painful. Have a nurse explain to you how to sharpen and test the needle. A properly sharpened needle is almost painless. Don't ask a young nurse how to sharpen a needle. She'll tell you to use disposable ones like she does. If you do, wrap them properly before chucking them in the garbage, or you won't be popular with your dustman.

Did you know that insulin has saved the lives of thousands of people and thousands of dogs? Did you know that insulin was developed at the University of Toronto by experiments (yes, vivisection) upon dogs? Some twenty dogs were operated on and subsequently tested. Without their sacrifice thousands of dogs who are enjoying normal lives would be suffering lingering deaths. Was it worth it? Ask the local anti-vivisectionists. Ask them to treat your diabetic pet without insulin.

PS: There is another sort which is called *diabetes insipidus.* The dog shows many of the same signs but the urine test is negative for sugar. Happily it too can usually be controlled by drugs.

Diarrhoea

Loose bowel motions. There are, of course, various sorts. The stool may be only slightly loose, very loose, water, mucous or even blood filled. Diarrhoea may be caused by unusual food, change of water, bad food, worms, intestinal obstruction, or more commonly it may be the sign of a general infection like distemper or enteritis. The only safe effective first aid is *starvation.* Cut off all food and fluids for twenty-four hours. In the case of young puppies allow only a tablespoonful or two of food every six hours. If the condition persists after twenty-four hours then you must consult a veterinary surgeon. If your pet has bouts of diarrhoea over an extended period you had better examine the diet. Is it too sloppy? Are you washing the bowl between meals as you would your own? Is the meat fresh and refrigerated? Is it half-frozen when served? Most people rush out and buy worm pills, and this is exactly the wrong thing to do. It may in fact accentuate the condition. I repeat – the safe treatment is starvation (any diseased organ wants rest) for twenty-four hours. Then feed only a tablespoon to a cupful of good quality raw chopped meat (depending on the size of your pet). If the condition persists take him along to the vet.

Diarrhoea in a puppy is rather more serious, and I would advise professional treatment at the earliest convenient time.

Diarrhoea accompanied by vomiting is serious too, and should certainly be seen professionally within hours. Feeding an animal, and particularly force feeding a vomiting animal, may cause complications and even death.

No animal is going to die in a day or two or three without food, so please don't let your sympathy overrule common sense. I go on about this because so many owners persist in feeding when we ask them not to.

The second most common failing of pet owners is medicating their pet for a day or two before taking it to the vet's. Surely one should know that treatment without diagnosis is cruel and dangerous.

Diet

It's impossible to cover in a few lines a subject so broad, but one can give the general idea and point out the common mistakes.

Young animals require most care. Before weaning they should have gradually been introduced to lapping milk and semi-solids. There are good enriched milk products on the market made especially for kittens and puppies. One of those products should be fed twice daily, and good quality meat, finely chopped, twice daily. After a few days you'll get the hang of judging the right amounts. Never leave food over from one feeding to the next. After a month or so you can cut down to three meals a day, and at about six months to one large meal and a small breakfast.

An adult only needs one meal a day, but some are happier with a second small one, and there's no reason why they shouldn't have it.

Many adults are starved one day a week and it's not a bad idea, but it only works with confined animals. A wandering animal will just mooch that day's meal off the neighbours, or tip over the garbage pail.

The kind of food depends, of course, on where you are. I have seen Chihuahuas thriving on little else but cooked corn, and Labradors and Newfoundlands on nothing but fish. I have seen healthy Poodles on a diet that was primarily spaghetti and other forms of pasta, and at the time of writing I know a pregnant French Bulldog of impeccable lineage that is looking well on a diet of Spanish paella – olives, garlic and all. She won't eat anything else.

The basic diet for dogs and cats is meat or fish, and to this you may add brown bread, cooked rice, biscuit, vegetables or table left-overs.

The things to avoid are seasonings, small sharp bones and sugar.

Every once in a while some new food fad makes the rounds of pet owners. Fido must have a half-pound of rice, or three tablespoons of beetroot juice, or three of those ubiquitous vitamin pills.

They do no harm and they do no good, but if it makes you happy, and because whatever makes you happy makes Fido happy, your veterinarian is unlikely to object.

The only deficiency you're likely to run into with an all-meat diet is calcium. Many adult dogs won't drink milk, and for such dogs I would suggest a calcium pill once weekly or a bit of bonemeal once in a while.

Many pet owners feed the same tinned food day after day, and although reputable brands are likely to contain all the essential ingredients, it is impossible to know for sure, unless you live in a country like America where the labelling laws require them to tell you. Tinned food is expensive and rather sloppy stuff. I would suggest you keep it by for weekends or emergencies.

The following list may be old hat to most people:

Milk: essential for young, growing, pregnant and lactating animals. Cow's milk is not as 'rich' as that of the dog. Many good fortified brands on the market.

Beef: the staple of many adult diets, and can be stretched out and enriched by adding almost anything.

Horse meat: as good as beef, and usually much cheaper.

Veal: especially valuable in older animals, and those suffering from kidney trouble.

Chicken: also good for kidney patients. Be careful of the bones.

Fish: quite adequate for all protein requirements. Be careful to remove all bones.

Fat of all sorts can be used to add to biscuit and meat and in dogs can constitute up to thirty per cent of the diet as fat is so useful for energy requirements. Pork fat doesn't agree with some animals.

Pork: many animals don't seem to take to it, but if they do there's no reason why it shouldn't be fed.

Tinned foods: expensive and sloppy usually. Useful as a stand-by.

Eggs: valuable protein, and may be used as part of the diet.

Vegetables: almost any vegetable except potato peel is acceptable, and helps to balance the diet.

Liver and entrails: very nutritious and delicious. Must not be used in animals prone to diarrhoea. Liver is useful in animals that are prone to constipation.

Bread: brown bread is a good filler and source of energy.

Rice: the same as bread.

Spaghetti, pasta, etc: the same as bread.

Sweet biscuits: chocolate, etc., in reasonable quantities are acceptable as rewards or treats for active pets, but no good for lap dogs as they're likely not to want anything else.

Tea: fed to dogs nowhere outside of England. The only nutritional qualities are in the milk and sugar. All right for active animals, but will put lap animals off their right meals.

Cheese: nutritious but may be constipating. Sick animals will often be tempted by strong-smelling cheese.

Beer and wine: we all know of some dog that needs his daily pint. If he can keep track of the licensing hours he deserves it.

Dieting

In this affluent era our pets suffer more from overweight than any other single condition. Cut down on the biscuits, the bread, the tea and fats. Make sure the neighbours aren't catering to his begging ways. If all that doesn't help consult your veterinary surgeon.

Digitalis

An ancient drug derived from the foxglove plant that is still the main drug in the heart armoury. It slows and strengthens the beat. The only reason I include it here is because dosage is all-important, and often people think if one pill is good two must be better. In fact two may mean trouble, so follow instructions.

PS: Some canine patients get bouts of nausea after they've taken the drug for several weeks or months. Your vet may advise that you skip it one day a week.

PPS: Cats simply don't tolerate the stuff.

Dislocation

Dislocation of the hip is the commonest, although in fact other joints may become dislocated. Automobile accidents are the commonest cause. They are usually extremely painful, even more so than fractures. The animal walks with the affected leg held up, and will react violently to any manipulation of the limb. If not treated it will become less painful after a few days and may make a false joint. At that stage it is very difficult to correct, and often removal of the head of the long bone is the only cure. If it is diagnosed and treated within twenty hours the chances of complete recovery are good. Many dislocations, however, will pop out again with the first real stress. The ligaments that were stretched during the accident take weeks to regain their tone. So if the beast gets home and jumps out of the car and gives a yelp of pain you had better turn right around and go back to the vet's. He might attempt strapping the limb, but with a really agile dog this doesn't work for long.

I suppose I should mention that I have seen the odd case where the combined efforts of three veterinary surgeons failed to return the hip joint to its socket. In those cases one is forced to leave it alone for some weeks to let the swelling go down and then decide if a piece of the bone should be removed to facilitate the making of a false joint.

The only prevention is keeping your dog on the lead wherever there is traffic about.

Summary: A limping animal should be seen by a veterinarian as soon as convenient.

Disposal

Most people are distressed by the problem of disposing of a dead pet. If they live in the country, or have a friend that does, deep burial is often the answer. In towns it's more difficult. Phone your veterinarian and ask him if he has arrangements to pick up and dispose. Many do. Most of the animal welfare societies will accept and dispose of dead dogs. Usually they are incinerated.

Distemper and infectious hepatitis (*hard pad*)

These are virus diseases that can strike any dog at any age, but the really dangerous age is weaning to one year. It usually starts with a fever, a bit of eye discharge, lack of appetite and sometimes vomiting. Very quickly the second stage takes over which may be pneumonia, diarrhoea or liver involvement. The form of the disease where the pads of the feet turn hard is rarely seen these days. During this stage

70

your vet will treat with antibiotics, liver replacement drugs and all sorts of supportive drugs depending on where the virus is striking. Your dog may then have an apparent recovery, and you will congratulate yourself on your choice of veterinarian or your nursing ability and your dog on his toughness. But the virus hasn't finished. It still has to work its way through the nervous system, and it is then that the real damage is done. If a dog that has been treated for distemper starts throwing fits, the outlook is very bleak indeed. Damaged nerve tissue rarely regenerates. Your pet has a better than even chance of throwing fits all his life, or at the best developing a constant twitch of one or more muscles. The whole point about the distemper-hepatitis complex is that they are virus diseases as opposed to bacterial diseases. Medical veterinary and chemical research workers, despite all the 'miracle' drugs, still have no drugs effective against the smaller viruses.

There have been for many years vaccines that will prevent these diseases. Properly used they are safe and near enough a hundred per cent effective. When you get a puppy (most people get a puppy at weaning time, between seven and nine weeks) take it around to your vet for its initial examination. This is best done before you take the puppy home. He will tell you how badly you've been done, count its fleas and its worms and maybe give it a first shot against distemper, hepatitis and the two sorts of leptospirosis. That first shot will have to be repeated two to four weeks later and preferably every year afterwards. I must note here that many vets still insist that a puppy should be twelve weeks of age before its first shot. Unhappily that regime leaves it without protection at the most susceptible stage. Tell him to check with his suppliers or with the manufacturers. They will confirm that 7 to 9 weeks for the first shot and 11 to 13 for the second is ideal.

One final warning about distemper. Buying a puppy from a shop window is very tricky. It's at a very susceptible age, and having been thrown in with other dogs it's likely to be harbouring the disease when you take it home. Club Row (near Petticoat Lane) is almost another word for distemper at our clinic, and I'm sure at many others. A puppy should be bought not from a dealer but from the owner of the bitch. Up till weaning the pup has the benefit of its mother's immunity. Then it should go directly into its new home.

Oh, and one final word. A vaccinated animal will have a proper certificate signed by a veterinary surgeon, and it will give the date of the vaccination, and the vaccine number. Don't accept anyone's word for it unless you see the certificate. There's no waiting period for the certificate so there's no reason it shouldn't come with the dog. *PS:* Country vets are lovely people but their experience of pets may be limited. A vet from Scotland phoned me one day. He had just bought a Bull Terrier puppy from a top breeder on the outskirts of London (Bull Terriers, incidentally, must be in the top ten of most vets' 'popularity league'). He thought he'd have a night out in London before he drove home. Could I kindly put the puppy up for the night in the surgery kennels? I explained that I'd be more than happy to oblige but I thought it was unwise to expose the puppy to such an obvious risk. 'What risk?' he asked. 'We see about a half dozen distemper cases a day,' I patiently replied. He was more than interested. He hadn't seen a case for years.

One can only conclude that limited experience is not conclusive. One must also point out that dogs who live in remote areas must be more susceptible to disease than those in built-up areas. Annual boosters for them may be a waste of time and money for many years, but if there is an outbreak you'll be glad you bothered.

Doberman Pinscher

Incredible as it may sound, this world-famous breed was developed only less than a century ago by Herr Doberman in Apolda, Germany, who set out with an idea in his head of what he wanted in a dog. He used German Pinscher, Rottweillers and the Vorstenhunde. Towards the First World War other people added Weimeraner to form the breed more or less as we know him today. If you really know what you're about the 'Dobe' is the supreme guard dog, but if you can't train him or afford to have him trained all you'll have is a nervous, vicious brute. I hope you end up in gaol if you allow one to become a rampaging killer. The breeders say there are no bad Dobermans, just bad owners, and to a certain extent I agree. One meets the most insignificant meek types parading a Doberman hoping, I suppose, that the public will accord the owner the respect befitting the dog. The dog, proud, alert and aloof when in the hands of a calm person, can be nervous, snippy and snivelling in the hands of a weak, nervous one. Of course, there are Dobermans that are shy and nervous and virtually untrainable, but reputable breeders with a reputation to uphold will ruthlessly weed them out. If you insist on a Doberman take your own sweet time finding an established breeder. There are no bargain Dobermans.

Remember too that this is one of the few breeds in which the bitches can be as aggressive as the dogs; remember too that their movements and reactions are faster than yours. This lesson was indelibly imprinted on me while I was still at vet school. While attending a hospitalized Doberman she suddenly leapt out of her kennel. There was only one place I could go. I spent the night in the cage while she paced outside.

Docking

The cutting of tails. A barbaric practice that is supposed to improve the appearance of certain breeds. Poodles, Cockers, Terriers, etc., are all born with that normal appendage, but fashion decrees that they must come off, and fashion decrees further exactly how many joints of the tail should be left. Ears were once cropped in England for the same reason, and they still are in America. I don't suppose the docking of tails will become illegal in England for a few decades yet, so in the meantime please have it done when the puppies are just a few days old and it's a quick, almost painless affair.

PS: The situation has changed in the last few years. At the moment of writing, the only country that has actually made docking illegal is Norway. And it doesn't look like anyone else is about to follow their lead.

In Britain it's all a bit of a muddle. Both the British Veterinary Association and the Royal College of Veterinary Surgeons (the vet's regulatory body) officially frown on the practice. In effect docking is considered unethical, although it's not illegal. Since the ruling, I have seen lots of puppies docked by vets but I have yet to hear of a vet who has been disciplined or struck off for doing so. The rationale of the vets who continue to dock puppies' tails despite the disapproval of their colleagues goes something like this: 'So long as it's not illegal people will do it themselves if we vets refuse to do it. It's less cruel if it's done by a vet.'

The breeders say, 'It's difficult to sell a Yorkie, a Poodle or a Doberman with a long tail. It's impossible in the export market. At the top end of the game many breeds would rapidly deteriorate without that market. We must dock to survive.'

Here in fairness one is bound to outline three further arguments put forward by the traditional breeders: most vets agree that dewclaws should be removed, yet docking is less painful; secondly, anyone who has ever tried to groom a matted long tail of any shaggy breed will realize that it's neither fashion nor cosmetics that decrees the practice. Surely shepherds don't dock lambs for frivolous reasons; thirdly, we don't care whether vets do it or not because any breeder

73

who specializes in, say, Fox Terriers or Poodles has done far more puppies of that breed than the average vet has seen. Finally, they add, with more than a grain of truth, 'If we were to export undocked puppies, the breeders in America and Europe would have to have them done before they could be exhibited. Docking a two or three day old puppy is virtually painless. Docking a half grown creature is a serious operation. So who is talking about cruelty?'

It would now appear that the vets are quietly quitting the campaign to have the practice declared illegal. As one said, 'Surely we have more important problems to discuss than puppy dogs' tails.'

Drinking

All animals should have a supply of clean water available at all times. People make the mistake with small dogs of not changing the water and cleaning the bowl. A fevered animal will often drink a great deal, and so will one with digestive or intestinal complaints. If your pet is drinking a bowlful and immediately vomiting it up, you had better consult your veterinary surgeon at the earliest convenient time. Cut out the water meanwhile. If your pet's water consumption rises over a period of weeks or months, you had better see a vet. A bitch with pyometra will drink excessively. Middle-aged and older animals with kidney trouble will drink excessively. Please do not attempt to control it by withdrawing the water. This is cruel and dangerous. It needs all that extra water because the kidneys can't do their job. You simply must get professional help. Only one word of summary: your veterinary surgeon may ask you to limit a pet's drinking for two or at the most three or four days, but he will never tell you to limit it for a prolonged period. If the water consumption can't be controlled by curing the primary condition, then the situation is very grave indeed.

Drooling

One of the unpleasant features of some Boxers and other short-headed breeds. It's due to the shape of the head which scrunches all the organs in the back of the throat, so there's nothing to be done about it except to keep your drooler away from people you're trying to impress.

If your normally non-drooling pet starts a bit of saliva dribbling one day and it gets more pronounced the next, you had better look at its teeth and see if there's a large bit of tartar or a bit of bone stuck between them. If you can't remove it, or if you see an inflamed gum, make an appointment with your veterinary surgeon.

If the drooling starts suddenly and is very pronounced look in the mouth and see if you can find the cause (like a large bit of bone) and remove it. If you can't, go to the vet's straightaway.

PS: Now that rabies has moved up the list of possibles and has almost moved into the list of probables, you might be better advised to leave the examination of drooling animals to your vet. Why do you think he carries so much insurance?

Dropsy

An accumulation of watery body fluid in the abdomen or tissues. It's almost always a sign of heart, liver, circulatory or kidney trouble, and its very serious indeed. It's not an emergency because it's probably been going on for days or weeks before you noticed it, but professional advice should be sought within a day or two.

Drowning

Pick the animal up by his hind legs and allow the water to drain out. Open his mouth and see that his tongue is out, and there are no obstructions like sand, mud or grass. Then apply artificial respiration.

Dyspnoea

Laboured or difficult breathing. Seen after some car accidents, in the pneumonic form of distemper, in pneumonia, in old heart patients, etc. The only home treatment, of course, is rest and quiet. Specific treatment depends on professional diagnosis.

Ears

People believe that only mites can invade the ear, but actually, in the dog, mites are seldom a problem. I have seen the ears of Cocker Spaniels almost closed by lice, and a single flea can cause a nervous dog to scratch his ear till he draws blood. Prevention is really a matter of grooming – checking to see that the visible portions of the ear flaps are clean.

However, a dog's ears may become infected from a number of causes besides parasites, and if the condition is neglected it can be very serious indeed.

What are the common-sense rules if you see your dog scratching its ears or rubbing them along the floor? First place the animal on a table under a strong light and have someone hold him. Look at the ear and see if there's something on it or in it that you can easily remove. Thorns, grass awns, tar, chewing-gum are all easily removed if they're in the external ear. Maybe the ear has been scratched or bitten by another animal. A soothing antiseptic lotion will help. If you can see nothing, warm a little bland oil like olive oil and pour it liberally into the ear so that it floats up whatever debris is down there.

Under no circumstances probe or poke into the ear itself. You don't know what you're doing because you can't see into the canal, and you may be shoving the object around the curve and so cause real trouble.

If the oil doesn't cure the trouble please don't buy those horrible things called canker pills or canker powders. I've never known any to do anything but harm, but then, to be fair, I must say that we see those cases where those pills and powders have caused such a mess that even the stupid drug peddler has realized veterinary attention was needed.

To summarize: See if you can locate the source of trouble and remove it. Otherwise try pouring in lots of oil. If that doesn't help seek professional attention.

Now a few words about that problem the Poodle and, yes, it's the miniature and toy I'm talking about. The poor things somewhere along the misbreeding line have got ear canals that are lined with hair, and few of them live out their lives without at least one episode of ear trouble. The hair either blocks the canal or traps bits of dirt that cause irritation and infection. Besides which they are funny contorted little ears – altogether not the sort of ear that nature intended a dog to have. You must be careful to pluck, not cut, those hairs at least once a month, and if it looks as if trouble is starting, get it to the vet's. He will probably use antibiotic or cortisone ointments or a combination of both after determining the source of the trouble. He may probe, using the otoscope or even give a general anaesthetic in order to clear the ear properly.

Don't be impatient. Often a month's treatment is necessary and, of course, if the trouble is the basic shape of the ear the condition may recur.

Many cases will not respond to medication, and then an operation called a resection is necessary (see below).

A bleeding ear usually looks worse than it is. Don't panic. Place a pad of gauze on both sides of the ear flap, and bandage right around the head.

If an animal walks with its head to one side the chances are that it has a middle ear infection. These are very painful and should not be neglected. Give a codeine or a couple of aspirins as first aid, and get in touch with your vet. Antibiotics will usually relieve the condition within hours and cure it in a few days.

Cropping An archaic practice still followed in parts of Europe and America. It consists of cutting off a portion of the ear flap of Boxers, Great Danes and other breeds so that the ears stand up. It's supposed to improve the appearance of the animal, but I've seen some that were made permanent nervous wrecks. The operation is only part of the story. Afterwards the ears are 'trained' in aluminium, cardboard or plastic forms for a period of days or weeks. Fortunately this barbaric practice is illegal in Great Britain.

Haematoma Actually a blood blister of the ear. Usually caused by a bite or a blow or constant scratching. Don't try to drain them yourself. They'll only pop up again. Your vet will try non-surgical treatment, and if that doesn't work he will give a general anaesthetic and then cut a rather large oval or maybe an 's' shaped piece out of the blister, drain and curette and then suture tightly. Even then it may recur and require another operation, but usually they are successful first time around. If one comes up suddenly don't panic – just wrap a bandage around the ear so that it doesn't flap and make an appointment with the vet. Incidentally, in case your vet forgets to tell you, most haematomas will permanently disfigure the ear flap. Those cauliflower ears that add character, but not dignity, to the dog's face are usually the after effects of a haematoma.

Mites These are wee crawlies just visible to the naked eye aided by a strong light. They are very common in cats, and we do see them occasionally in dogs. In puppies purchased from pet shops or neglected homes, the condition may be very advanced and cause nervous symptoms like walking in a circle or falling over. If your pup's ears look filthy have the veterinarian check them and do the initial cleaning which does require a fair bit of probing. He will probably give you a bottle of oil containing a mite killer which you pour into the ears very liberally. The oil will float all the mites and the skin debris out of the ears. Check the pup's ears from time to time to see that they haven't become reinfested.

PS: Many dogs begin scratching their ears shortly after the family acquire a kitten. A kitten may be heavily infested with ear mites without showing any signs of discomfort. Yet a single mite may set up an irritation in the ear of the dog which requires weeks of treatment.

Conclusion: If your dog has ear trouble take the cat to the vet at the same time.

Resection This is a rather involved operation done on dogs in those cases in which medication will not clear up a long standing ear infection. The dog is given a general anaesthetic, and the hair on and around the ear is clipped and shaved. The area is then disinfected. Usually a fold or two of the ear flap is removed, and as it's an area that bleeds freely many pressure sutures are required. (These stay in for ten days or two weeks after the operation.) Then the main part of the operation begins. It's rather tricky and involves a fair bit of judgement, because what the surgeon is trying to do is cut down and remove the ear canal down to the point where it curves towards the ear drum – and to do this without narrowing (and if possible widening) the opening. He stitches down at the new opening, and if everything has gone well the dog has a healed and serviceable ear in about ten days. During this period he must not be allowed to scratch at the operation site. Most surgeons keep the area dressed and ask you to come back daily or every second day to have the dressings changed. When it's all healed the stitches are removed, and in nervous dogs this requires another general anaesthetic. Altogether the operation is a time consumer from the vet's point of view, very expensive from the owner's point of view, and a thoroughly unpleasant experience from the dog's point of view. Believe me no vet looks forward to it, and we would much rather you brought your dog along in the early stages of its ear trouble when medication just might work. Of course, many members of some breeds like Miniature Poodles are almost condemned to ear trouble from birth, and then the surgeon must rectify the ear that nature never intended a dog to have.

Eczema

I'm sure it's unkind, but many doctors envy the skin specialist because their patients never die and never get cured – or so it seems in many cases. Eczema is an irritating itchy condition of the skin that drives a person or animal so frantic they scratch the area until it bleeds and subsequently becomes infected. A tiny irritating spot one day becomes a great red one the next, and in three or four days a scabby and purulent mess. Some veterinarians of eminent rank state that ninety per cent of all skin conditions are secondary to either fleas or lice, and although I've seen eczema cases in which I could not find either fleas or lice I believe it's the common-sense starting-point. Examine the animal under a strong light and patiently fold back the hair at several places until you see either the wee jumper that is the flea or the slightly faster crawler that is the lice, or the eggs or droppings of either. Use a powder on the dog (there are several good ones on the market), and clean out the animal's bedding, powdering that too. Examine the dog again in a day or two and repeat the inspection in a week. In the summer a bath made for the purpose is preferable. Do not omit the bedding or the area where the animal sleeps. If you have a dog and a cat and only one has eczema, check both for fleas and lice. If the itch persists in one area apply a soothing calamine lotion – several times daily. I believe that is as far as the layman should go in home treatment, and if there are no results in three or four days I would trot the ailing beast off to the veterinary surgeon's. Incidentally, nothing is quite so infuriating to the vet as being called on Christmas Day or early Sunday morning for something that you've been treating yourself for a fortnight, so use your common sense. But aside from the vet's feelings, an eczema that is allowed to run on can become complicated and much more difficult to cure.

The veterinary surgeon will use simpler remedies at first, depending on the sort of eczema it is, and then if those don't work he will go on to the cortisones, antibiotics and more severe drugs, but don't be angry or impatient because he didn't use the strong drugs right off the bat. It's always better to cure with a simpler drug if at all possible.

Now for a few general observations.

Don't let your pet get overweight. Fat dogs seem to get eczema more easily, more severely and for longer than animals in good condition. Secondly, an exercised and tired animal will be more likely to sleep or rest quietly than a bored one. Often an animal will scratch just out of general boredom, so get out in that park and walk. It will do you lots of good too. Thirdly, cut out those biscuits and candy treats. Fourthly, eliminating one item from the diet sometimes seems to help. Fifthly, long-haired dogs must be groomed daily and excess and dead hair removed.

During treatment, if the animal persists in scratching, use bootees on his feet so that he can't open the skin with his claws.

Your veterinary surgeon is a busy man and may forget to tell you to apply what lotions and creams he gives you to the skin and not to the hair. Most people rub the stuff around on top of the hair where it can't do any good, and just forms a caked mess under which the infection flourishes. Rub the goo into the skin itself and leave as little as possible on the hair.

Finally, and this applies to any external medication, put it on just before exercise time. By the time you've returned from the walk it will have dried in and done most of its work. The dog will have forgotten that he really did intend to lick the nasty stuff off.

Elbow dysplasia

This condition is a malformation of the bones of the elbow and doesn't cause the animal any trouble in its youth but usually leads to arthritis later. It is thought to be congenital, that is, the animal inherits the condition and is born with it, in the following five breeds – Alsatian, Bloodhound, Newfoundland, Bassett and Irish Wolfhound. As there is a similar condition in man which ends in the same painful and crippling arthritic joint, veterinary researchers in the States are tackling the problem with the aid of funds provided by agencies interested in the human aspect. The veterinary research will, of course, try to standardize X-ray and diagnostic procedures so that breeders can know with certainty what parent stock is transmitting the condition. The applications to human medicine will not be immediately apparent, but like all scientific research it will just sort out one more piece of the jigsaw of our ignorance.

Electric shock

BE CAREFUL. If an animal is lying flat out beside an electric cord (they *will* bite at them), don't touch him until you've switched off the current. Many animals urinate when they are shocked and you may step in the pool, which is an excellent conductor. Then apply artificial respiration and have someone phone the vet.

Elizabethan collar

Two half circles of cardboard or plastic or wood are laced together around the animal's neck so that it can't scratch at its ears or eyes.

Elkhound (*Norwegian Elkhound*)

One of the many, many nice things about Norway. This 23kg (50 lb) hunter is attractive, virile and has a perfect disposition. Like the Norwegians he's happiest out of doors. As in all long-coated breeds you must pay attention to his coat, particuarly in summer, if skin complaints are to be avoided.

English Foxhound

As English and as ancient as the hunt. If you have a fair bit of money and about thirty years you should be able to produce a fair pack.

English Setter

Many people's idea of beauty in a dog. The Irish Setter is more popular in Britain now, but the English Setter is still widely used in the United States and Canada. Height about 60cm (2 ft), weight about 27kg (60 lb), coat flat and silky, feathered legs and tail. Colour white with a wide spectrum of markings. Highly recommended.

English Sheepdog (*Old English Sheepdog, or Bobtail*)

This ancient breed is becoming more and more a hairy curiosity. I know they are wonderful companions, but is all that hair really necessary – particularly around the eyes where it causes so much trouble? From my side of the veterinary table they lose much of their attractiveness, and become plain stubborn eczema cases. Unless you are prepared to comb and groom daily you shouldn't have one.

English Springer Spaniel

What a multitude of types this name covers: the tall, big-boned, too often thin-chested show type, the shorter but stronger field type, and all temperaments from Spaniel docility to inbred hysteria. Choose the breeder you buy from as carefully as you would a tailor. If you keep your Springer in an overheated flat, comb and brush him daily. Don't allow him to get overfat. Like all field dogs, he'll develop every sort of neurosis and skin trouble if he's not getting enough exercise.

Enteritis

This is a general term meaning inflammation of the intestines. There are many varieties and many causes. The symptoms you will recognize are either diarrhoea or vomiting. In both cases the only safe first aid is starvation and rest.

Entlebuch Mountain Dog

The smallest of the four breeds of Swiss Mountain Dog. He's black, white and tan, stump tailed, a herding dog, and averages about 11kg (25 lb). I've never seen one outside of Switzerland, and he's the possessor of no outstanding characteristics that are likely to bring about a sudden export demand.

Entropion

Do you think all those folds of skin on the faces of Pekinese, Boxers, Pugs and English Bulldogs are cute? Somebody must think they are, because many breed standards specify those folds, and some judges and breeders value them highly. I can't dispute their historical or aesthetic value, but I can tell you that it predisposes to a condition called entropion in which the eye lids do not lie smoothly at the edge of the eye where they belong but roll sloppily within the eye so that the hairs of the lids cause a constant irritation. There is so much extra skin that the lids are practically forced into the eye. The correction of the condition involves a rather delicate cosmetic operation in which the surgeon judges just how much skin to remove so that the lids will lie exactly where they should. Sometimes a second operation is necessary. The only after-operative care required is some ointment in the eyes as the surgeons will direct, and preventing the dog from scratching or rubbing at the stitches. Bootees or an Elizabethan collar are often helpful. About seven to ten days is required for complete healing.

PS: At a dog show you may note a judge or another breeder closely examining a dog's eyes. Do you think they're trying to measure intelligence, establish rapport or gauge soulful expressions? Nothing so complicated. They're trying to see the scars of an entropion operation. When it's well done it only leaves a thin line above and below the eye. One assumes that if either the sire or the dam have had to be surgically corrected the progeny too may suffer. Amazing how many champion poodles and chows, among others, carry those tell-tale marks. Don't take my word for it. Look for yourself.

Escalator

It might seem self-evident, but many people don't realize their pets should be carried up and down moving stairs. They can and do get their toes caught and torn. First aid in case of bleeding consists of a pressure bandage starting above, and including the injured foot.

Euthanasia

Painless and gentle death usually done by an intravenous injection, which actually puts the animal to sleep first and then stops the heart. Usually done in the case of incurable illness or viciousness. Some veterinary surgeons prefer using chloroform or ether to induce sleep. and then stopping the heart with an injection. In the case of tiny puppies many people prefer to save the veterinary fees and drown the animal. As anyone who has ever seen a drowning creature can testify that method is only slightly less cruel than burning. I would suggest that if you can't afford fees, take the unwanted litter along to a welfare clinic. Make sure it's one that has a vet in attendance and that it's done by injection. Some use electrocution apparatus. Others use decompression chambers. Despite all the so-called scientific evidence that these methods are painless, I prefer to believe the evidence of my own eyes. If those methods are painless so is the mediaeval rack. The reason I know the injection method is painless is because I've experienced it a few times. The difference between anaesthesia and euthanasia is not all that great. Fortunately most anaesthetists are aware of that fact. If you're in an isolated place or a country like Spain where humane standards are low and you would rather do it yourself to make sure, I would suggest that (with a little effort) you can find a friendly chemist who will let you have enough sleeping pills to do the job.

There are still some men around, of the old school, who prefer to shoot their own horses and dogs if it becomes necessary. With dogs the point to place the gun is slightly above the mid-line between eyes and ears, with the line of fire down into the head rather than back towards the spine. That method is safe only if the dog is absolutely still (as he may be after an automobile or shooting accident). If the animal must be held, then of course you must aim from the back of the head towards the muzzle. Unless you know dogs and guns, better leave the job to someone who does.

Evissenc

A greyhound type native to the Balearic Islands, but widely distributed throughout Spain where it is used as a rabbit hound.

Eyes

If both eyes are squinting or discharging, the chances are that the animal has a general illness and the eye symptoms are only a part of the picture. For example, a puppy in the early stages of distemper will usually have a thickish discharge at the corners of the eye, particularly in the mornings. You can bathe them until the cows come home and only make them worse. So do look at the animal carefully and see if it's showing any other symptoms. If it's just a wee chill or it's been hanging its head out of the car window, it'll probably pass off by next day. If it's still miserable on the morrow phone the vet. If only one eye is affected look carefully under a good light, and see if there's a bit of grit floating about. Animals with protuberant eyes (what the breeders like to call a bold eye) like Pekinese or Pugs will pick up any dust or cigarette ash that happens to be around. One of the better solutions to bathe an eye with is salt in water (teaspoon to a pint, boil and let it cool). Pour it liberally on the eye to float off any foreign object. This same solution will soothe a scratched eye until you get to the vet's for some ointment.

Ointments Please do not try to save pennies by using some tube of eye ointment that Aunt Martha left behind. Eye ointments have a limited life. There are many different sorts for different conditions and the wrong sort may do harm. For example, applying a cortisone eye ointment to an ulcerated eye will retard healing. An old eye ointment may have become contaminated and introduce infection. Right. You have the ointment as prescribed by the vet, but you can't seem to spread it over the eye as easily as he did in the surgery. Give yourself a fighting chance. Place the animal on a table, have a friend hold him. If your pet is an incorrigible Corgi or an untrained Alsatian you may have to take extra steps, as described under *Restraint*. Then place the thumb and index finger of the left hand above and below the eye and, keeping the tube nozzle a bit away from the eye-ball, squeeze a drop into the corner of the eye with the other hand. Close the eye with the thumb and forefinger of your left hand. This spreads the ointment over the whole eye. You'll be able to do it quicker than reading this once you've got the idea.

Emergencies I know a doctor (of humans) who copes with emergencies daily with the calmness born of knowledge and experience, yet when he dropped some hot cigar ash on the eye of his wife's King Charles he went frantic. Its cries of pain and hysterical scratching at the eye put the helpless man right off his stroke. Obviously the first thing to do, whether it is a chemical burn, or a scratch or an insect or ash, is to wash the eye repeatedly with salt water (one teaspoon to 6dl (1 pt), boil and cool, or just as it is in an emergency). Salt water is very much like tears in composition, which are the eye's natural defence. It's a two man job so get someone to hold the animal (the police will help if you're alone) while you bathe the eye. If the pain persists and he's rubbing the eye get an Elizabethan collar, or put some bootees on his feet while awaiting the vet. If you're miles from a vet but have a co-operative medical friend, ordinary human cocaine drops applied every two or three hours will control the pain until you can get to a vet. A codeine or two will help as well.

Protruding eye-ball Pekinese, Pugs and other breeds with prominent eyes may actually have the eye knocked out of its socket by an accident or even through sheer fright. Soak a cloth in warm water and hold it over the eye, and get to a veterinary clinic with all possible speed. Sometimes the eye can be saved.

Note: All breeds with protruberant eyes need regular attention. Bathe with saline. If you're rich have two dogs. They'll clean each other's eyes.

Severe bleeding from the eye or lids Place a soaked cloth tightly over the whole eye. The animal won't panic if you're not pressing his throat or nose and if he can see out of the other eye. Get to the vet's.

Other conditions These include a host of abnormalities from blocked tear ducts (which cause that constant watering so common in miniature poodles and dachshunds) to inturned eye lids (see *Entropion*), to ulcers, cataracts, opacities, etc. It is downright cruelty to watch your pet's eyes degenerate or to try treating them with remedies so freely sold by those that aren't prepared to follow the case through to its conclusion. In other words give your pet and the surgeon a chance by getting it to the vet's early on. For example, there is a condition called detached lens in which the lens starts floating freely in the eye fluid. The animal has a starry blank look. If it is seen and diagnosed within forty-eight hours an operation to remove the lens has a fair chance of ensuring some sight from the eye. Delay usually means the loss of sight and sometimes the eye itself must be removed.

Consultation Eye surgery is a specialized field. Although veterinary surgeons can cope happily with emergencies or with 'routine' operations like blocked tear ducts, entropions, etc., few of them can be genius enough to specialize in everything including eye surgery. Your vet will send you along to a colleague if the condition warrants it. In London or Philadelphia where there are veterinary faculties this is a fairly simple procedure. In small or remote places many vets will utilize the services of a human eye surgeon. The vet will do the anaesthesia and his colleagues from the field of human medicine will do the surgery.

Surgery in the canine eye is much more difficult than in the human eye because the canine eye bleeds more, and it bleeds more easily. Moreover, it is difficult to rest or bandage the canine eye properly.

Fainting (*loss of consciousness*)

This is easily differentiated from a fit because in the latter there is a great deal of uncontrolled movement first. Fainting may follow over-exertion or over-heating but is usually seen in older dogs with heart conditions or in younger dogs of extremely nervous disposition like some of the white Miniature poodles. Don't pummel or push at the poor beast's chest, and never try to force brandy or water into it. Allow it to lie quietly for a few moments, on its side with its hind quarters slightly elevated. It should come to in a matter of moments. Allow it to rest quietly for the rest of the day. Don't exercise it. In a younger animal it may never happen again, so forget it unless it does recur, at which time you had better make an appointment with your

85

vet. In an older animal I would suggest a veterinary consultation within a day or two.

PS: If you yourself are on the queasy side, do your vet a favour and stay in the waiting room while he does the necessary behind a door. I can assure you I've had to see to more fainting humans in my surgery than animals. One was a local police sergeant. As I was inoculating his Pekinese puppy he turned various hues of yellow and white, staggered outdoors but didn't quite reach his car. He fell against the bumper. He was well and truly out so I had him carted off to the hospital. When he returned three weeks later he apologized to the nurse as he handed her the Peke, 'Do you mind if you take him in for it's second shot? I've shovelled bits of people off highways without thinking anything of it, but when it comes to animals I'm a bit soft.'

False pregnancy

If your two year old bitch suddenly becomes over affectionate or mopey or starts crawling into unusual places dragging your favourite kimono behind, there's a good chance that she's pregnant. If she was kept on a lead through her heat period and absolutely did not get out on her own there's a good chance that she's pseudo-pregnant. In other words, nature intends a female of breeding age to have offspring and when we prevent it the barren female often goes through all the changes of pregnancy. Her temperament will change, her breasts will swell, her tummy will fill out and she may make milk, choose a corner for a nest and even go through the motions of labour. In America bitches are spayed (the ovaries and uterus removed) as commonly as female cats are spayed in England, but for many reasons the British prefer to leave their bitches entire, so one may be faced with the problem of pregnancy or phantom pregnancy twice yearly from the time of the bitch's first heat until advanced old age.

There are two ways of treating false pregnancy. The first is by an injection or two of a hormone. This usually clears up the condition in a day or two, but many veterinarians believe it is rather severe and may lead to trouble like pyometra later on. However, the veterinarians who do use the hormone injection method point out that a bitch who has had several phantom pregnancies is likely to develop a pyometra no matter how you handle her, and there is some statistical evidence to prove their theories. The more conservative treatment is basically to forget it unless there is such a flow of milk or so much abdominal swelling that the bitch is uncomfortable. Then we prescribe flushing pills along the lines of epsom salts and cut her water intake to a bare

86

minimum. This usually stops the milk flow in four or five days. If a bitch has three or four false pregnancies in a row and if they are severe your veterinarian may suggest spaying as the only real answer.

False teeth

As the dog doesn't chew his food but bolts it down, teeth are not really necessary. Many people ask about it because the fitting of false teeth to old sheep to prolong their breeding lives has had such publicity. Valuable guard dogs who have lost their teeth as a result of an accident or decay may be fitted with teeth, because without them they are much less useful. In the Alsatian or Boxer the veterinarian has a relatively easy job, but I'm afraid in the Yorkshire Terrier, madam (and their teeth may go very early because of their abnormally narrow jaws), the results wouldn't be satisfactory. Manchu would rather have soft foods than those funny bits in his mouth.

Feeding

What to feed is covered under *Diet*. How and when to feed is really a matter of common sense. My dog isn't very hungry at six o'clock, but develops a ravenous appetite at four in the morning, and if he had his way my life would revolve around his stomach. Fortunately, dogs have learnt to adapt themselves to our ways, and if you follow any sort of regular schedule they will soon accommodate themselves to it. Every boarding kennel receives a long list of instructions with every dog. Fido likes a biscuit at tea time and two saucerfuls of tea at dinner time and chicken on Sunday. Ming will eat nothing but halibut poached well. Christine (Dachshunds have the most extraordinary names) simply cannot eat from anything but monogrammed plate. And so it goes. Christine, Fido and Ming are homesick and miserable in the kennels. They refuse the food for twenty-four hours. Then at the next regular meal time ordinary meat and brown bread mixed in an ordinary bowl are brought around. Fido barks in anticipation, sedate old Ming gives a gracious wag and Christine knocks ingratiatingly on the front of the cage. Down goes the food, the bowl is licked clean, and everyone settles down happily. The point is that bad feeding habits are always a result of the owner's indulgence and there is no animal, however pampered, which can't be taught to eat regular food at regular hours. The principles are simple. Regularity – about the same time every day, whether you feed once or twice. Cleanliness – bowls, both watering and feeding, should be washed daily. No leftovers – after about ten minutes or so a dog's bowl should be removed and the contents thrown away. If there's a lot left over every day you are feeding too much. Don't try to save food from day to day without refrigeration. Don't worry if an animal skips its food for one day – especially in hot weather. Don't indulge every regular request for titbits. Don't feed an animal off your own table. Scraps from the table may be used as a substantial part of the diet but they should be fed at the animal's feeding time, not yours.

Feet

If an animal is lame or holding up its leg examine the foot, because that is where the majority of lamenesses originate. We wear shoes which prevent our feet from being cut by glass, sharp stones, or nails, or from being burnt on hot sand, concrete or hot ashes, or frozen by ice and snow. The wonder is that accidents to animals' feet are not far more common than they actually are. The first thing to do in the event of trouble is to look carefully at the foot. I know it sounds obvious but it's positively amazing how many animals are allowed to go around in pain because their owners simply didn't have a good look. Put the beast on a large table, lay it on its side, and with the aid of a good light check the pads, between the pads and the nails. A bit of grit, a thorn, a bit of glass, a grass awn, all can be vey painful. Usually they can be removed easily if the animal is properly restrained. Stubborn bits can be eased out after bathing the foot with warm salt water. A bit of antiseptic ointment, a bandage, repeat the bathing the next day and all should be well. If the foot is cut, bandage it until you can get to a veterinarian who will decide if stitching is necessary. Pads heal slowly because of the constant pressure, but the earlier they are sutured the better the chances of healing. Broken or cracked nails should be packed around with cotton and the foot bandaged until you can get to a veterinary surgeon's.

Cracked pads Common in city dogs. Prevention is walking on grass rather than concrete. Sometimes a bit of olive oil will help the pads heal, but usually bootees for a few days are necessary.

Interdigital cysts These are infected areas between the toes which can be quite difficult to heal. They are common in Sealyhams, Scotties and other wire-haired animals. Pekinese too have more than their fair share. The only prevention I know is grooming the hair of the foot and cleaning at least twice weekly, and more often if the animal is walking on gritty earth. See also *Awns*. Home treatment consists of bathing three or four times daily in warm salt water or a warm solution of epsom salts.

In all foot troubles a bootee or a bandage for a few days will often allow nature to heal the lesion.

Field Spaniel

The breed is rather rare, which is unfortunate, because it has most of the virtues of the Cocker and fewer of the faults. It's rather larger than the Cocker (up to 16kg (35 lb) or even 18kg (40 lb)), slightly shorter in the back and lower to the ground, but otherwise you can hardly distinguish the two breeds. Its temperament is where the Field Spaniel shines. You have less chance of getting a neurotic if you choose the Field Spaniel. Why? Simply because its unpopularity has kept it out of the hands of ignorant or unscrupulous breeders. If kept indoors the breed can go to pot. Any working dog wants lots of exercise, and any long-haired animal needs daily grooming.

Finnish Spitz

Looks like a cross between a Chow and a Fox, but actually is an ancient Finnish hunting-dog who is a combination of pointer and setter, and is raised for hunting anything up to and including bear. I should have thought it was a natural for western Canada and the western United States where so-called sportsmen shoot anything that moves and quite a few species (like owl) that don't, but I've never seen a Finnish Spitz out there. Weight about 16kg (35 lb), stands about 45cm (18 in), and its colour varies through several shades of cream to red.

Fish-hooks

Puppies will try to swallow anything, so do your fly-tying where they are not. If an animal gets a fish-hook caught in its mouth get to a vet straightaway. Under general anaesthetic it's usually fairly easy to remove them. Unfortunately, many fish-hook accidents happen in places remote from veterinarians and the other amenities of modern life, and you'll have to get it out on your own. The only things I can tell you that may be of help are:

1 Get someone calm and strong to hold the animal.
2 Get the best light you can.
3 Get a pair of wire cutters or pincers.
4 Get a sharp knife and boil it and allow it to cool.
5 Don't try to pull at the hook. Try to push it on until you can feel it under the skin. Then cut down on to it. Then cut off the head or heads of the hook. Then push back the other way.

Fits

Can take many forms. Commonly the animal loses its sight and awareness, gnashes or champs its teeth, and froths at the mouth, its body tightens, shivers or convulses and it may go through running motions.

Note well that an animal in a fit will not recognize anything – even its master. It will bite and hang on. In short, even your lovable affectionate pet is dangerous during a fit. Don't talk to him. He can't hear. Don't run about with brandy or water. It will do no good.

Throw a few old blankets or pillows into a closet or small room without sharp edges. Edge behind the animal and grab it by the skin of the neck just behind the head. One hand each side. Hold it firmly. In this position he cannot hurt you. Small agile dogs you grab with one hand on the neck and the other on the loin, and stretch. It all sounds cruel but it's not and it's the only safe way.

Place the animal in the closet and leave it. The fit will pass in a few moments or half an hour. Allow the animal to rest quietly. Take it along to the vet's next day.

He will try to determine the cause of the fits. In puppies it may be worms. In all animals it may be spinal or brain damage as a result of a virus disease like distemper. The treatment and prognosis, of course, depend on the diagnosis, which may not be immediately reached.

Flat Coated Retriever

Some people say that both the Labrador and the Flat Coated Retriever were developed from Newfoundland-Gordon Setter crosses. Others say that Newfoundland-Labrador-Setter crosses were the origin of the Flat Coated Retriever. Whatever the breed's origin it hasn't had a very illustrious history because it's never really caught on with the sporting fraternity either side of the Atlantic. There are a few breeders in America (you name it – America has it) but I don't know if there's anyone breeding them in Britain on any scale – stands about 60cm (2 ft), weighs about 35kg (70 lb), whole black in colour and rather thicker than the Labrador. Its coat is smooth or flat, hence the unimaginative name.

Flatulence (*gas in the bowel, breaking wind*)

This unpleasant condition is often present in overweight dogs of advancing years who are fed one large meal daily. A dog of eight or nine who looks his age or more and who just isn't up to much exercise may be better off with two or even three smaller meals. If cutting down his weight and the size of his meals doesn't help you may try adding charcoal to the diet. Check the ingredients in his food. There may be just one ingredient that isn't agreeing with him. All that, of course, is only applicable to dogs who share your sofa and possibly your bed. There are millions of happy, healthy dogs who live on tripes, leftovers and whatever they can catch or steal, who emit sounds and odours that are beyond embarrassment. Their owners are equally happy and (God willing) healthy. They stay indoors and let the dogs get on with it somewhere else.

Fleas

Fleas move around quickly in wee crawls or long jumps. One flea can drive some animals to distraction. To see a flea you need patience and good light. Nature has blessed them with a camouflage called protective colouration. They tend to merge into the browns, greys and blacks that most of our dogs favour these days. Look for them in the lighter coloured parts of the coat or in the more sparsely covered areas that polite people don't mention. Little specks that some would dismiss as dirt are in fact flea droppings. They're about the size of the dot at the end of this sentence.

There are many powders and sprays that will kill adult fleas. At the time of writing one of the cheapest, most effective and safest is Malathion. It's the same stuff as I use on my roses, but for many reasons it's labelled 'unsafe for animal use'. I use it on our pets but of course I avoid the mouth and eyes. As I would with talcum powder.

For some strange reason collars, sprays and strips containing far more dangerous compounds are sold in every pet shop. A veterinary toxicologist friend of mine (name available on request) told me that the mortality rate in his rat colonies rose one third after the introduction of these new-fangled kinds of organo-phosphorous compounds and cousins.

For what it's worth, I tell you I don't trust collars and strips. I'd sooner bathe, powder, dust and brush.

Whatever method you choose repeat it in a week or ten days. Don't forget to vacuum thoroughly and stick the bedding in the spinwash at the same time. The adult flea is easily eliminated, but the eggs can hang around a long time – they can survive a year off the host.

Incidentally, fleas are a bit fastidious about who they choose to charm. Dog fleas tend to prefer dogs; but I can tell you from personal experience that some of them take a long time deciding they've hopped on the wrong train.

Then, too, some people discover exactly how many fleas they've been accommodating only when they get rid of their pets. Try it yourself next time you go on holiday. Put the animals in a boarding establishment. Return a day early. Spend the night in the house without your pets. Spend the next day counting flea bites.

Foreign bodies

To the veterinary surgeon any object in an animal that doesn't belong there is called a foreign body. A grass seed in a dog's ear, a fish bone in its mouth, a tennis ball in a Poodle's stomach, a mass of indigested bones in the rectum, gun-shot in a Retriever's shoulder, are all examples. The commonest are balls, toys, stones, bits of wood, usually swallowed during the excitement of playing. Needles and thread are commonly swallowed. Obviously every case presents its own problem in both diagnosis and treatment. The only advice I can give you is to keep small objects out of harm's way. If your animal starts vomiting and you haven't seen his rubber bone around you had better assume he swallowed it. Please don't complicate the vet's problem by treating your dog with some tonic for a week while it steadily loses strength. Also please try to tell the vet the truth as closely as you recall it. That will often save extra X-rays.

What do we do about it? Fish-hooks are removed easily once the animal is anaesthetized. The same goes for most grass awns. Gun-shot is usually dug for (with the aid of anaesthesia and X-rays) but sometimes is best left alone to work itself out.

Swallowed objects can be a simple nuisance or they can be danger-ous and cause death. I've X-rayed a tennis ball in a Labrador's stomach and decided to operate the following morning, only to be greeted at the kennel door by a madly wagging beast with the tennis ball at its feet. It was quite willing to play that funny game again. Usually, however, even something as small as a golf ball will move down the gut and cause an obstruction. Needles, if pointing the right way (eye end towards the tail of the dog), can be left in and the progress down the gut followed by X-ray. Open safety pins, however, must always be removed surgically. Sometimes bones can be gentled along with oil or reached by enema.

The surgery in such cases involves opening into the abdomen, locating the object in the gut and then exposing the portion that is involved. Cutting into stomach or intestine is very hazardous because any spillage at all can cause peritonitis and death. The bowel either side of the foreign body is clamped off, the area surrounded with gauze

92

pads, and then the incision into the bowel is made. Everything that then comes into contact with the foreign body or the inside of the bowel is discarded as it is used. The inside lining of the bowel is sewed together and then even the rubber gloves changed for a fresh sterile pair.

Sometimes the bowel is so inflamed or even bruised and dying that a portion of it must be removed. Then a coupling is made, using only healthy bowel.

Why do I go on with these boring details? Because almost always we get the same dog back a few months or a couple of years later with a similar problem. I know that some dogs simply will swallow things, but it can be curbed by training, and it is the owner's responsibility to keep tempting objects away. Often, however, the owner's attitude is one of jocularity. 'Look what nasty old Ranger did. Nasty old Ranger going to have an oppy-woppy-ration. Isn't he?'

What comments would you make to such people?

Fox Terriers

The smooth-haired sort led the popularity parade about a generation ago both here and in America, but one doesn't see many today. It's one of the few sorts of dogs that popularity didn't destroy and I don't think you'll go wrong in choosing one.

The wire-haired sort is still quite popular, and if you avoid the spindly ones with those fashionable hind legs you may be able to get a dog without hip problems. You see, that straight hind leg so beloved by show judges doesn't allow the stifle joint to act as a cushion or spring for the hip. As a result the socket of the hip joint takes the full force of every jarring step. That, of course, is an over-simplification of a rather complex problem. but it should be enough to indicate to you the care necessary in choosing a wire-hair.

Pedigree and show points have little relationship to an animal's chances of a healthy life. In fact, in the wire-haired, the better the dog from a show point of view the worse his chances from the point of view of health. That long head that seems to have been stretched in just fifteen years of selection may have something to do with the number of neurotic wire-hairs we see.

If you have a wire-haired dog of any sort pay particular attention to grooming the coat and keeping the hair between the toes from clumping.

PS: Although terriers (like all our dogs) are descended from wolves, unlike wolves they don't easily share a canine community life. Most would rather fight than eat. Man has selectively bred them for unbridled aggression. You may keep a pack of beagles or a herd of deerhounds, but if you don't like bloodshed limit your Fox Terriers to duets or trios.

PPS: On a personal note may I add that we bred a smooth-haired Fox Terrier called Laurel. He's got so much style that no judge can pass him without adding another rosette to his collection. Some people say he's almost as good as the immortal Snuffbox. His littermate, Hardy, is an OK dog, but nothing spectacular. When a prospective buyer came around to view the two pups we told him, 'Laurel is obviously world class. Hardy is no better nor worse than run of the mill. Laurel is twenty pounds more.' I don't think the money mattered much to the buyer. But few of us can refuse a bargain. In the event Laurel went back to Miss Beck. Long may she and Laurel reign supreme. *Moral:* there are a lot of truly professional breeders in whom you can place your trust.

Fractures

Sometimes it's perfectly obvious to the layman that a leg is broken, but in other cases the animal appears perfectly all right except that he holds up one limb. In some fractures the animal is only intermittently lame. I would suggest that all lamenesses that don't clear up in a day or two or that get progressively worse should be seen by a veterinarian. An animal that laps liquids but will not eat solid food may have a broken jaw.

Fractures in themselves are not emergencies except in so far as they are painful. Twenty-four hours doesn't usually make much difference in the outcome of the case. In fact, most surgeons prefer to let the swelling subside before attempting repair. So please don't panic. Don't attempt to bandage or splint. You'll probably do more harm than good. Give the animal an aspirin or a codeine if you have one. Allow him to rest comfortably in a basket or bed. Some injured animals will drag themselves off and hide, so do restrict the area. Then get on the phone and find an open veterinary clinic. Amazing how many people rush an injured animal into a car without any idea of where they are going or if the veterinary establishment they are going to is actually open. If it's two o'clock in the morning and the dog goes to sleep (he won't move the leg because of the pain that movement will cause) you go to sleep too. Incomprehensible as it sounds the vet is probably asleep already. Lest this sound cruel, ask any friend who has broken a limb how long he lay in hospital before a surgeon started working. Most ski-ing accidents happen some hours from the closest

X-ray unit and surgeon, and they get cleared up OK. I'm not trying to say that a fracture isn't serious. It is, but the picture isn't any different in the morning. Now as to the actual repair. This is really a matter of the surgeon's judgement. He may use plaster, pins, plates or wire. In some fractures he may advise euthanasia. We don't advise euthanasia because our techniques are not as good as those of our counterparts in human medicine. In fact, in some sorts of fracture repair veterinarians pioneered the way. Pinning was first practised by American veterinarians before the war. Unfortunately, though, one cannot immobilize an animal for weeks and weeks, which is necessary in some fracture therapy. An animal that breaks bones in two separate limbs has a very rough go. How can he keep weight off both? Pelvis fractures require as much nursing as doctoring, so if you're not really attached to the animal say so at the outset.

The following examples are presented not as a handy dandy home first-aid course but as information that may help you understand what is happening and how you can best nurse the injured animal after he's returned from the veterinary hospital.

Fractured jaws Holes are drilled on either side of the fracture, and usually on the opposite side of the jaw. Stainless steel wire is inserted, the bones moved into place, and the wire tightened to keep the fractured ends together. Torn flesh is sutured together with material that will dissolve in a few days.

The animal must be given broths and meat soup only for a week or ten days. The wire is usually removed in ten days or a fortnight. Please do come back when told. It's cruel to leave it in longer than necessary, and it makes the removal more difficult.

Fractured shoulder blades These are usually slow and painful in healing, but fortunately it's a well-protected bone and so it is rarely fractured. Sometimes wire is used to pull bits together, sometimes a plate of steel inserted and screwed in, and sometimes it's left to heal on its own. It all depends on which parts of it have been shattered. Rarely does it mend absolutely perfectly, and the dog may be left with a shoulder that will cause pain and lameness from time to time.

Fractured humerus The large bone in the front leg between the knee and the shoulder. This is usually mended by inserting a stainless steel pin into the marrow of the bone and uniting the two fractured ends. The pin must be a tight snug fit in order to eliminate all movement.

Stitches come out in ten days time. The pin is removed in about three weeks.

If the bone is fractured and shattered the two ends may be brought together with the pin and then the shattered bits wired into place around the pin.

Fractured radius or ulna, or both These are the twin straight bones of the front leg and fracture is fairly common. We see a lot in puppies who attempt too high a jump or who are dropped.

If it's a fairly clean break and the bones are still in line plaster will usually do the job. If it's more complicated then one usually uses a plate of stainless steel. This is about the width of the bone and about 10cm (4 in) long. It has holes in it for screws. The fractured ends are brought together, and the plate placed over the fracture. Then it is screwed down tightly. A couple of screws either side of the fracture will usually hold. The screws must take a good bite, because with any loosening at all the fracture won't heal. Sutures are taken out in ten days. The plate is removed in three weeks to two months. Some surgeons prefer to leave it in. Some surgeons will plate and then plaster the leg as well.

Fracture of the smaller bones Of the lower limbs. These may be wired into place but usually plaster is used. Healing should take place in a fortnight. The plaster may be changed then and the second cast taken off ten days later.

Fractured femur The big one of the hind leg. This is almost always pinned these days. The pin usually removed in three weeks or a month but some are left in.

Don't panic if you see the pin push through by itself. Restrain the dog from licking at it. Phone your veterinarian and ask him when he wants to see it. He may replace it with a larger pin, or if there is a good callus he'll remove the pin and forget about it.

Fractured pelvis An all too common fracture. We generally don't operate on the canine pelvis because we can't put our patients to bed for a couple of months. Nursing is all important.

The animal must be helped to stand every four or five hours while 'he does his business.' If a blockage occurs you must take him back to the vet's. Keep the diet fairly sloppy.

Note: Plaster of Paris or other hardening agents used as casts seem to be irresistible chewing objects for their canine owners. They must be covered with elastoplast the day after they're put on. You wait a day to allow the plaster to dry.

Most plaster casts are removed in three weeks, but if they're chafing the skin take the dog back to the vet, who will change it.

Prevention The two commonest causes of fractures are motor accidents and falling or jumping from open windows. If you simply will not use a lead then train your dog to look before he crosses. Don't allow a nervous dog to sleep near an open window and never never lock an animal in a room with an open window. Quite a large number of fractures are caused by dogs jumping or falling out of people's arms. It's common in puppies, so do take care.

French Bulldog

There is some controversy as to whether this breed is derived partly from the English Bulldog, but most authorities believe it to be a completely French development of dogs originally brought from Spain. Be that as it may be, the breed as we know it today has the Bulldog characteristics of loyalty and doggedness, but it doesn't have the obvious physical drawbacks of the English Bulldog or the Boston Bull. An excellent testimonial to the rational French, it has the powerful chest, the bowed front legs and strong jaws, yet none of these characteristics are over-developed to the point of being deformities as they so often are in the English Bull. Its head is not so round as the Boston Bull, and this might be the reason the French dog has fewer breathing problems. Its nose can function as a nose and not as a cute button on the end of a case of snuffles. Although the French Bulldog has narrow hips they're usually not so narrow that the bitch can't have a normal delivery. I wish I could say the same for its English and American cousins. If you like the Bulldog temperament and wish to avoid veterinary problems choose between the French Bulldog, the Bull Terrier and the Staffordshire Bull Terrier.

Gastritis

Inflammation of the stomach. I don't know how you could easily tell it from enteritis, which is an inflammation of the bowel. If an animal is drinking a great deal and vomiting afterwards you might suspect gastritis, but it could equally well be kidney disease or distemper. Until you get professional advice the only safe home aid is starvation and rest. Don't pour any so-called soothing broths down the distressed beast's throat. They will only come up again and all you will have done is aggravate the condition.

Summary: If you suspect gastritis don't give or allow food or liquid.

Geriatrics

That branch of medicine (both human and veterinary) which deals with changes wrought by age. Like yourself, your pet (whether dog, cat or budgie) is subject to the degenerate changes of old age. Black hair, especially around the mouth, turns to grey then white, and corresponding changes occur in the heart, the head and the limbs. How old is old in the animal world? Like ourselves, animals show wide variations. One dog may be old at eight, another remains sprightly at eleven, but generally speaking dogs of the larger breeds show the slowing of age at seven or eight, and the smaller breeds at ten or eleven. Fourteen is a ripe old age indeed. I emphasize that there are wide individual variations. Every vet has a favourite old patient who at sixteen is brought in regularly for his check-up and heart pills. Your veterinary surgeon will point out to you what is best for your ageing pet. Generally he will emphasize that his habits are fixed, and that the pattern of his life is to be disturbed as little as possible. In other words, because you realize one rainy morning that faithful Fido can't hear you so well and is a little creaky getting up in the morning, don't cut out the biscuit he's always had and start pouring brandy down his throat. Any changes you and your vet decide are necessary must be brought about slowly and gradually. If he's overweight his diet should be reduced over a period of weeks, not days. Instead of a three-biscuit snack after that walk, reduce them to two and then one. Instead of a two-mile run make it a two-mile walk. Cut down the opportunities for excitement and the reasons for stress. Field dogs particularly have to be weaned gradually from their activities. Don't change his diet except on your vet's recommendation. He will probably want you to cut down on indigestible elements like fibrous roughages. He may add calcium or other elements to the diet. A constant supply of fresh (often changed) drinking water is more important then ever. Avoid at whatever cost boarding your aged pet in kennels. In particular an older pet who is being treated for heart or kidney disorders should not be put in kennels, with the exception of animals with some heart conditions in which your vet may decide that a period of enforced rest in kennels would be of benefit. Remember to leave a slip of paper with four simple headings to help the kennel staff: first, the animal's name, secondly, what he usually eats, the amounts and time of feeding, thirdly, his exercise periods, and lastly any particular foibles or quirks. And don't forget the old helpful business of leaving his favourite pillow or toy. Finally, a sad and cautionary note. No medicine and no surgery will make an old pet into a young one. In older animals we can relieve and we can postpone but we seldom cure. The regenerative powers in aged animals is limited. We can provide comfort, relief from pain, easing of his last months or years, but more than that medicine cannot do.

Gestation

This is the period of pregnancy, i.e. from conception (assumed to be first copulation) to delivery. In dogs it's about sixty days, with a range of two or three days either side. Usually only two routine check-ups are required. One early on at which time your vet may decide to worm her if she hasn't been done at the proper time of one month before breeding. He will advise about calcium, cod-liver oil and milk. The second visit should be made about fifty or fifty-five days on, just to make sure all is going well. At this time you should ascertain just how your veterinarian handles difficult confinements. Some prefer to visit at the home, and others prefer to have the bitch brought in to the surgery. Find out, too, about evening and weekend arrangements.

Gingivitis

Inflammation of the gums or sore gums is a common condition in older animals who have been on soft sloppy diets, or whose teeth have been allowed to get filthy and tartared. The neglected animal should be taken to the vet (by appointment for this job please) to have the tartar removed. The gums should be rinsed with salt water after meals for a few days. Use a bit of cotton, dip it in the salt water (a teaspoon or two to a pint) and wash down each side of the mouth. If the gums are too sore try sodium perborate (available at your chemists) or glycerine and honey for a few days, then go on to the salt water. Some gums and teeth are so badly neglected that a course of injections of penicillin or other antibiotic is necessary to reduce the inflammation and infection before the mouth can be opened without pain.

Glenimaal Terrier

I hope this wonderful Irish dog never becomes so popular that the dealer-breeders find it worth their while. Now it is unspoiled, absolutely fearless, and compact, weighing 13·5kg (30 lb). Aside from a slightly narrow mouth he has no faults. If you buy an Irish champion you can be sure he's done well in the field as well as on the show bench. How many wire-haired Fox Terrier champions have ever been worked?

Golden Retriever

Similar to the Labrador, but slightly rangier in appearance. If you like that golden coat, which is halfway between chestnut and cream, then by all means exercise your preference. This, in fact, is what many people who are more interested in appearance than field sports do because there is little doubt that the good old-fashioned Black Lab is still the best worker. I suppose it's because there are many more of them, so that one can be more selective and cull more rigidly. The Golden Retriever is a separate breed and its origin is distinct from the Labrador.

The story goes that in the 1850s a Scottish lord bought a troupe of circus dogs which he took back to Scotland. His training, the Scots air, an admixture of Bloodhound to develop the nose and another hundred years of selection produced the modern Golden Retriever. Being a lazy person I've never bothered to check on the truth of the story, but it's a nice one and this is certainly a nice dog.

Gordon Setter

As the name suggests, it's of Scots origin. It's a great field dog, and a real one-man companion dog. Although there are exceptions the breed as a whole is definitely not good with children. Slightly larger than the average Labrador, its colour is black with tan markings. Some specimens betray the partly Collie origin by the lie and wave of their coats.

Grass

Dogs will search out succulent green shoots to supplement their diet. It's a perfectly healthy thing to do provided the grass isn't covered with those ubiquitous poisons called chemical sprays. Carnivores in their natural state eat their entire prey and relish the grass-filled stomachs and intestines. In other words, vegetables are a valuable addition to a carnivore's diet and that is the reason your pet relishes those tender shoots.

There is another reason for grass eating, and that is to induce vomiting. The animal is then not selective at all – indeed may choose long tough fibrous leaves – and may do so in what I can only describe as panic. It looks a bit like an alcoholic reaching for his early morning shakes stopper. If this sort of grass-eating followed by vomiting is repeated two or three times in the course of the day, or if it's a daily occurrence for two or three days, I should consult your veterinary surgeon so that he can attempt to find the reason.

Great Dane

Everyone knows just how impressive this ancient breed can be. The best types are found in Germany (where they were largely developed) and in America. The bitches weigh 45kg (100 lb) and more, and the dogs 54kg (120 lb) or more. They can and usually do carry this well-distributed weight majestically. Take note before you buy one that nothing in dogdom can look quite so pitiful as 45kg (100 lb) of bone and muscle skulking nervously behind the sofa, and few 'domesticated' animals can be as dangerous as a very large dog who through shyness or hysteria or lack of training is unpredictable. Unfortunately unscrupulous breeders in the past flogged 'shy' puppies, and the breed has been given an undeserved bad name. Choose your breeder carefully. Have a look at the dam and the sire if possible. Please devote ten minutes a day (until he is well into adulthood) to training your Dane. Incidentally, Great Danes are not long-lived dogs – eight or nine is an average life expectancy. They are noteworthy too for very large litters. A final word of caution. If you are vaguely thinking that it would be nice to have a huge dog, please remember that huge dogs can and have killed people. A few years ago a pair of Great Danes pounced on and killed a woman so quickly that a policeman who was standing by could not prevent it. In other words, if you know what you are about, get one. If it's a whim then do some serious thinking before paying the deposit.

PS: I know a clever young man who buys old Rolls Royces in England and sells them in California. He has two equally fashionable Danes. When either has pups he provides beautifully typed pedigrees that are completely fake. He sells the culls of the litter first and at top prices because, as his patter goes, they're show quality. The best he keeps to the last just in case one turns out well. *Moral:* Next time you buy a Rolls get a new one.

Greyhound

What can I say about these dogs without getting into trouble? There are two sorts. The racing sort and the show types. Personally I prefer the appearance of the former. If you are interested in going into the racing game, you had better be very smart (in which case you probably won't), very rich (in which case you'll probably prefer horses), very lucky (which everybody is going to be – tomorrow), or very much not my sort of person. It's uncanny how Greyhounds resemble thoroughbreds in appearance and temperament, and visiting a racing Greyhound kennel is like visiting scaled down racing stables, except that the smell of hay is replaced by that of meat bubbling away in huge cauldrons. There is always a group of penniless 'stable-boys' or 'kennel-men' trying to get together enough money for a bet on that afternoon's 'sure thing,' and often there is the little hierarchy of trainers and 'head-lads' who really know what the score is, and occasionally the hapless and helpless owner who pays the bills and wonders what's going on.

But if you're interested in that lot you're not likely to be reading this book. The Greyhound follows almost entirely by sight. His troubles are usually leg and feet because of the tremendous pounding they get. Greyhounds are kept muzzled, not because they are dangerous to people (most make very tractable pets), but because they may turn and pull their mate to pieces (and so quickly it's over before you've realized what's happening), and only a fool will take a pair of unmuzzled Greyhounds out on the lead unless he knows them very well.

Whether Greyhound kennels abound with fools I cannot say. Two years ago for ten days I visited daily a large track with the then official veterinary surgeon of that track. The following three episodes occurred during that period. A kennel-man took six Greyhounds out. In each hand he held three leads. They started in on each other, and before they were separated one dog was dead, one bleeding to death and one had to be hospitalized for serious injuries. The kennel man had simply forgotten to muzzle the dogs.

The second episode was reported by phone. Two lads were told to bathe a dog. They picked up a barrel of pure carbolic and poured it over the dog. The dog died in agony. Both 'lads' went to hospital to have their burns treated. The arm of one of them was described as being like a piece of liver. They hadn't been told to dilute the disinfectant – or something.

The third event was really what Orwell would have called 'no-see seeing.' One of the favourites did very badly in a race. He stumbled more than once. Next day he was still sort of stumbling, or at any rate he wasn't really steady on his legs. The dog had no illness to which the official veterinarian or I could attribute his condition. The track official who discussed the matter with us decided that the poor dog had probably been overtrained and an official report would not be necessary, and it seemed a shame, he said, to go to the bother of a blood or urine test for something so negligible. The official veterinarian has only three choices. He can resign, which really accomplishes nothing because his successor just has to go through a long initiation into the mysteries while the same old thing continues, or he can continue to try bit by bit to civilize the natives. Or, of course, he can create a scandal, and watch his bank balance disappear while people congratulate him on his courage.

Do you want a Greyhound as a pet? Most kennels have one that has knocked a joint and can't race any more or just isn't up to breeding standards, and they'll be happy to let you have one. They've been inoculated and raised properly with a balanced diet, and most of those retired racers make most appreciative pets. It will take a few weeks of patience to break any bad habits they've picked up in kennels.

Two further reservations about Greyhounds as pets. First, they will fight other dogs. Secondly, they are one of the few breeds that can out-run a cat. Unless you are prepared to fence your Greyhound in you are going to be very unpopular.

Griffons Bruxellois

If you want a cuddly wee beast that hasn't had the brains bred out of it, this would be the ideal choice. They come in the large size 5·4kg (12 lb) package, and in the economy size weighing in at about 3kg (6 lb). They are alert and Terrier-like, and despite their size have competed successfully in obedience trials with Alsatians and Dobermans.

Grinding of the teeth

This is almost invariably a sign of pain, and if you can't determine and eliminate the cause I would suggest an early visit to the vet's.

Groendael

This jet black Belgian shepherd is a first-class herding, police and army dog. Fortunately, in Belgium, field trials are quite as important as the show bench, so the breed's intelligence has every chance of surviving. Elsewhere it has never been a popular breed so only the genuine enthusiasts have kept breeding kennels. If you are thinking along Alsatian lines you should consider the Groendael, because your chances of getting a good dog are better than with the Alsatian. About the same height as the Alsatian but weigh less.

Grooming

This isn't a very fancy or difficult business. It's just a matter of helping your pet keep clean and sort of tidy. A short-haired dog like a Boxer, a Dalmatian, a Staffordshire or the average cross-Terrier mongrel only need a brushing once or twice a week. Four or five minutes will remove all the dead hairs and scurf. Wire-hairs require combing and a brush down. Long-haired dogs require more attention and more often. Any animal that is moulting should be groomed daily. Use a soft but firm bristled brush that won't scratch the skin. Use a cloth over the face if the animal objects to the brush over the bony bits.

Get the beast used to the idea from an early age. Hesitant ones are best held by one person while a second does the work. Do it on a table and use a good light. A spread of newspapers will collect the debris.

Grooming should include a look between the toes and pads, combing out or removing any knotted hair there, a check to see that the nails aren't too long, and a look under the tail to see that there aren't any soiled mats of hair or anal glands swelling up. Every two or three months check to see that the teeth aren't being covered with tartar.

After a wet walk the animal should be dried off, and a while later combed and brushed.

Guard dogs

A guard dog is a dog that can do just that. You're only fooling yourself if you think your Fifi is a guard dog just because she barks. Fifi is just a warning dog. A determined person (and most intruders are) can silence Fifi with one well-placed kick. We see dogs in the clinic – usually belonging to shopkeepers or publicans – who have been injured while trying to protect their owner's property. Naturally they include some Alsatians, Airedales, Dobermans and Boxers, but at least with those breeds it's more of an even battle. It's grossly unfair to employ a dog weighing under 27kg (60 lb) as a guard. There is one notable exception to the 'only large dogs can guard' business and that is the Welsh Corgi. They're not my favourite breed by a long way so I can't really be objective about them, but it would take a brave or foolish man to try to get by one. Unfortunately, though, the Corgi has more chance of getting injured in the process than a really large dog. Also, a big dog can pull a man down and hold him. The Corgi can only corner his prey.

The best guard dogs are our best patients. They are quiet, well-behaved and co-operative. They have been thoughtfully selected and carefully trained. They are happy as only working dogs can be. I recall an absolutely huge Alsatian that is still working for the London Police Department. He is almost all black, weighs 45kg (100 lb) without a bit of fat, and has the biggest set of teeth you ever saw. He came in with his handler one midnight just pumping blood from a severed artery. He had stepped in a broken bottle and then jerked his foot out. The handler had applied a tourniquet and a tight bandage which probably saved the dog's life. Anyway the point of the story is that that huge dog, although in pain and weak with loss of blood, lay quietly at his owner's command. He was given injections and sewn up and it wasn't even necessary to hold his head or tie a tape around his muzzle.

Many ordinary people have large guard dogs who although not so highly trained as the official Police dogs, are every bit as companionable and handleable. The essence of the English system of training Police dogs is that they live with their handler during training and afterwards live with the handler and his family as an ordinary dog would. Nobody can say that this decreases their efficiency in their work.

The worst sort of guard dogs (if I can dignify the victims of human stupidity with that term) are those poor beasts who have been confined and chained and teased and starved, until they are nothing but surly snarling teeth attached to a shrunken digestive tract. I don't think there is a special department in Hell for the people who do such things to dogs, so one should bring the full force of the law to bear on them while they are alive. If the laws can't cope they should be strengthened.

If you want a dog for guard purposes be prepared to spend up to £100 for the pup, and double that amount to train him and yourself. He will give you eight to ten years of faithful service, and will ask for nothing but his food. If he's not worth the outlay you have damn little worth guarding.

Guide dogs (*seeing eye dogs*)

If you have a few roubles kicking around loose, and you would like to help both animals and people at the same time, you might consider giving to the association that provides the guide dogs. The special relationship that exists between a blind person and the guide dog cannot be described without getting sentimental and sloshy. From the veterinarian's point of view the guide dog is the ideal patient. He has as much trust in man as his master must have in him.

Guide dogs get so attached to their blind masters that they simply start to waste away if parted for any length of time. The problem of when to retire an ageing guide dog is heartbreaking, for it usually means euthanasia. The blind person cannot cope with two dogs in the street, and the retired one's life of waiting would be quite impossible.

A few common-sense hints to help the blind and their guides. A dog cannot read, so if they are standing under a bus stop sign that says the bus doesn't stop there on Sundays, please go up and speak when still a few feet off and explain the situation. If you see the pair of them hesitating at an intersection offer your help. The dog knows when it is safe to cross the street, but if it's a new neighbourhood he can't be sure if it's the right street. And please, please, whatever you do keep your own dog away from the guide dog. The latter is trained to mind his own business, and it's unfair to subject him to the sniffs of yours. The guide dog has a job to do, and much as he'd enjoy a visit and a good old introductory smell, he's much too conscientious to return the courtesy.

To return once again to money. There are a lot of blind people in this affluent year of Our Lord who don't have a guide dog because there isn't enough money. Let me assure you that there are no happier, better balanced dogs than the guide dog, and a contribution to the purchase and training of one could be your testimonial to the highest relationship yet achieved between man and dog.

Gun dogs

There are volumes of books and lifetimes of labour devoted to the dogs who work with the hunter. If you are interested in any of the sporting breeds (and there are dozens of them varying from the now all but wrecked Cocker Spaniel to the almost unspoilable Labrador) may I offer the following suggestion. Buy from a breeder who is interested in the field performance of his dogs rather than accomplishments in the show ring. I am perfectly aware that a great field dog may also be a great show dog, just as high-performance dairy cows more often closely approach the show ideal than do the indifferent producers. Obviously the ideal is a champion both aesthetically and practically, but where one can't reach the ideal I would sacrifice the show points every time.

You see, I would rather have a dog who responded to training, who could walk and run as nature intended and who wasn't a neurotic, than one who looked as the wee clique of judges thought he should look. I don't want to be drawn into the current backroom controversy about who are competent dog judges, but I do state that there is less room for human error judging in the field than there is judging on the show bench. It is quite obvious that the Cocker would not have deteriorated to the pitiful state he's in today, if field performance were the criterion of excellence.

Most of the people I meet couldn't care less about who thought what about Champion Love of Silk Ears. What they want in a gun dog is a trainable, workable dog, who can live a normal life and won't chew the children into small pieces. All I suggest is that they're more likely to find that dog in the field than at the show.

We usually see gun dogs in the clinics out of hunting season. Then they are brought in suffering from all sorts of complaints, but usually nervous eczemas. Of course we dispense what we think might help, but as the cause is usually boredom the cure must wait till the next season's game is plump enough for the shot.

Retired gun dogs can get grotesquely fat and smelly and itchy. Diet must be watched and exercise kept up and grooming becomes more important than ever.

Haematoma

Blood blister. They usually come up suddenly as a result of a blow, and they are normally painless and rather firmer than abscesses. They may be drained with the aid of a boiled needle if they are very small, but they do have a tendency to pop up again. Those that do pop up again should be treated by bandaging to prevent further damage until you can get to the vet. He may cut into the blister, strip out the lining and suture the whole mess down, but usually he will try bandaging first, because it's better if it absorbs naturally. Any fair-sized haematoma will leave your dog's ear looking like that of a retired boxer (see *Ear haematoma*).

Haemorrhage

We've all been exposed at one time or another, either in boy scouts or in the army or at school, to first-aid courses. The instructor (who has read it all in the manual) emphasizes that the first thing one does is to determine whether it's an artery or a vein that's been cut. Arteries bleed bright red and they pump out lesser or greater waves while veins bleed a steady ooze of darker coloured blood. For veins you put a tourniquet below the injury, for arteries above. That's all very nice except: 1, I have never been able to tell the difference between the brighter red blood and the darker blood; 2, usually it's a great mess of blood and one can't see if it's oozing or pumping; and 3, how do you put a tourniquet on a hip, a penis, a nose or an ear?

Everyone acts differently in an emergency and I don't suppose that many people will remember my method of dealing with bleeding, but for what it's worth here it is.

The first thing I do is protect myself from injury. This is partly selfish, but it doesn't really help the situation if everyone involved is adding blood to the scene. I grab the animal by the scruff of the neck, and holding him on either side of the neck raise him on to a table. While still controlling his head I get someone to tie a cord (or a necktie) around his muzzle and knot it behind his ears. Only then do I feel free to look at the wound.

Unless the source of blood is obvious and easily tied off I then put anything – a torn shirt, a handkerchief, even a package of tissues – on the wound and hold it there with as much pressure as I can apply.

Then I take a breather and try to assess the damage and how best to deal with it with the materials available. Often someone knows a source of bandages close by. In England almost anyone will rip a pillow case or sheet in strips to help an animal.

If it's a freely bleeding wound you need not worry about iodine or peroxide or boiling up the dressings. Leave that to the vet, later.

Take the strips of cloth and wind as tightly as you can around the wound. Go well above it and well below it. Lay the strips as flat as you can.

Leg wounds are fairly simple. You simply wrap round the leg. Body wounds you must go round the whole belly or chest.

To stop an injured tail bleeding you usually have to wrap the whole tail in tight bandage.

A bleeding scrotum is very difficult. One places a pressure bandage on the bleeding area and ties it in by criss-crossing strips over the back and around the hips.

An injured bleeding penis should have a tight pressure bandage tied in place by strips right around the body. The same goes for a bleeding breast or nipple.

I don't know of any effective first aid for a bleeding tongue or gum or tooth. One needs anaesthetics and ligaturing material to deal with those.

A bleeding ear flap should have a bandage placed on both sides and the flap bandaged flat to the head by winding strips of material round and round the head. One must be careful not to wind too tightly or the animal will not be able to breathe freely.

Bleeding around an eye can usually be controlled by holding a bandage to the wound while getting to the clinic. The dog may not panic if it can see out of the other eye.

I leave the most serious to the end. The dog's natural way of killing other dogs is by slashing open the jugular or the carotid. These huge vessels lie in the furrows that run along either side of the throat in the neck. It might just be possible to save an animal that's had its jugular ripped open, but I've never heard of one surviving more than a few long seconds. Certainly if the carotid were opened death would occur in a few short seconds. However, many dogs get their throats slashed and the big vessels remain intact. The area, though, is one that bleeds freely and a pressure bandage can save a life.

All the above are simple emergency measures to save the animal from bleeding to death. One gets the pressure bandage in and then gets hold of a veterinarian. What would he do if he had no equipment with him? Very much as I've outlined, with a bit more precision and a surer touch than yours. He would then take the animal to a proper place with proper equipment for dealing with the situation.

Usually the animal is anaesthetized and the bleeding vessels located and tied off. The area is cleaned up as much as possible and then the skin sutured. A bandage protects the wound and an antibiotic injection is given to combat infection. If the animal has lost a lot of blood a transfusion is given. Sometimes other injections are given to help the blood to clot. The antibiotic injections are repeated daily for a few days, the dressings changed every day or twice a day, and a week or ten days later the skin sutures are removed and Rover is ready to go and get into trouble again.

One more thing. There is no effective first aid for bleeding from the nose or the anus or for internal bleeding. Keep the animal quiet and calm. Wrap it in a blanket and get it to the vet.

Hair

See bathing, brushing, clipping, eczema, grooming, hairlessness, licking, scratching.

The more there is the more care is needed, but generally five minutes of daily combing and brushing will make your pet glow like a film star at her latest wedding.

Hairlessness

Total baldness is rare, but one does see the odd case in Yorkshire Terriers and other toy breeds. Partial baldness is more common and one attempts to find the cause before starting treatment, but don't blame the vet if the first course of injections has no result. If there were a simple answer to baldness doubtless our colleagues who practise medicine in the human world would tell us about it. The common causes of baldness are over-strong solutions of drugs and soaps, scratching due to fleas or lice, ringworm, mange and burns,

109

constant licking for nervous reasons and continually lying in front of the fire. We find that grooming, dusting with insect powder and lots of outdoor exercise effect cures in a number of cases. Fat animals are prone to all sorts of trouble, including bald patches. It's amazing how many animals get a nice new coat of smooth hair when they lose a few pounds.

Harness

Very small dogs with short necks like Pekinese, neckless beasts like Pugs, very fat lap dogs like those one sees in Brussels or Paris, and guard and guide dogs are usually provided with a harness rather than a collar.

Harness should be removed after every walk. It should be washed and saddle-soaped weekly.

Most people buy harness when the animal is still growing and they just don't seem to notice it getting tighter and tighter. The poor dog probably thinks all that squeezing is the price he has to pay to go for a walk.

Harrier

The hound bred to chase the hare – an activity that man and the hound have practised together for a couple of thousand years. There are packs in Britain with 200 years of well-recorded history behind them. I don't think the Harrier makes an ideal city dog or family pet, but people do keep them, and what's more they even put them on a show bench. I suppose we can look forward to Miniature Harriers. They won't be able to run very fast or see very well, but you'll be able to carry a pair in your shopping basket.

Heart

We are seeing more heart conditions than formerly, and that is quite understandable. Our animals, like ourselves, have more chance to live into ripe old age as more and more of the infectious diseases of youth come under control. Then, too, as the area of concrete increases and that of green decreases, there is less opportunity for exercise and therefore many more over-weight pets. The heart has to do that much more work to feed blood to all that additional weight.

If your ageing pet is slowing down and isn't really eager for his constitutional, or if he coughs after going up the steps, you had better have a check-up. Many ageing animals are living quite at ease with the aid of digitalis and other drugs.

If your middle-aged fat pet has what you think is a fainting fit it may well be a heart attack. Don't use brandy or water. Allow the animal to rest quietly. Reassurance is about all the help you can offer. Don't make him move for an hour or two unless he wants to, and take him along to the vet later on.

Again prevention is the answer, and although we still have many unanswered questions we do know that overweight is a contributing factor. Please don't kill your pet with kindness. Avoid those treats and starch filled biscuits unless every calorie is walked off.

There is a unit doing heart research at one of the American veterinary colleges which, although it has been in full operation for only a few years, has already come up with some interesting observations. Boxers and Alsatians get more than their fair share of heart trouble. Male Cocker Spaniels have heart trouble eight times more than female Cockers. Some families of dogs are almost certain to produce a puppy or more in a litter with heart trouble.

Why do trained scientists spend their time studying heart diseases in the dog when they could be working on human heart problems? The simple answer is that science and medicine know no boundaries. A problem solved in canine medicine may lead to a solution in human medicine.

Heat

Bitches normally have two seasons or heat periods annually. Some breeds, Chows for example, may have their first heat at five or six months, but eight or nine months is more usual. Some bitches may not come on heat until they are a year or a year and a half old. It's nothing to worry about.

How can you tell when a bitch is on heat? Her vulva (the external sexual organ below her tail) will be swollen. Coming from it will be a discharge. It will be blood tinged and varying in colour from a light pink to a dark red. All the male dogs in the neighbourhood will drop around for a visit. If they're not allowed in they'll leave calling cards in the liquid form such canine occasions call for.

The bitch will bleed about a week before she will accept the male. The period she will accept the male is usually about eight or nine days but it can vary from five to twelve. The important thing to remember is that the danger period is after the blood has stopped. To be on the safe side you should keep the bitch strictly confined for three weeks from the first sign of blood.

If you wish the bitch bred, the male should be presented two days

111

after the end of bleeding and again two days later if the first meeting was unsatisfactory.

There are injections available that are given one month before the onset of heat and that will prevent heat for six months. Ask your vet if he thinks they're safe. I don't.

PS: The birth control pill for bitches is now widely accepted as safe and efficient provided it is used exactly as instructed. I think the instructions include the phrase, 'at the onset of heat'. I know lots of people who wouldn't notice their house was on fire. Vets advise those sorts to have their bitches spayed. Many vets also think it advisable to allow a bitch one normal season before putting her on the pill. Some breeds that seem to have more 'cycling' difficulties than most include Scotties, Basenjis and Chows. Your vet might think otherwise, but I'd be inclined to save the pill money and buy an extra lock for the door. Incidentally if you've got a surplus of the pills don't chuck them. They're also used for treating some sorts of cat eczema and occasionally have been known to turn randy, vicious male dogs into tractable darlings. Try a handful on your boyfriend!

Heat stroke (*sun stroke*)

We're in little danger here if those long range forecasts are right, but if Chang Fu and you have retired to Cannes or Miami, you had better use a little common sense at high noon. If it's a really hot day and an animal lies down panting, loses consciousness and starts breathing very rapidly in short gasps, it may well be heat stroke. There usually isn't time to find a thermometer and take the temperature, which will be 40°C (105°F) degrees or up. First aid consists of getting the animal into the coolest shade nearby, and very quickly. Ice packs all over the body, or if there is no ice available running the coolest water available over the animal will alleviate the condition. Ice or cold water in the rectum will lower the temperature rapidly. A salt water injection is indicated (in Mediterranean countries a chemist will do it) or a bit of salt in water (a few drops at a time in the mouth or rather more in the form of an enema) will also help.

Speed is the essence in treating heat stroke, so do all that and then try to contact a vet.

PS: Dogs left in closed automobiles suffer the same syndrome. My brother-in-law, John (who isn't as stupid as he looks) tells me it's better to smash the windscreen. It's usually insured whereas the small windows on the side are not. Remember too that most dogs consider the family car an extension of their own territory. When they come to life they may resent your presence. Establish an escape route and live to be the heroic rescuer yet again.

Heating

The best sorts of artificial heat for an orphaned litter, or for an animal you are nursing through sickness, or for an ageing thin-skinned lap dog are either a properly insulated electric bed, a really warm room or, failing those, a polystyrene-bead pillow. Hot water bottles tend to chill during the hours they're needed most. Infra-red bulbs give light as well as heat so are not conducive to proper sleep.

We often see and treat burns caused by animals lying too close to an electric or coal fire. Young animals or large boisterous ones like Boxers can and do cause accidents by knocking over the heater, so take the appropriate precautions.

Dogs will sit by the hour staring into a fire and it doesn't seem to bother most of them, but we do get the odd one with eye trouble because of the habit. If your pet has the habit and runny eyes, see if a screen doesn't cure the condition.

Animals who lie for hours by the fire sometimes develop a dry scurfy skin and even eczema. The cure is obvious.

Hernia

A condition in which an organ or a part of an organ that belongs in one part of the body is moved into another part of the body. For example, if a bit of bowel pokes through from behind the abdominal muscles where it belongs and lies just under the skin. There are many sorts of hernias, but most of them are either caused by accidents or the animal is born with them. They are corrected surgically by poking the organ back where it belongs and sewing up the hole it came through. The commonest hernia is an *umbilical* hernia. It's often seen in kittens or puppies. You see a swelling at the belly button or umbilicus. Turn the animal on its back. If the swelling disappears then it's a hernia. The bit of bowel has gone back where it belongs. Often these heal on their own, but if it persists or gets larger you must show it to your vet. A similar swelling up inside the thigh is called an *inguinal* hernia, and is common in bitches. There is a great deal of evidence that both these types of hernias are hereditary, or that at least the tendency to those hernias is hereditary. Obviously an animal with an hereditary hernia should not be used for breeding, but it's amazing and disgusting how many people who can and do know better can't overcome their commercial greed. They breed animals with hernias and sell the offspring to unsuspecting people. I was presented once with an ageing white Poodle bitch. The old age pensioner who had bought it for three guineas (all she could afford) was under the impression it was a puppy. She was worried because it had a large swelling high up on the inside of its hind leg. The swelling was an inguinal hernia, and the bitch was so old that the operation would be tricky. In addition the bitch needed several teeth removed, and she had evidence of kidney disease. The person who had sold that bitch to the old lady had sold litter after litter from the bitch, and when she was no longer capable of rearing a litter had flogged her like a used automobile. And, of course, all the puppies would be good candidates for hernias. Moral of the story: Know who you are dealing with.

Another type of hernia is called a *diaphragmatic hernia*, and it usually occurs after an accident like falling off a window ledge. In this case the bowel, liver or stomach pokes through a hole in the diaphragm into the chest cavity. The animal appears all right. It may even eat. But its breathing is very, very fast. The operation to correct this condition is one of the more difficult ones, and you mustn't be too optimistic.

Hip dysplasia

The hip joint is located in the middle of that thick pile of muscles and fat that you sit on. The long bone of the leg ends in a round ball that fits into a concave hole or socket in the pelvis.

If the long bone's round end fits nicely into its socket as nature intended there is no problem. But if the socket for some reason or other is flattened, or if the end of the long bone is square rather than round, then obviously the joint is going to crack. There will be pain and swelling and the animal will become lame.

In the last few years we have been seeing more and more dogs with lame hips, and many of them are grouped together for convenience under the term hip dysplasia.

Alsatians seem to be afflicted with the condition more than the other breeds, but that may be only because there are more Alsatians about. We see the condition fairly frequently in Labradors too, and I have seen examples of the disease in the Bull Mastiff, the St Bernard and Pyrenean Mountain Dogs.

Many authorities believe the condition to be hereditary or at least that the predisposition to the condition is hereditary. There are study groups and committees looking into the problem.

The first item, of course, is to define the problem. What is hip dysplasia? How many degrees out must the joint be before it is considered pathological?

You might think the answer is obvious. If the animal is lame and the joint is out a bit, then that is hip dysplasia. But many apparently normal animals have hip dysplasia that only show on X-ray. Why worry about them? Simply because it is thought that if you breed two such animals together the offspring will almost certainly have hip dysplasia.

All that doesn't interest you if old faithful Rover can't make the steps. What can we do about it? All too little, unfortunately. We can relieve the pain, of course, and often we can manage to minimize the period that the animal is actually completely lame, but we cannot cure the condition medically.

The only real answer is to determine which animals are transmitting the condition, and not breed from them or their offspring. It's a problem for the veterinarian and for the breeder, and only by research by the former and consultations with the latter will the condition be eliminated.

PS: If you are contemplating the purchase of a puppy of any large show breed and the vendor says, 'Hip dysplasia . . . Never see it. It's been invented by the vets,' I would be inclined to make my apologies and look elsewhere. I would, however, be prepared to look at puppies whose breeder explains, 'We've always bred working dogs and so far as I know none have ever gone down with h.d. So we haven't bothered. Look at old Maud over there. She's fourteen and still retrieves like a puppy. Wouldn't think she was a great-great grandmother, would you?'

History

To you history probably means war and peace and the messes man has made. To simple-minded people like myself and other veterinarians it means the story of your pet. He can't talk, but if you want to be helpful you can simplify our problem of diagnosis by answering the questions simply and directly. How old is he? Say 'two' or 'three' or 'five,' not 'when did Aunt Sophia fall off the sofa?' When did he eat last? What did he eat? When was she in heat? Has it been inoculated against distemper? Has she had puppies? Has she been spayed? etc., etc. Of course we can answer most of the questions ourselves, but it does save time to get an accurate history right at the beginning of the examination.

Hives

Some people call them shingles. They look like little bumps under the hair of the body. Bits of the cheeks or the skin around the eyes or ears may be swollen. The bumps may be very itchy, but usually, they don't seem to bother the animal at all. They are the result of an allergy, like reaction to insect stings. They are dangerous only if the animal is having difficulty in breathing. If the animal is panting for breath or turning blue rush to the vet, because an injection of adrenalin or antihistamine is crucial. In the mild ordinary cases bathe the spots with sodium bicarbonate or just wait for a few hours. The swellings often go down on their own. If they don't the veterinary surgeon will give an antihistamine injection and some pills to go on with.

Holding (*while examining or treating*)

Handling a dog so that you don't hurt it and so that it can't hurt you is really a matter of experience, but until you have that experience be warned that most animals (your pet included) will revert to its natural instincts of biting and clawing if it doesn't like what you are doing.

Dogs of medium or large size are easily held by grasping the neck folds, one hand on each side, and controlling the head firmly. If the dog is an Alsatian, Great Dane or St Bernard you had better get an appropriate sized man to hold him. I don't know how you hold a Bull Terrier that doesn't want to be held. The strength in their necks is unbelievable. Fortunately most really strong dogs are usually amenable to their owner's words of encouragement.

Small dogs like Yorkie, Chihuahuas and Maltese Terriers are usually held with one hand on the neck, the other on the loin. Sometimes it takes two people to hold a small dog. One holds the neck, the other holds the feet. Some are best held by wrapping them in a towel. Pekinese are a problem, and each one has to be handled differently. Generally I support the chest with one hand and hang on to the hair of the neck with the other. Fortunately (because their mouths are so malformed) their bites usually aren't severe.

Highly nervous dogs may have to be given an injection before they can be handled. These cases are often held with a noose on the end of a pole while getting the tranquillizing injection.

All dogs who bite should have a bandage wrapped around their muzzle (see *Tape*).

Finally, a well-trained dog who respects and trusts its owner is usually no problem at all.

Hounds

There are Greyhounds with a few thousand years of history behind them, and aristocratic Russian Wolfhounds and graceful Irish Deerhounds and Foxhounds that have been reared for many generations in the kennels that grace Maryland and Virginia and the gentle English downs.

Smaller versions called Lurchers are commonly advertised in the English press. There are as many definitions as varieties but whippet-greyhound-terrier crosses seem to be the most acceptable by the fraternity of gypsies, cockneys and north-country types who speak their own unique version of the English language. As geneticists might say, neither the owners nor their dogs breed true. Many, however, are blessed with hybrid vigour.

There's another kind of hound that's found throughout the American continent. It is usually a lanky under-fed mangy sort of a hound weighing up to 31kg (70 lb), brown or tan or grey in colour, long in the leg and long in the muzzle with sharp hungry teeth, and of a variety within that general type that defies description. Most of those that I've seen look like longer, lankier, hungrier Greyhounds, but some are squarer in the head and blockier in the body.

Almost always these hounds of no traceable ancestry belong to some chap who 'does a bit of farming, and odd jobs that jes happin to be going and all the huntin' that's worth huntin'.'

On the prairies of the Dakotas and Saskatchewan they honour their hounds with the title Coyote Hounds. North of the border they don't pronounce the final e. Farther south and in the foothills the hound becomes a Big Cat Hound, or a Lynx Dog or sometimes, optimistically, a Mountain Lion Hound. Across the continent he changes his name and his occupation In the south the most common designation is Racoon or Coon Hound, and of course lots of people call them just plain Hound Dogs.

By and large these hounds aren't really notable for anything except hunger, laziness, mange and an absolute fear of their owners. However, there are some packs which, whether by accident or design, are eminently suited to hunting the game found in the area. Increasingly the more 'settled folk' in the hunting areas are taking an interest in these hounds, and by selection producing some acceptable hunters. Sometimes the strangest people are brought together by their mutual interest in hounds.

One of my friends-cum-clients down Yucatan way kept a pack of hounds that he claimed were equally good at 'circling' deer or tracking jaguar or running down wild pigs. All I ever saw that pack do was scratch, although I must admit they would make a great noise if you turned them loose. Their owner, too, spent most of his time scratching, although occasionally he would look at the pictures in some old magazines.

Once I had to make a trip to New Orleans, and my friend asked me if I'd take one of his hounds along and trade it with a fellow up in Mississippi, who, so he had heard, had a really admirable kind of hound. 'How would I find the fellow?' I asked. 'Oh, that's easy,' my friend replied. 'You just go up to Mississippi and say you're looking for Bill Faulkner. His hounds are famous all over.'

Husky

A general term used to describe the dozen or so breeds of Spitz-like dogs found in the far north. The breeds vary widely, and there is even a lot of variation within them. There have been a lot of crosses with wolves, so one sees huskies that vary all the way from almost pure timber-wolf to the shorter compact Baffinland, Greenland or Malemute, that look so Spitz-like.

In the north of Canada distemper has taken its toll, and in the last ten years rabies has appeared. The aeroplane has become a common sight in the far north. The Eskimo with the building of the DEW line (Distant Early Warning) has become a labourer and a mechanic. All too often, since his contact with the whites, he has become a thief and his woman a prostitute. The mistakes made with the American Indians are being repeated with the Eskimos. We are replacing their well-tried ways with the worst of ours. I know this is a handbook about animals, not people, but it is relevant because in the 'civilizing' process the husky is becoming nothing but a yappy whining beggar of a camp follower instead of the hardworking, courageous and independent co-conqueror of the north so well described in the journals of the explorers. Lest I call down the wrath of my friends and colleagues in the Canadian Department of Agriculture, let me hasten to add that not only are they aware of the problems but have for many years devoted their efforts to the survival of the northern dog. It's an almost impossible task because the society that produced that dog is passing from the scene.

PS: The oil fields and their pipelines are finishing the alteration job on the environment. The only note of optimism for the Husky is that many people who work in the north have enthusiastically taken to the type. Quite wisely they devote their energies to working competitions rather than beauty shows. One must also add a note of sympathy for outdoor northern dogs who are transplanted to southern suburbs.

Hysteria

The causes of hysteria are many, and only through a thorough examination can the cause be determined.

Some dogs, particularly white Miniature Poodles, seem to have a built-in nervousness that easily turns into hysteria, and there is no cure. One can only control the symptoms with dope.

First aid consists of soothing them in a quiet place. If they are dangerous at these times you had better place the animal in a padded closet (see *Fits*).

We used to see a condition that was called 'canine hysteria'. It was discovered that it was caused by one of the bleaching agents used to produce white flour. I can't remember what it was supposed to do to humans. It probably made us all a little crazier. Anyway, it is against the law to use that particular bleaching agent, and canine hysteria as a disease entity has disappeared.

Ice

Soft living city animals may get painful jabs and cuts in their feet from sharp particles of ice or bits of snow, so do remember when you're out for one of those brisk walks in the winter that your dog will follow you no matter how painful the path. Home aid consists of bathing with cold water to get the foot clean, drying it and apply a bit of vaseline, olive oil or medicated ointment.

Snow or ice in the ear can be painful. Melt it out by pouring lots of warmed oil in the ear.

Illyrian Sheepdog

Yugoslavian herding dog. It looks like a collie with a rather squarer head. About 27kg (60 lb) I've never seen the breed but I have treated one for ear trouble by correspondence. Treatment at long distance is quackery, but in this instance it worked, and I have received an invitation to visit Dubrovnik. Please note that this service is available only to Illyrian Sheepdogs.

Inbreeding

This is the crossing of a closely related pair in order to ensure that certain characteristics which both have shall be possessed by the offspring. In other words if you cross a very small Poodle with its very small sister or mother you will be almost certain to have a litter that will not grow into large adults. The drawback is that not only are the desirable characteristics emphasized but the undesirable ones are too. The features that both parents possess in common will be emphasized in their progeny. For example, if you cross a smallish nervous white Poodle with a bit of extra hair in its ears to its sister with similar features, you are quite likely to get a litter of small white Poodles that are highly nervous and have ears almost plugged with hair.

But, please, every time you see a groomed curly coat attached to a bundle of nerves don't jump to the conclusion that all inbreeding is bad. In fact it's only by inbreeding (or line breeding, which is really the same thing only much slower) that a breed may be improved and desirable characteristics fixed so that they recur in the succeeding generations.

If you cross litter-mates, father to daughter or son to mother, and vigorously cull all their offspring that show undesirable characteristics, and then breed the survivors to each other, you will have a litter with very few undesirable characteristics and many of the desirable ones.

If you keep repeating the process, each time weeding out those animals that don't reach your ideal then you will have animals that not only look as they are supposed to but also carry the genes in their make-up to ensure that their progeny too will look like the ideal.

I know it sounds complicated, but let me assure you that it has been demonstrated thousands of times with both plants and animals.

If you mistrust science – which is really nature observed – may I suggest that many vigorous wild species practise inbreeding. Many wild animals stay in small compact groups or herds generation after generation.

The Rocky Mountain Goat will keep a harem that includes his mother, two or three sisters, several daughters and a few males that are weaker than he and are never allowed to breed the females. After he has kept the herd intact a few seasons and is surrounded by grand-daughters that are also his wives, he ungraciously surrenders his position to the most vigorous son or grandson. Anyone who has ever seen the Rocky Mountain Goat cannot accuse them of nervousness or lack of vigour.

Why then do the public and some dog breeders distrust in-breeding? It's simply that in many cases breeders have selected for the wrong characteristics. They have often weeded out the large vigorous pups and kept the small ones. After four or five generations of breeding the runts to the runts they have something that is small enough for grandmother to carry in her shopping bag, but for all the similarity it has to a dog, grandma might just as well be given a transistor radio with bad breath and a set of teeth.

The breeders who have misused the principles of inbreeding fall into a few broad categories:

1 Those who genuinely want to found a new variety of very small dogs, and simply will not accept that a species can only be shrunk so far and yet retain anything like normal health. 1kg (2 lb) Chihuahuas, mini Dachshunds and sleeve Pekinese are only three examples of creatures that could not reproduce themselves without man's help.
2 Those breeders who will produce anything for which there is a market, and who couldn't care less what faults go with their products. Apricot and white Poodles, distorted Bulldogs, dish-faced Pekinese with flat noses, and the other scores of dogs who have had some saleable feature accentuated to the detriment of the dog as a whole, are all monuments to human selfishness.
3 Breeders who out of sheer ignorance or poverty buy culls from other breeders. I know a woman, indescribably filthy in herself, who comes in with the most pathetic assortment of white Miniature Poodle bitches – the offspring of other bitches that she has bought at bargain prices. They and their daughters are bred to litter-mates that the woman has not yet sold. I find it incredible that a human as appallingly ignorant, stupid and avaricious as she is can find customers for the pups, but as long as one professes oneself an animal lover all normal standards of judgement are apparently suspended.
4 Breeders who out of sheer laziness breed their bitches to the closest stud even if it happens to be a litter-mate of no particular virtue.

May I offer some advice to anyone who is really interested in improving a breed? Inbreeding is the way to do it. Go to the closest university and hire (their time is worth money) the services of a geneticist. If you can't find an academic who is interested in helping, inquire at the nearest large poultry farmer. Many poultry farms today are gigantic outfits that got that way because they employ trained minds. You'd be surprised how many poultry breeding problems are worked out with the aid of computers. I can assure you that the chicken that converts 1·3kg (3 lb) of grain into 450g (1 lb) of gain wasn't arrived at by the hit or miss methods of the average dog breeder.

Outline to your expert what you want in your dogs. He'll know or be able to find out which of those characteristics are dominant in that particular breed and which are recessive. He'll give you a fair idea of the genetic make-up of your parent stock and how to improve it.

It matters not at all whether your expert knows a West Highland White from a Cairn or a Doberman from a Dachshund for that matter. He can soon find out, and the guiding principles of genetics are the same whether it's sweet peas, chickens or dogs.

Don't pay too much mind to those cliques of doggy types (similar to horsey types without whips) who would have you believe that knowledge is sacred, secret and fraternal. What they are peddling is a collection of prejudices. You stick to principles that can be stated in a nice orderly fashion, and that don't have to be shouted in false fellowship or whispered in corner conferences.

Indigestion

It may be caused by spoiled food, unusual food, food too hot or cold or undue excitement at feeding time. The animal usually salivates, moves its mouth like a human with nausea, and vomits. The treatment is starvation for at least twelve hours but preferably twenty-four, and half-diet for a couple of days. If the condition persists or if it's a too common occurrence you had better take him along to the vet.

Injections

Many medicines are not as effective when given by mouth as when they are injected. Some simply cannot be given by mouth. In some cases we choose injections because the animal is so difficult to handle that we can't get close to its mouth. No matter what sort of injection is used the animal must be restrained firmly because it is bound to dislike the strange sensation, and it will react with teeth and claws.

The commonest ways to inject medicines are:

1 Subcutaneous, i.e. under the skin (usually the folds of the neck or behind the shoulder).
2 Intra-muscular, i.e. into the muscles, usually the thick muscles of the hind leg or of the shoulder.
3 Intravenous, i.e. into the vein (usually the vein that runs along the front of the front leg or the side of the hind leg).

If you are injecting an animal yourself, as you may well do in diabetes, under the direction of your veterinary surgeon, you will probably be using the subcutaneous route.

Prepare everything beforehand. This includes cleaning, rinsing and boiling the syringe and needle. Then load your syringe with the material. Then get the animal. Minimizing his waiting time makes it easier all round.

A fairly quiet animal may be held with one hand behind the neck while you inject with the other, but a calm assistant makes the job much easier. Some animals will have to be taped and properly restrained.

The most important point from the animal's point of view is a properly sharpened needle. Ask a registered nurse to show you how. PS: Most people now use the disposable sort. They're made to be used once and then discarded. One cannot boil them. They can, however, be sterilized in those formalin cabinets that barbers are meant to use or in more sophisticated apparatus. A lot of people simply rinse them under the cold water tap while taking care not to touch the needle or inside bits. If you produce an abscess at the injection site, either you're being too parsimonious or your washing and re-assembling technique is at fault. Why not waste the pennies and save your dog a lot of pain? Use a new one every time.

Introducing

When you produce a new addition to your family of pets, it is usually wise to keep the newcomer in a separate area for two or three days. If this is difficult you must at least feed the newcomer separately until you're quite sure jealous fighting scenes won't occur. All the animals should be kept on leads during the first few hours of physical contact.

That bit of advice is as true and as cheap as most generalizations. Please temper it with common sense. One simply does not introduce an Italian Greyhound to a houseful of Terriers without trepidation. Alternatively many people have proved that you can take a stray kitten into a kennel of guard dogs and within seconds it will have the warmest bed and the best food.

Most animal behavioural students agree that within minutes or hours a hierarchy must be established. Once each animal knows its place the chances of bloodshed are minimal. The growls and hisses are mainly display. Personally I have found it advantageous to keep well out of the way while keeping a wary eye on the proceedings. I've never had to interfere.

Incidentally, that new beast may be covered with wee beasties, or it may be full of worms, or it may be suffering from distemper or hepatitis, so please have your vet check it *before* you take it home.

If all this is just too tiresome for words, then stop on the steps for half an hour and apply flea powder. Once you get fleas in the house you've lost half the battle.

Irish Setter (*Red Setter*)

Many a pint has been drunk disputing the relative merits of the Irish, the Gordon and the English Setter. These discussions usually prove that man's capacity for self punishment is unlimited. Two things cannot be disputed about the Irish Setter. The first is that it is one of the most beautiful dogs in the field. The rich chestnut coat of a well-conditioned setter cannot be equalled. The second is that when you get an eccentric one he can be very looney indeed. It is just an opinion of mine, and not a verified one, that elderly Irish Setters get skinny to the point of emaciation. I wonder if many owners of the breed would bear this out?

Irish Terrier

Why are the Irish so partial to chestnut and red? Their Terrier may be one of three variations of red. He is almost too game a fighter, and will tackle anything else in the dog line, so buy a stout lead. He is usually dependable in human company, is middle-sized and very attractive in colour. I don't know why he's not more popular outside Ireland.

Irish Water Spaniel

Possibly the oldest Irish breed, he is superb in the water and would be much more popular if it weren't for his appearance, which some people describe as mongrelly Poodle. If you want a Spaniel that works well in the field but quickly learns household habits you could do worse. He weighs about 27kg (60 lb), and is covered in tight little purple-brown ringlets.

Irish Wolfhound

If you want to make a lasting impression go visiting with half a dozen of these wiry beasts. They are almost a yard high, and that doesn't include the head which is carried eagerly and proudly. They are a graceful, very strong and very fast hound. I should think you'd have an interesting experience raising one in a flat.

PS: I must mention Rosy, the only member of the breed I've lived with. She was as gentle as only giants can be and sometimes incredibly stupid. About once a week we'd have to stitch her up because she never learned not to follow cats or rabbits straight through a barbed wire fence. I think she did learn to close her eyes because that was the only part of her anatomy that remained unscarred. We finally gave her to the artist Vera Haggerty who lives in a place that isn't surrounded by barbed wire. There she died suddenly and painfully of torsion of the stomach – a condition many large breeds are prone to suffer.

Italian Greyhound

A graceful, almost too delicate, dog that was in fashion three centuries ago both in England and on the Continent. It looks like a scaled down Whippet, which as you probably know looks like a scaled down Greyhound. They are thin skinned and fine haired, and I've seen them lying in front of the fire shivering. They sometimes belong to the kind of woman who ties them outside a shop even when it's raining while she goes inside to choose the joint. I know because I've seen it. If you own one please get a properly fitted blanket and plastic rain coat. Incidentally, many of the dogs that you see in court paintings of Tudor and Stewart times are Italian Greyhounds.

Itch

I think the common sense approach is to try one or two dustings with a flea and louse powder or a defleaing bath if the weather is right. If the itch persists you had better get professional diagnosis, and not let the condition get complicated.

Iviza Hound (*Ibizan Hound*)

A middle-sized hound common throughout the Balearics. Used as a rabbit hound and as a companion. In Spain a companion dog is fed by the owner and runs loose the rest of the time, avoiding the stones and kicks of the populace.

As for being a rabbit hound, this is why the Ibizan Hound is reputedly able to spring 2 metres (6 feet) in the air while hunting in order to see which way its prey has gone.

Jack Russell Terrier

This was a well-established breed noted for its high spirits, its ability in the field as a hunt terrier and its gameness. It was developed by Parson Jack Russell who selected primarily for sporting ability but also for a distinctive long-backed, spotted-faced, wire-coated type. They bred true to type and found enthusiasts throughout England but particularly in the west country.

Today the Parson Jack stands a little over 30cm (1 ft) high, still has the long low look and usually the spotted face (black tan or lemon on white) and weighs up to 7·7kg (17 lb).

There are a great many more owners of Jack Russells than there are real Jack Russells. Why? Because any small Terrier with a patch over its eye or its ear can be sold today. The public, God bless them, think that a patch or a spot makes the puppy a true Jack Russell and if it's a Jack Russell it must be good. I agree that a Jack Russell must be good, but the vast majority of pups that the dealers are flogging are just mongrel Terrier-types that have been selected for colour alone. The sporting ability they might have is purely accidental.

Note: The Kennel Club doesn't recognize the breed.

PS: If you want something along the same lines that you can be sure is more than just a mongrel Terrier then look at either the smooth-haired Fox Terriers (who are recognized as purebreds), or have a word with the local hunt; Hunt Terriers may not have papers but they've got the guts, stamina and character typical of a breed bred for a specific job. In other words they are what the so-called Jack Russell is meant to be.

Japanese Spaniel (*Chin-Chin*)

Taller, slightly more elegant than the Pekinese from which it is descended, this breed is fairly well known in America, particularly on the west coast. It has the same faults as the Pekinese – protuberant eyes, malformed mouth, crooked legs, etc. – but none of them to the same extent as the Peke. It has a disdainful snotty look and spirited but delicate action. If I may be allowed a strictly personal preference then, illogically, I prefer the Peke.

However, I must add that one is much less likely to meet a strictly commercial Chin-Chin breeder. Almost invariably the people who sell this breed are genuine enthusiasts.

Jaundice

A yellowing of the tissues which we usually see in the eyeball or the lips, although I've seen a white Poodle where the yellow showed dramatically through the hair. Usually caused by bile duct obstruction or by liver infection or more rarely by blood infection. Jaundice is a symptom not a cause of disease, and the exact diagnosis of the cause requires all the skills of the clinical veterinarian aided by the laboratory.

Jaw

Dislocations and fractures of the jaw are fairly common. An animal who falls a fair distance usually strikes its head sharply and a jaw fracture may accompany the invariable concussion. Fortunately they usually heal quickly and without complication. A general anaesthetic is given and the dislocated jaw snapped into position or the fractured jaw wired into a position. Soft lappable foods must be given for two weeks. In case your vet's assistant forgets to tell you, the wire in the jaw must come out in two or three weeks.

Jealousy

This can be just as operative in your pet as in an elder child when the new baby is brought home, so do make a fuss of the established pet when introducing a newcomer to the house. Some dogs never seem to get over their jealousy of the new baby. If there is any indication at all that your dog means to follow his envy through with physical action you had better, and quickly, find him a new home. Meanwhile, don't leave him alone with baby.

Keeshond

The Dutch version of the ubiquitous Spitz. Very loyal, not inclined to shyness, and possibly a little too quick to use its teeth. The main drawback is the amount of grooming necessary. It stands 45cm (18 in) and weighs about 18kg (40 lb). Colour various shades of grey.

It has been noted in the past that Keeshonds get more than their fair share of epileptics. Recent research has shown that many members of the breed carry a recessive gene for the condition, and if those dogs are mated to another carrying the same gene the resulting offspring will be likely to have fits on and off through life. I only mention this because of the sensible attitude of most Keeshond breeders. They have recognized the problem, have asked researchers and veterinarians to look into it and are following the recommendations to get rid of the condition.

Kelpie

The short-haired Australian herding dog. They weigh about 13·6kg (30 lb) and stand about 50cm (20 in). They are a very alert looking dog with the spirit of a wild animal. The breed resulted from the judicious crosses of imported working Collies with the native Australian Dingo.

Like all breeds that are worked more than they are shown, they have developed no real faults. However, they are now becoming popular on the show-bench in Australia, and unless the people down there are more sensible than their English or American counterparts we can expect the show modifications that lead to trouble.

Kennel Clubs

The American Kennel Club in New York, its older cousin in London and other kennel clubs keep a register of pure-bred dogs. They lay down standards (or ideals if you prefer) and grant championship status to dogs who win in those shows whose rules and judges they approve.

I think many show standards are wrong. In too many cases the breed standards lead to illness and crippling. Is this the fault of the kennel club? No, not at all. Kennel clubs on both sides of the water, like clubs everywhere, are no better or worse than their members. They must be guided by the best known, or the most experienced (or sometimes by the most vocal or influential) experts and lovers of each breed. Some breeders have the wrong idea of perfection in their dogs. Some have the right idea. Gradually ideas and ideals change. The kennel clubs are usually not instrumental in those changes. They merely record them.

If there weren't official kennel clubs it would be necessary to invent them. Without a regulatory body the only standards would be those set by the buyers of dogs. All of us would be in the same helpless position as the uninformed customer of a pet shop in the slums. No one could be sure what a puppy would look like when it grew up.

Finally, most of us mistakenly believe that the Kennel Club in Britain doesn't recognize some breeds recognized by the American Kennel Club. No, it's not true. Like all well-established aristocrats neither club is a snob. The Kennel Club in London, though, only maintains a separate Breed Register for those breeds in which 150 or more dogs have been registered in a three-year period. The Tibetan Mastiff for example has been known and defined in Britain for half a century, but there have never been enough around to make a separate registry, or granting of championship status worthwhile. Mexican Hairless, Coon Hounds, Walker Tree Hounds, Malamutes and Belgian Sheepdogs can all be registered in Britain. If any of them gets popular enough they'll have their own little registry, but for the present the poor dears have to be satisfied with being 'Any other breed'.

PS: The years have rung some changes. Some breeds have grown in popularity, others have declined. The Kennel Club, however, wrestles with two problems no one would have predicted fifteen years ago. Both are the result of social and economic changes which few dogs really understand.

First there are things called unions. The people who actually do the work of filing all those pedigrees and taking the money are being organized. You know the scene. One out – all out. Collective bargaining means collective strength. This book is not a political polemic and I'm simply not prepared to pass judgement. In my limited experience I'd sooner be an organizer than organized. Whether the outfit is working or on strike you're still being paid. And good luck to you. Exactly why I want my son to be either a plumber or a lawyer. But as I said dogs simply don't understand the subtleties.

Secondly there is a fact that only men are allowed to rule the Kennel Club. I'm talking about the British one which is the progenitor of all the Kennel Clubs everywhere. The current excuse is that the Kennel Club is really a gentleman's club. The dog side of the business is really not quite so important. Or so it might seem to those of us who are merely allowed to peek through the window.

I have only one question to ask. If you took the ladies out of the dog game what would be left?

Warning to the gentlemen: Enjoy your privileges while you may, because your days are numbered!

Kennels

If you are investing in kennels I would suggest that you first read three or four books on the subject. Secondly, visit and if possible work for a while at each of three or four established kennels, and thirdly, but most important, find an architect who shares your enthusiasm. Don't try to save a few pounds by doing without an architect. He can usually save you more than his fees and set you up better than old Jock down the road. I assume that you're not going into the thing blind, but have had two or three breeding bitches for a couple of years and you wish to expand. If you've been living in town and decide – because of Aunt Emma's legacy – that you can make a pleasant living in the country just because you 'love animals', let me warn you against it. Kennel management requires as much business sense as manufacturing frocks. Please get as much experience as possible before investing any sizeable capital.

Kerry Blue Terrier

I've never seen one that wasn't a real character. They are all Terrier and something else beside. You must take them in hand and start training them early, else they can be dangerous snarlers. If you can afford it try to buy one in Ireland where they must still work if they are going to be exhibited. I can't describe their coat which is like nothing else in dogdom, but it is easily scissor-trimmed and does not shed freely. Breed enthusiasts maintain they are marvellous with children, but I have known untrained nervy Kerry Blues that couldn't be trusted not to injure themselves. An angry and uncontrollable animal will break its teeth barging against an obstacle. Don't be dissuaded from getting one. Just raise it properly, train it and you'll have a superb pet.

Kidneys

The kidneys are the filters of the body. The blood passes through them, the waste products are sieved out, and the blood is allowed to go on circulating in the body. The waste products and the surplus fluid of the blood form urine. The urine goes down the tubes called ureters to the bladder. When the bladder is full, or partly full, the urine is passed to the outside through another tube called the urethra. The urethra passes through the penis in the male and the vagina in the female.

There is a lot of difference between the urine of one normal healthy animal and of another normal healthy animal. The diet of the animal and the amount it drinks will determine the colour and the thickness of the urine. If an animal is restricted in its water intake but not in its diet, then obviously the same amount of waste products must be passed in a small amount of fluid. One then sees a thick darkly coloured urine. An animal that drinks a great deal is going to have a lighter, thinner urine.

Now, if the kidneys become diseased so that they don't filter the poisons or waste products out of the blood, the body will try to make up for it and make the kidneys' job easier by diluting the blood. How is this done? There is only one way, and that is to drink more water.

That is why if your pet suddenly increases its water consumption, say from one bowl a day up to two or three, and if he keeps it up for a few days and it's not because the weather is hotter or he's exercising more, then you must suspect kidney malfunction and get him along to the vet.

There's one main reason I enter into this detail in a general book like this, and that is because many people mistakenly cut down an animal's water because they think it can't be good for it. In fact often the only thing that is allowing the kidneys to function is the increased water consumption. A veterinary surgeon may ask you to cut down your pet's water intake for two or three days, but please don't misunderstand him. No one will recommend a permanent limit on drinking.

The other common symptom of kidney disease – and this we see in cases of long standing – is rotten teeth. The bad teeth are a result of the kidney disease and very rarely a cause.

Kidney malfunction is usually a one-way thing. We don't usually get cures, but we can and do relieve the condition a bit, and we can and do dispense pills and advice about diet that can keep an animal fairly healthy for quite a period.

The diet is usually mainly white non-oily fish, veal, fowl or rabbit meats, all of which have less waste products for kidneys to filter out than do the red meats. All the water the animal can drink. We sometimes advise boiling the water.

A final word. There are many different sorts of kidney disease, and only clinical examinations aided by the laboratory can determine which one your pet has. The drugs used depend on the sort of kidney disease it is.

It is both stupidity and cruelty to attempt treatment with tonics, proprietary drugs, advice of friends or shopkeepers, or those well advertised vitamins.

King Charles Spaniel

They look and act like the Cocker, but since they've never been as popular as the Cocker one isn't as likely to run into nervous ones. If you like the Cocker disposition but are afraid of getting landed with a snippy nervous Cocker you should consider the King Charles. Unfortunately though, there are physical drawbacks to the King Charles all originating in the funny twisted head which shortens the jaw and shoves the eyeballs out. Try to get one that looks more square-headed and 'normal' than the real show type. Lately some unscrupulous breeders have been catering to the demand for even smaller house dogs by breeding the runts of the litter to each other and producing something that looks halfway to a Pekinese. Cute as they may be, these creatures that have been chosen for smallness alone are almost certain to be trouble. If you own a King Charles, groom it at least once a week and pay particular attention to those long ears and to the hair between the toes. At the first sign of eye trouble consult your vet.

Summary: If you want a small, dependable, affectionate breed that is attractive in looks and disposition and quite capable of living a hearty outdoor existence look no further.

King Charles Spaniel (Cavalier)
(*called the Cavalier King Charles Spaniel*)

This is the larger variety of King Charles and has lately become more popular. It is supposed to be closer to the original type that existed even before Charles II popularized the breed.

I prefer the Cavalier variety because they are sportier dogs than their smaller cousins, and are more likely to have a nose and eyes and mouth that function properly. The Cavalier King Charles is about 30cm (12 in) high and weighs up to 9kg (20 lb). The King Charles is about 5cm (2 in) shorter and averages about 4·5kg (10 lb).

Komondor

The shaggiest, woolliest, sheepdog you ever did see. A large 80 lb Hungarian, he doesn't mind cold or wind, but he just can't stand strangers.

Kuvas

The most popular (pre-War) of the Hungarian breeds. Originally bred as a sheepdog, but his pure white coat attracted town dwellers, and he is now used as a guard dog in addition to being a good children's and house dog. About 31·5kg (70 lb) and 60cm (2 ft) high, and he looks not unlike a smaller, neater St Bernard.

Labrador Retriever

Was developed originally by crossing imports from the 'New World' with English breeds. This all-rounder is *the* superb retriever, and his pre-eminence is recognized. He's a good watch dog, guard, police or guide dog, and absolutely perfect as a family or house dog. He'll swim in any weather or water; but do use a little common sense. If he lies in front of the fire fifty weeks of the year, don't push him among the ice-floes on your fortnight's holiday.

We are beginning to see a lot of hip dysplasias in the Labrador, and when the problem becomes sorted out by the veterinary profession, and recommendations are made, I am sure that the Lab breeders (sensible dogs, sensible breeders) will be among the first to make whatever changes are necessary. There is growing evidence that hip dysplasias are congenital. That is, if either the dam or the sire have the condition the puppies are more likely to have it. The solution, of course, is not to use such animals for breeding purposes. The Labrador is one of the few popular breeds in which most show champions have also been proven in the field. This has probably somewhat limited the incidence of hip dysplasias, because lame animals can't work well, and the breeder or owner wouldn't be likely to breed from such an animal.

The Lab stands about 55cm (22 in) high and weighs up to 31·7kg (70 lb). In a city practice one sees many Labs that weigh 36kg (80 lb) and even 45kg (100 lb). These poor creatures are being killed not by kindness but by stupidity. If you have allowed your dog to become a caricature of the breed get him along to your vet's and start him on a supervised diet.

There is also a Golden or Yellow Labrador which is the same as the Black in all respects except colour. Unfortunately it's never been as popular in the field as the black and many more strains have been bred for generations just for show or for companion purposes. As a result one is more likely to run into physical or nervous problems with the Yellow. I hope I'm not discouraging anyone from getting one. I'm just saying that you have to be more careful, and know more, in choosing a Golden.

Both the Black and the Golden Labrador are streets ahead of most other popular breeds in their chances of living healthy unneurotic existences.

Three hours of daily hard exercise will keep a Lab in tiptop form. If you can't stand fresh air don't inflict your indoor existence on this breed.

Lactation

This is the provision of milk by the nursing mother to her growing litter. During this time she needs lots of meat, calcium or bonemeal supplements, and all the water and milk she can drink. If a mother isn't 'dropping' her milk within a few hours of giving birth she may need an injection by the veterinary surgeon. If she suddenly dries up before the litter is weaned you had better call in the vet. Some milking mothers require a bit of extra attention like clipping off the excess hair around the teats, or applying a bit of oil if the teats are raw or cracked. If the growing litter is scratching the mother you should trim their nails. When you wean the litter it should be done gradually by increasing their food and therefore decreasing their dependence on the mother's milk, which will slow down. At actual weaning time cut

133

out all fluids from the mother's diet for twenty-four hours. This will help 'dry her off', to use the dairyman's term.

Laiki

The name used in Russia and Finland to describe the many breeds of Spitz type used in their far north as either sledge or hunting dogs. It's a generic term like Husky, and like the Husky the Laiki varies considerably according to its area and purpose.

Lakeland Terrier

An attractive derivative of the Black and Tan Terrier. This 7·7kg (17 lb) dog was originally bred not to chase the fox but to go in after the hounds and kill. He's still occasionally bred for that purpose, and when he is, he's a tough little customer. Lately the Lakeland has become popular as a show dog, and has been refined more than a little in the process. He's always been narrow-chested – purposely bred this way so that he could squeeze through narrow places – but you don't have to be a scholar of anatomy and physiology to realize that you can only narrow a chest so far before you impair the breathing process. Some show breeders have just about reached the limit.

Laryngitis

The owner usually reports an animal with pharyngitis and laryngitis as having a bone stuck in its throat. The afflicted animal does indeed seem to be trying to cough an obstacle out of its throat. The animal, however, will usually drink and eat sloppy foods, which of course it could not do if in fact a bone were stuck back there. In acute or severe cases the temperature will be high (up to 40·5°C, 105°F), and a virus is usually the cause. Antibiotic injections are needed. Often cases that are not so severe may recover in a day or two with just a bit of cough syrup. a codeine at night, and the feeding of a soft, easily swallowed diet. The condition is common in miniatures of all sorts, and I have seen Miniature White Poodles that start coughing every time it rains for a few days. You can well imagine that in the English winter they have barely recovered from one bout before they come down again. Prevention is largely keeping the animal from getting wet and chilled. A plastic raincoat and a thorough drying after walks is necessary. Animals kept constantly in overheated rooms without proper circulation of air are, of course, prone to the condition. Finally, in puppies laryngitis is usually one of the symptoms of a serious virus infection, and it simply must not be neglected.

Legal

Lawyers are no more intelligent than you or I, but the law is what they have studied and worked at so presumably they know more about it than your grocer, the publican or the lady down the road who collects for the RSPCA. If you have a legal problem, listen politely to the free advice then phone your lawyer. If you have an uncontrollable snappy dog which you don't have the time or inclination to train, you deserve all the harsh words you're going to hear.

Leptospirosis (*canicola type*)

This is not one of the distemper family, but it's usually classified with distemper because some of the symptoms are the same and because dogs are often vaccinated against leptospirosis at the same time as they are done against distemper.

It's caused by a wiggling family of germs called spirochaetes which are very difficult to find and identify, so in fact many cases of leptospirosis are never properly diagnosed and some sick animals that don't have leptospirosis are diagnosed as having the disease.

In practice this doesn't matter as much as you might think, because the treatment of it and distemper and hard pad is usually symptomatic; that is, the vet treats the symptoms as they occur.

The important thing to remember about leptospirosis – and your vet will point it out to you if he has the slightest suspicion – is that it may be passed on to man and to cats. The urine and faeces of sick animals will contain the germ, so every care should be taken that children don't grub about where the animal has voided. If you are nursing an animal suspected of having leptospirosis don't handle its excreta with your bare hands, and wash after every contact.

How do most dogs get the disease? The theory is that they get it by their natural habit of sniffing where other dogs have been.

The obvious lesson is not to take puppies for walks where other dogs go until a week after their final inoculation.

What are the symptoms of leptospirosis? They vary widely, but usually there is some vomiting – first of white froth and later of bile. There is often a great deal of stomach-pain, and because of this the animal tucks up his middle, arches his back and moves reluctantly with slow, choppy, stiff steps. Within a day or two it becomes very ill, dehydrated or dried out and unless it gets fluids either into its veins or under the skin will rapidly weaken and die.

With early treatment the outlook can be fairly optimistic and most cases are recovered within about two or three weeks.

Note: The above applies to the common type of leptospirosis, known to scientists as canicola. A rarer type, which occurs in dogs and humans, and which is usually fatal, is transmitted by rats. It is known as the icterohaemorrhagic form. All rat-catching terriers and hunting dogs likely to be in contact with rats should receive inoculations against this type.

Lice

There are about 2800 species of lice. Most, however, are 'host specific'. So if James comes home from boarding school with a headful of the creatures there's no need to rush Rover off to the vet's. Lice are commonly associated with filth or overcrowding. Buy a mansion and take a bath. Unlike fleas they normally spend their entire lives on the hosts, hence they are easier to control. One uses insecticidal shampoos, dusting powders and cold cream ointments containing various products like rotenone or some of the pyrethrins. Usually the first sign that an owner sees is a bald spot or intense itching. Examination usually reveals the eggs clustered on the hairs of the ears. May I repeat? There's no need to panic. In our salubrious society they're much easier to control than fleas.

Licking

If any animal licks and licks at one particular place on its skin, you had better have a look. It may be a scratch, or a foreign object, or an abscess starting. You can bathe the area with warm salt water, but if some medication like an antiseptic ointment is necessary there's no point in putting it on unless you bandage as well. In fact you must be careful what you do put on, because the animal is quite likely to continue his obsessive licking and many skin medications can cause stomach upsets or worse. I use a lot of gentian violet on those places where an animal just seems determined to lick a wee nothing until it becomes a big something. Gentian violet has the virtue of drying in quickly and often it will stop the irritation. Put it on before a walk or before feeding time. By the time the walk or the meal is over it will have dried in and done its work. Poodles and Cockers can get a positive mania for licking between their toes. Try trimming out the hair, applying gentian violet, bandaging for a day. If it doesn't clear up in a day or two take it to the vet. An animal may lick at its behind. See if its anal glands are causing the trouble. If a bitch is licking her vagina and it is not as simple as coming on heat, then you had better take the beast along to the vet. It may be a pyometritis, which is very serious.

A male dog that continually licks at its penis may set up quite a messy condition, and this is better seen by the vet straightaway because it may be bladder stones or something equally serious causing the trouble.

Liver (*as food*)

Nutritionally excellent. May be fed raw, boiled, baked or fried or any way you can think of. Your pet won't appreciate the subtle differences between horse, beef, sheep or pig's liver unless you teach him to, so buy the cheapest. Liver is inclined to have a laxative effect, so don't feed it daily unless it's only a portion of the meat in the diet. In those animals that have chronic constipation, or an animal that has a constricted bowel as a result of an internal operation, your vet may ask you to feed liver daily. It will help keep the bowels open. In animals with diarrhoea or a tendency to looseness, liver, of course, should not be fed.

Liver disease

One of the common complaints of man, and especially the Frenchman, is cirrhosis of the liver. This is a hardening of the liver caused by replacement of liver cells with hard fibrous cells. Few dogs drink more than the odd beer or sip of wine, but all the same vets do see the condition.

It may be caused by a virus infection, or it may be just one of the degenerative conditions associated with ageing.

There is no effective treatment, but injections of liver extract may help.

We see a lot more liver tumours in dogs than doctors see in man. They are very difficult to diagnose as they don't show on X-ray until they are advanced. If a vet suspects liver tumour – and it is high on the list of possibles in dogs over eight or nine – he may confirm laboratory findings by doing an operation called an exploratory laparotomy. This simply means that he wants to open up the abdomen and have a look inside. He will explain to the owner that he's simply not sure and that it may be one of a number of conditions, some of which are curable.

When he opens the abdomen and finds a cancerous liver he will usually decide not to let the animal wake up from the operation. Its chances of recovery from the condition are nil, and the few months of remaining life would be painful.

Am I an advocate of euthanasia for men with incurable illnesses?

It may be old-fashioned but nothing frightens me quite so much. Why then can I so glibly advocate it for animals? Simply because man has assumed the responsibility for them. He has decided which species he can hunt and eat, which he can raise and slaughter and eat, and which he wishes to take into his home. Man has taken the dog and cat into his home and often they become part and parcel of his family and his life. We decide in exactly what manner a dog or cat should live, and in what manner it should die. We decide how many of a litter shall be allowed to live, and whether they shall be allowed to breed or even retain their sexual organs, and I believe that we must also decide, unpleasant though it may be, how long they should live.

Lungs (*as food*)

There is a lot of bulk and fibrous connective tissue in lung and comparatively little feeding value, but if it is cheap and you have the patience to handle the bulk it is not a bad filler.

Lung disease

Commonly seen in younger animals, where it is a complication of a virus like distemper. The symptoms are, of course, various degrees of difficulty in breathing. The only effective home treatment is rest until the animal can be seen by a vet.

Since the advent of penicillin the word pneumonia seems to have gone out of fashion. It has certainly lost the terror once associated with it. So much is this so, that people today can be told their dog has pneumonia and usually they will then ask, 'Can he go for his walks?'

No, he can't go for his walks. He must be kept indoors, warm and dry and rested. Our new drugs will kill the germs or most of the germs, but they won't heal the lungs. Only time and rest can do that.

How do you rest the lungs? By not dashing about and making them work harder. You lie in bed. If the dog won't lie in his basket then you can restrict his exercise by putting him in a small area.

If he's coughing do you rush to the chemist and get a cough syrup? No. Because it may contain alcohol or some other substance that will counteract the antibiotic with which your vet is treating your dog.

Lung tumours

Smoking is one of the few vices that dogs simply cannot be taught. Nevertheless we do see lung cancer in the dog. It's not the growing problem that it is in the human, and we see more of it in the bitch than in the dog – additional evidence, if any is needed, to add to the case against the cigarette. I smoke as I write this and regard it as an unjustifiable and certain risk.

Unfortunately there are no reliable statistics to indicate whether city dogs are more prone to lung cancer than country dogs, but one suspects from the grime one sees in their lungs that they are.

We diagnose many cases of lung cancer in bitches who also have mammary tumours, and the pathologists tell us that in fact lung tumours are usually 'secondaries' from the breast. If we excise the mammary tumours at the right stage there is less danger of the tumour appearing in the lungs.

If we suspect lung tumour and confirm its presence by X-ray, then we don't usually operate on the mammary tumour because it would just cause the whole thing to flare up.

What does one do with a pet who has a suspected or confirmed lung tumour?

Your vet will outline a regime of limited exercise, diet and pills, and will ask to see the animal for a check-up every week or so.

Some dogs will go on for months or even years without pain and with little discomfort. However, a point must come when he will advise you that euthanasia is the only humane answer.

PS: Please read the first sentence again. It is correct; they cannot be taught. They can be *forced* to smoke; to our eternal shame there have been experiments conducted in Great Britain during which the hapless Beagles had no alternative. I have done the vet column for *The Sunday People* (the paper that reported it all – and followed it up) for many years. I am a firm believer in vivisection. I believe the benefits to animal and man are greater than the suffering inflicted on the few. But scientists are not gods. In this case (and I'm sure in many others we don't know about) the suffering inflicted can never equal the benefits.

Conclusion: I would like to be in charge of the body that licenses every single experiment. The first thing I'd do would be to hire a librarian or similar type to prove that it has all been done before.

Malignant

A dreaded adjective meaning bad. Usually refers to growths or tumours that are incurable.

A malignant tumour is usually fast-growing and spreading, and thus difficult to cut out completely. It usually has metastases or secondaries, which are little offshoots that can appear in other parts of the body. These secondaries can in their turn grow quickly. The malignant tumour will prevent the organs they invade from doing their job, and thus cause varying symptoms. Gradually the malignant tumour takes over more and more of the healthy tissue until it kills its host.

Mallinois

A Belgian herding dog, wire-haired, or more accurately coarse-haired, 60cm (2 ft) high and weighing about 22kg (50 lb). He looks like a kindly, smaller Alsatian and he can be trained as a police or guard dog, but he's really superb at working cattle or sheep.

Maltese Terrier

A most attractive toy that originated and has been known in Mediterranean lands for some four centuries. He's got long silky white hair, weighs 3kg (7 lb) or less and is as hardy as a Pekinese, and that's saying a lot. He's a very spirited independent cur, and every one I've seen would as soon claim your finger as your friendship. Don't get me wrong; they're devoted to their owners. If you don't like combing long hair don't get one.

Incidentally, the Maltese is another of the smaller breeds where the standard specifies 'the smaller the better – 1·3kg (3 lb) ideal'. If you are interested in a healthy pet then I would remind you that show standards are often foolish, and from a veterinary point of view the larger the Maltese the better.

Mammary tumour

Cancerous growths in the breast. They usually start as small marble-like nodules under the skin. Some misguided people think they are abscesses, and will advise you to put liniment on them or lance them or some such cruel and dangerous nonsense. Leave them alone! If they develop in a young or middle-aged animal your vet will probably have them off without further ado. In an older animal more judgement is needed, and you may be advised to do nothing about them unless they grow quite large or start opening and draining. The danger of course, is that they may spread – this sort of tumour usually produces 'secondaries' in the lungs – and tumours that spread are incurable. Please don't let a growth get larger and larger just because you're afraid that the vet will advise euthanasia. There is a time when mammary tumours are easily removed and your hesitation may well make it too late. In other words, attempt no home treatment. Rely on your veterinarian's judgement.

Mammitis (*mastitis*)

An inflammation of the breasts that arises after pregnancy (and some-times after false pregnancy) and if untreated can be most painful. Often the swelling will localize into an abscess or abscesses and the accumulated poisons will try to break out and drain in the form of pus. Prevention is largely a matter of clean bedding and clipping the hair between the breasts, and of washing and drying the breast. Strong aggressive puppies may have to have their nails clipped. Chapped teats may have to be oiled. But despite all your care mastitis may de-velop, and the only effective home treatment is bathing with warm salt water. Antibiotic injections are your vet's usual treatment, and they usually clear the condition up in three or four days. A codeine is indicated if there is pain. Incidentally, did you know that after a few hours each new-born puppy will choose a teat for itself? If one of the litter dies its particular teat should be partially milked out twice daily for three or four days. If a large, growing litter is constantly worrying at the bitch, one may use a many-tailed sling bandage to protect the area. Take it off only at specified nursing times.

Manchester Terrier

Also called the Black and Tan Terrier. Developed in the north of England, and it's still best known in Lancashire. About a hundred years ago it was very popular, but then the pendulum swung and the breed was almost extinct for a while. Today there are many good breeders of this 37·5cm (15 in), 7kg (16 lb) ratter and family dog.

There is a toy weighing from 1·3kg (3 lb) up to 4kg (9 lb). It is an exact replica of its larger progenitor, and has been known as a breed on its own for over a hundred years.

Mange

There are different mites that can invade the body and cause skin trouble, and if neglected the lot of the hapless animal is miserable. I consider that neglect includes those well-meaning fools who try all sorts of remedies until the condition becomes very serious and then they consult a veterinary surgeon.

The diagnosis of mange involves the examination of a scraping from the skin under the microscope, that is unless the clinical signs are clear cut. The symptoms you will notice first are itchiness, loss of hair, reddening of the skin, and possibly thickening of the skin. The vet will dispense or prescribe the appropriate medication, but he may omit to give full directions. These include:

1 Boil the animal's bedding at weekly intervals. Do this for three weeks – or longer if the condition doesn't clear up.

2 Clean (soap and rinse) the animal's collar and harness.

3 Don't allow contact with other animals.

4 In long-haired or wire-haired dogs you may have to trim the hair around the infected areas.

5 Make sure you get the medicine on to the skin and not just layered on the hair.

6 Dispose of the cotton or cloth after every application.

7 After every application clean the area or table where you are treating the animal.

8 Wash your own hands well afterwards.

9 Don't use drugs other than those dispensed. They may neutralize the one dispensed.

10 If you see no improvement in four or five days, for heaven's sake go back to the same veterinary surgeon, and tell him so. Changing vets will only put your animal back to where he started.

Marremmani

The most beautiful of herding dogs. Seen everywhere in Italy, but hardly recognizable south of Naples because there he's usually semi-starved, as indeed are many of the people. He's snow-white, weighs 31·7kg (70 lb), and can work well in the mountains but isn't so thick furred as to be uncomfortable down below in the valleys. Lately there has been a lot of talk about the breed's intelligence, and some enthusiasts are 'pushing' the breed abroad. I suppose someone will start the fashion to breed them smaller and smaller, and produce yet another neurotic testimonial to city life.

Mastiff

This precursor of the Bullmastiff was in Britain in Caesar's time. There aren't many around today, but then it doesn't take much Mastiff to make a lot of dog. They are quite the most enormous beasts in dogdom, and no words can describe their appearance, which makes even the largest of most other breeds look like miniatures. Unfortunately their great size makes them prone to limb and joint problems.

If you own a large butcher's shop and a small bakery, you'll find it easy to keep a pair.

Mating

Dogs seem to have little difficulty in finding partners and consummating the relationship if they are running free. Trouble begins when man tries to pair them off. It is terribly annoying when your prize Shih Tzu is sent off to be mated to another Shih Tzu and absolutely refuses to take notice, and then the moment a careless person leaves the door open she runs out and gets bred by the one-eared short-haired stray down the road. Patience, common sense and experience are all that is necessary. This is one phase of animal care where I would suggest you do listen to the advice of experienced breeders, and if possible work along with them for a while. The occasional maiden bitch of nervous disposition may be helped by a tranquillizer which your veterinarian will dispense.

The only rule I would remind you of is that old one about always mating a virgin female with an experienced male and *vice versa.*

Incidentally, the best time to diagnose pregnancy is three to three and a half weeks after breeding. At this stage your veterinarian can feel the pups as wee bumps. Before and after this stage it's much more difficult.

Measles

For some reason I can't understand, vaccine made from the virus that causes measles in humans protects dogs against distemper. We are told by the manufacturers that it has advantages over the older distemper vaccines. They claim that it can safely be used during an outbreak, that it works even on suckling puppies because the distemper antibodies they receive from their mothers don't interfere with the immunizing properties of the measles vaccine, and that it builds up resistance much faster than ordinary distemper vaccine. The more conservative manufacturers who stick to the distemper vaccine say, in effect, 'We have tested the measles vaccine, we dispute the other people's results, we don't think it gives adequate or lasting protection, it certainly doesn't protect any more quickly and, furthermore, we are perfectly capable of making it and would if we believed in it.' Certainly you'd have to be pretty well versed to sift through the conflicting evidence. In my ignorance, I have an uneasy feeling that manufacturers of measles vaccine push their case a bit hard. If you're already making a product and an additional market is available it would be bad business not to jump in with both feet. Personally I put my trust and my orders with the outfits that provide the old-fashioned sorts. Distemper is too nasty a disease for short cuts or economies.

Meat

In all its forms meat is the staple diet of our dogs. Nutritionally there is little difference between breast of lamb and prime Scotch Sirloin – that is, kilo for kilo of actual muscle meat – so you buy as economically as you can. Tinned meat is no better than fresh, and usually has additives and water to cheapen its cost, or balance it – the term used depends on whether you are a buyer or a manufacturer. Commercial kennels, the Greyhound people and knowledgeable owners add brown bread to the meat of adult dogs to make it go further. An active outdoor dog can use lots of fat in its diet. A working Labrador, for example, could obtain about a third of his energy from beef drippings. Pork and pork fat doesn't agree with many dogs. Raw meat is perfectly all right. Your dog will love it if you haven't spoilt him. In France they put a raw egg on raw meat, and the people eat it and it doesn't make them vicious or give them worms. Tripes should be cooked. All bones should be removed or used to make a broth. If your pet is getting meat almost exclusively, you must add calcium to the diet.

Meat juice

Made by squeezing or grinding meat. It is a valuable help in nursing sick animals who aren't interested in eating but will lap a bit if encouraged.

Menstruation

Occurs only in the human and some of the higher primates. Bleeding in the bitch occurs at the opposite end of the sexual cycle, namely, when she is in heat and ready for impregnation.

There is a vice in some dogs which consists of their attacking, and often injuring, a woman who is menstruating. Fortunately it is rarely seen. I know of no cure, and we advise that a dog with this vice should be put down. If you have such a dog and are very attached to it and absolutely refuse to have it put down, castration may be tried. If that doesn't effect a cure, the dog will have to be permanently kennelled.

Metritis

Inflammation of the womb. See *Pyometritis*.

Milk

The milk of the bitch contains more fat than does that of any other domestic animal. The cow has only between three and five per cent fat in her milk whereas the bitch has between nine and ten per cent.

Bitchs' milk is richer in all solids except milk sugar. Her milk in fact contains twenty-five per cent solid matter as compared to the cow's twelve or thirteen per cent. How the puppy 'formula' of adding sugar and water to cows' milk began I can't understand, but the fact is that thousands of orphan puppies have been raised on various dilutions of cows' milk. It's no testimonial to cows' milk, but rather to the toughness of dogs. If you can't get a proper commercial bitch milk formula because you are in some forgotten outpost, you might do better raising those orphan puppies with the milk of either the ewe (six to seven per cent butter fat, twenty per cent total solids) or the goat (four to five per cent butter fat, fifteen per cent total solids). If you must use cows' milk, then use the following formula:

Take equal parts of evaporated milk and water to make 3dl ($\frac{1}{2}$ pt). Add a tablespoon of sweet syrup, an egg yolk and a drop of cod liver or halibut liver oil. Mix well and keep in the refrigerator between feedings.

After the puppies are on solids you can gradually shift to straight cows' milk.

Weaned puppies or adult dogs with diarrhoea should have restricted liquids and no milk at all until the motions firm up.

Adults vary in their desire and need for milk. Our Professor of Medicine (bovine, equine and that sort) used to lecture us about the vice of adult milk drinking. He said the adult stomach just wasn't meant to cope with milk. He praised the virtues of whisky and practised what he preached. Some friends of mine haven't been able to make up their minds so they dilute their milk with whisky.

Mongrel

An animal of unknown ancestry. The mongrel will usually have some of the good features and some of the bad of both its parents, and it's quite impossible to determine in advance which features of its ancestors it will retain. The idea of pure-breds is to fix or predetermine certain features. If you cross two dogs who are good retrievers you are quite likely to get a puppy that is a good retriever. If you breed two mongrels you may get a puppy that is a good retriever, but chances are that you won't unless one or both of the parents was that way inclined.

Mongrels are more like the majority of people in that they breed by inclination rather than logical selection. Just as there are lots of wonderful people so there are wonderful mongrels. We are inclined, however, to attribute to mongrels virtues they don't possess. I think it

145

unlikely to find a mongrel more trainable than a good Alsatian, stronger than a bull terrier or faster than a Greyhound. Nor is there the slightest grain of truth in the common saying that mongrels are more resistant to distemper than pure-breds. A mongrel requires as much care and feeding as a pure-bred, and if he's ill he requires the same treatment. The one place where most mongrels outshine the pure-breds is the city. I suppose there must be a considerable amount of selection by survival, because one does see city mongrels negotiating the most difficult crossing with more ease than the people. If you're contemplating the purchase or acquisition of a mongrel, I only have two bits of advice. First, the size of his pad is a fair guide to how big he'll grow. If a wee ball of fluff has feet the size of a match box, don't believe the vendor when he tells you it's half-Pekinese. Secondly, read carefully the section on distemper, and don't believe anyone who tells you the dog has been inoculated. I have found that many people who deal in mongrels will tell you any story, and sometimes produce some phony certificate to back it up.

PS: The sort of people who used to parade up and down King's Road with an Afghan, a Borzoi or a pair of Weimaraners have been succeeded by a generation of trend setters who believe that the only fashionable breed is a non-breed. And the scruffier the better. They would have you believe that they survive epidemics in which all the 'fancy pure-breds' died. Mostly stuff and nonsense. Any worker at any veterinary surgery or any animal welfare organization can confirm that the vast majority of animals that die – or are killed – on their premises are mongrels. Partly because they were acquired by unthinking people; partly because they were unsuitable for the purpose for which they were acquired; and partly because they are too ugly or too nasty or given too much to roaming.

Conclusion: I know I've spent much of this book detailing the faults of pure-breds. But if you go to an experienced, conscientious breeder – no matter what the breed – your chances of buying a canine lifetime of pleasure are quite high. The majority of people who acquire mongrels regret their decision as the puppies reach adolescence. This is not a personal opinion. Over a quarter of a million are killed in Great Britain every year. Think about it.

Name

Call your cat anything that pleases you. They'll ignore it unless it suits them not to, and, complex or simple, a cat always seems to recognize its name. A dog's name, though, is an integral part of its training. As dogs must be trained in order to be happy – it's those who don't know what their owners want who are nervous – the name must be one that can be easily repeated in training. The name should be instantly recognizable and distinct. It should be short, sharp and hard. It should have one syllable only, and it should have only one soft or vowel sound. Some examples of good training names are Spot, Pot, Mig, Mag, Jack, Jill and, of course, the commonest training name of all – Damn.

Whatever name you choose, use it from the first day no matter how old the puppy is, and stick to it.

Incidentally, don't use the name to admonish. They'll associate the name with punishment. Use 'NO' to express disapproval. Use the name only to tell the dog that a command is coming.

Neapolitan Mastiff

Undoubtedly an ancient Phoenician breed brought to perfection by the Caesars of Rome on the salubrious beaches between Salerno and Eboli. If you believe that, you may also believe that the Pekinese have not been eaten in Peking, and Bali is overrun with Balinese cats. The facts are that no Balinese cat has ever seen Bali, there are few, if any, Pekinese left in China and you could spend a lot of time in Naples without seeing a Neapolitan Mastiff. I know 'cause I've been. There they can't afford to feed their children.

I expect nasty letters from irate breeders. All I can say is that I've nothing to say against the breed. I think it's an imaginative name for a breed that I can't distinguish from any other Mastiff.

And as the authoritative A. Croxton Smith wrote thirty years ago, 'Breeders seem to have concentrated more and more upon getting immense size, and great bulk usually brings the evil of unsoundness in its train. I have seen plenty of perfectly sound Mastiffs, such as could move well and were really active, but latterly the proportion of unsound ones has been alarmingly heavy, for it is extremely difficult for breeders to get soundness in alliance with bulk.'

Nervousness

We see three kinds of nervous pets. The first sort are accompanied by nervous owners. The second sort are those that have never been trained. The third sort are examples of neurotic strains or breeds.

If your psychiatrist is having no success in treating you, your veterinarian can do little for your pet because it is reflecting your assorted manias. I'm not trying to insult you, but it must be obvious

147

to even the most casual of observers that most dogs will react to situations as do their owners. If you jump when there's an unexpected noise so will Antoinette. If you are frightened in the tube or go to pieces when guests come, don't expect Veronique to remain calm and aloof.

The only advice I can give you is to avoid the more active breeds of dogs. Avoid Cockers, Miniature Poodles, Chihuahuas, Corgis, Smooth Collies, Alsatians and Dobermans. Get an Afghan or a West Highland White and expect real trouble. There are lots of breeds of more even temperament. Among the lap dogs the Pekinese is least likely to become a nervous wreck just because you are. The Griffon is often too clever to follow your stupid ways. Pugs and French and English bulldogs are even-tempered. The big Standard Dachshund, although temperamental, is often sensible enough to cope with a crazy master. Bassets will often go to sleep while you are throwing your daily tantrum.

Generally speaking, the larger the breed the better it can cope. The Standard Poodle (what we are beginning to call the Giant Poodle) must be one of the most intelligent and sensitive of all dogs, yet it often manages to live with mad people with no apparent ill effects. It's very difficult to make a nervous wreck out of a Labrador, although I must admit to knowing two who are misery itself. I should think it virtually impossible to transfer your neuroses to a Bloodhound. The Great Pyrenean is a mountain of equanimity. But you get the idea. If you are taking tranquillizers then get a dog with a built-in tranquillizer.

Secondly, you must know that any dog who is not trained will be nervous in new situations. He doesn't know if he's supposed to sit or bark or chase his tail. He may manifest his nervousness by hiding under a chair, running into traffic or snapping at anything that moves.

If a dog is taught only one command, that of sitting when told to, a lot of unpleasant situations could be avoided. The untrained dog will work itself into a frenzy of excitement over trivialities like visitors or visits to strange places. If he will sit on command and is encouraged to stay down for five minutes while he surveys the situation he will usually realize there is nothing to be afraid of, and he may then act like a civilized creature. (See *Training*).

The final category of nervousness is that of some strains within many breeds that are almost destined from birth to be edgy, neurotic and unhappy. Every breed contains some bad families, but some breeds appear to contain more bad strains than good. I would suggest caution in choosing a Corgi as a family pet. Working Corgis are a pleasure to know, but most Corgis we see today are from families so abnormal that if they were humans they would be behind bars. The Alsatian, the world's greatest working breed, numbers among its representatives some of the most terrifying creatures.

White Miniature Poodles have more than their fair share of canine imbeciles and neurotics. Pomeranians, a generation ago, got such a reputation for their ridiculous temperament that they all but disappeared. The Cocker Spaniel is fast following. The long and narrow-skulled Collie is a mental mess. Some strains of Scotties are sure to be neurotic and there are some mad Cairn families.

The list is almost as long as the list of breeds. But I repeat. Some breeds are more likely to contain nervous strains. Choose the breeder carefully. Have a look at the dam and the sire too, if possible. You will have your dog for ten or twelve or more years. Take an extra week in choosing it.

If you are saddled with a nervous dog and despite everything you love it, then take extra time and train it properly. Even the worst of them can be improved with training. They will be happier for it, and they won't be a menace to you or your neighbours.

Neuter

A male that has been castrated, or a female that has been spayed.

Newfoundland

Some experts tell us that it originated in Europe and was developed in Newfoundland. Others state that it originated in Newfoundland by crossing imported dogs with Eskimo breeds. The imported dogs used were St Bernards, some experts claim, and others say they were Pyrenean Mountain Dogs. No one has advanced claims for the Pekinese.

Whatever its forbears, the Newfoundland is an all-black massive dog. He's a powerful swimmer with an instinct for pulling people out of water, and he was once famous and romanticized for his life-saving feats. A New Brunswick friend of mine was reared with a Newfoundland. He tells me that he had to tie the dog at home whenever he went swimming, because no sooner did he or his friends get in the water than the shaggy beast would jump in and pull them out.

We don't see many around any more because meat prices keep rising and gardens get smaller.

If you have the space and the money and children who can't swim, it's an obvious choice.

149

Niam Niam

A Basenji-like breed kept by the Niam Niam tribe in the Sudan. A few were once imported to Europe, but its chief virtue is as a bit of one-upmanship to silence people who start talking about Angmagssalik Huskies or Teechichi Aztec Sacred Dogs or Phu Quoc Ridgebacks.

Night blindness

This may be the first symptom of the condition called Progressive Retinal Atrophy. We now know that this is an hereditary condition and it's seen in many strains of certain breeds of dogs.

Night blindness is usually noticed in the first year of life, and gets slowly worse. Gradually day vision goes too. There is no cure.

Prevention consists of not breeding from affected animals.

Norwich Terrier

A wire-coated grizzled little Terrier weighing several kilos. Developed about a hundred years ago in Norfolk by selective breeding between imported Irish Terriers and native British Terriers. He was a hunting Terrier and I have no doubt that he could still be, but like most of the Terriers today he's a flat-dweller. As a result he's often bred for show rather than performance, and we do see some specimens that can barely waddle across the surgery floor.

Take your time in finding a conscientious breeder, and you will be able to choose a dog that has fewer faults than most of the smaller breeds.

Nose

Bleeding from the nose is usually caused by a sharp blow or by running a twig up a nostril while hunting. Fortunately it generally stops pretty quickly, but if it doesn't an ice pack on the bridge of the nose sometimes helps. Whatever you do never never stuff the nostril. It will just start the beast sneezing and make the nose bleed worse.

Dogs that sneeze and sneeze may have a bit of grass or an insect stuck in the nostril. If you can't remove the object easily don't go poking with tweezers because you'll damage the delicate lining.

Eczemas on the nose can be a real problem. Whatever you put on the dog immediately licks off. Cod-liver oil helps some, and even if it doesn't, it won't do the animal any harm.

Older Spaniels often get a scaling or drying condition of the nose. Home aid consists of applying olive oil or liquid paraffin. After a week of home treatment, if the animal is no better let your veterinary surgeon have a look.

Nursing

Good home nursing is an important element in successful treatment. A good nurse doesn't fuss. He or she does what is necessary and then allows the patient to rest. The following outline may fill in some of the blanks in your experience.

1 Make sure the ill animal is not in a draught. Get down to floor level yourself to make sure. Many homes are warm at waist level but blow chilly at foot level. Build the bed or box up with old blankets or newspapers – anything at all to make sure it's warm. Remember that the healthy animal can move out of the cold, but the ill one may just be so lethargic, doped or weak that it cannot.

2 Wrap hot water bottles very well and secure the wrapping with safety pins. Burns may be caused by exposed hot water bottles. Try to change them often enough to keep the temperature constant.

3 Never force food or brandy. Your patient isn't going to starve in a day or two. Follow the veterinary surgeon's advice about what foods to try. A little coaxing and encouragement may get the animal eating.

4 Water should be available always. Change the water at least four times daily. Small amounts may be spooned – gently – into the animal's mouth.

5 Quiet and dim lighting are conducive to sleep and proper rest.

6 Three or four times daily the animal should be carried to a pile of papers and supported while it defecates or urinates. Slight pressure over the bladder (squeezing gently with one hand each side of the tummy just ahead of the back legs) may encourage it to overcome its scruples and urinate indoors. Some animals will not do their business inside the house. They must be carried out to the garden.

7 If the patient is lying flat out and is disinclined to move you must turn him over every two hours. This helps to prevent pneumonia.

8 If the bedding gets wet or soiled it must be changed.

9 If the animal is ill more than two days you must groom it, or else it will start to lose interest in living.

10 Nasal and eye discharges should be wiped away and the nose and eyes bathed gently with warm salt water (teaspoon of salt to a pint of water, boil and allow to cool). A bit of olive oil will prevent drying.

11 If the hind end becomes soiled and matted you must wash and dry it. Any mild soapy water will do. It is best to just wipe down the area with a damp cloth and then with a dry one.

151

12 Give pills and injections as close to the stated intervals as possible. Many modern drugs depend for their effect on their level in the blood, and this can be kept constant only by regular doses.

Nymphomania

The bitch is on heat more or less all the time. Usually they are very nervous or vicious as well. There may be a constant bloody discharge.

The cause is cysts on the ovary, and although there are injections that will relieve the symptoms the only real cure is spaying, i.e. removing the ovaries.

Obtaining a dog

A considerable number of people don't buy their pets. A neighbour has kittens or pups to dispose of, a friend dies and there's no one to take over, your child just appears with an animal, a stray firmly chooses to settle on your doorstep, the neighbours emigrate to Australia and can't afford the sixty quid to take the dog, etc., etc.

Lo and behold, you've got another member of the family. Make no mistake: it's a new responsibility you're undertaking. And once you do, the law says it's your responsibility.

The butcher will assume an added importance. You will be seen at odd hours in your kimono and slippers cooing into the darkness. You will discover parks and neighbours you never knew existed. You will leave parties earlier and you will plan a weekend outing like a military expedition. Corners of your home will take on a new aspect.

Unless you've made up your mind, and firmly, don't accept any pet for 'a trial' or 'for a day or two'. You'll find that with each passing day you're less able to part with it, and some people just don't have the time or the money or the space to care for an animal properly. If the pet that is thrust upon you is middle-aged or old, you will likely be spending time and money at the vet's. In most cases I think it's unfair for people to pass on an animal that is well beyond its prime. They have had the best years of its life and want you to take over when the problems begin. Many animals are unhappy with the new environment and never do adjust.

Don't be sentimental and foolish about it. You're not doing the animal a kindness by half-heartedly taking it on or by being too soft to refuse. Almost every week people who have had animals thrust upon them suggest to us that the animal has some condition for which 'it should be put to sleep'. They would like to pass the burden of

152

responsibility on to the vet. It's really a difficult position both for the reluctant new owner and for the vet.

Of course, if you're really enthusiastic about it there's no reason why it can't be a good thing. The only firm advice I can give you is as follows. Find out the age of the animal, whether inoculated or not (assume it's not if there's no certificate), its sex (amazing how many people don't know), whether neutered or entire, when it was last on heat, if its heat periods are regular, if it's had a litter or litters, what its normal regime or diet and exercise is, what training it's had, whether it's bitten or snapped at adults, children or other animals (most owners lie about this), its bathing and clipping routine, where it's normally boarded during holidays and last but not least its veterinary surgeon. If the owner is going away write all the answers down, because you'll wish you had.

Ask the veterinary surgeon for some tranquillizers to help the animal settle in to your home. It should, of course, only be taken out with collar and lead.

If possible try to get the old bed or blanket so that it has something familiar in the new place. Put it at once where you intend the animal to sleep. Don't punish for any reason (except biting) until you're sure it accepts its new home.

Finally, if you already have a dog make sure the new one is healthy before taking it home. Make an appointment with a vet to see the animal before you go home. There's no point in bringing fleas or lice or worse to a clean place.

Orphans

Raising orphan pups or kittens is a laborious job if there isn't a foster mother available. Any bitch or cat that is in milk will do, and quite often a cat will raise a pup or two and bitches occasionally accept a kitten. If the foster mother still has her own litter and you reckon there's enough milk to spare for an orphan, you must be careful in introducing the orphan. Often the foster mother will reject or even kill the intruder. Rub the orphan all over with milk from the foster mother or some of the droppings from the natural offspring. Do this after the foster mother has been kept from her own litter for a couple of hours. Then when she lies down to give suckle hold the orphan or orphans to the spare teats. Repeat a couple of hours later. Usually three trials will persuade even the most snobbish of nursing females to accept the orphans.

If there's no foster mother available then use one of the substitutes

153

formulated for human babies, or better still, if they're obtainable, one made specially for puppies. If the foundlings are very small or young use a medicine dropper with wee holes in it rather than one with just one large opening. Later a baby's nipple and bottle can be used. Wash and boil between feedings. The temperature of the formula should be that of the body, and test as you would for a baby. Frequency of feeding is more important than amounts. Never feed more than a drop or two at a time. Wait for swallowing and then go on. Small, young animals get fed about every three hours, and the interval gradually lengthens to six hours. A rough general guide is a teaspoonful at a feed for an animal weighing 100g ($\frac{1}{4}$ lb); four tablespoonfuls for an animal weighing 1kg (2 lb).

After a couple of days you'll be an expert at it because raising orphans is more of an art than a science.

If no milk substitutes are available you can try raising puppies on cows' milk (see *Milk*).

New-born animals are very susceptible to temperature change. They must be kept in a draught-free box in a warm room. A well insulated hot water bottle changed when it cools is a great help. Change the bedding often.

Finally, a simple point that if neglected can lead to trouble. Puppies when they wake will want to start suckling. If there's no mother around they will start in on the limbs or ears or tails of their mates. This can and does lead to the most awesome sores, which get infected and can even kill the puppy. Unless you're making it a round-the-clock job you'll find it easier to raise orphans separately. Each will have its own box and area and each its own hot water bottle.

Os penis

The dog has an actual bone in his penis, and although that's an interesting enough fact it doesn't really matter medically or surgically.

Otitis

Means inflammation of the ears (see *Ears*).

Otterhound

A rough-coated hound that must be loved for his courage, because of looks he's got little. Stands about 60cm (2 ft), weights about 29kg (65 lb), and almost no one is interested enough to breed them these days.

PS: The otter itself is rapidly facing extinction. The real reason is the changing environment. Build a factory or a housing estate beside a secluded stream and the only thing it will nurture is garbage. Although the desecration of the countryside continues, otter hunting is now illegal. However, mink who have escaped form fur farms have become a pest. In a generation or two the Otterhound will be called the Mink-hound.

Ovario-hysterectomy

(See also *Spaying* and *Pyometra*.)

In the human, often only the diseased uterus is removed. The ovaries may be left in, so there is no basic hormonal change. The person's personality is unaltered. In animals the ovaries are almost always removed with the uterus, so the animal does in fact become a complete neuter.

Many veterinary surgeons used to believe that it was a good idea to leave one ovary in. They felt that the hormones elaborated by that ovary were beneficial. Some veterinarians still believe in the benefits of a partial ovario-hysterectomy, but I follow the majority in thinking that both ovaries are best out. The bitch who has all the psychological changes of heat but few of the physiological ones is a problem to herself and to her owner. Often the remaining ovary becomes cystic and must be removed anyway.

Overshot

The upper jaw protrudes beyond the lower. It's a characteristic some cartoonists would have us associate with decadent aristocracy. I can't tell you if it's common among decadent coal miners or cartoonists, or veterinarians for that matter, but it is seen in some strains of Fox Terriers, Collies and Greyhounds among others. It's not a good thing because the affected animal doesn't have a proper bite, and tooth trouble in early middle age can be expected. Sometimes the lower fang teeth push up and ulcerate the upper lips or the upper fang (or canine) teeth rub against the lower lips.

There is no cure for an overshot jaw. One must recognize the condition and not breed animals with malformed mouths.

Overweight

Most dogs will get as fat as you allow them to. You put it down and they'll eat it. No matter what your rationalization is you must be told (better by me than by your neighbourhood veterinarian) that it is cruelty to overfeed. A bloated animal isn't happy, it doesn't enjoy its walks, it gets all sorts of ailments and it dies in middle age. If you really have a fat balloon on your hands, better get it to your vet who will outline the dieting procedure and prescribe some drugs to help.

How can you tell if an animal is overweight? Just as you would a man. His belly is flabby. His chest is rounded. There's a roll of fat along his back. He doesn't walk; he waddles. And usually he's always begging for more.

Some breeds are more liable to become fat than others. The Dachshund can look like a balloon mounted on four twisted frank-furters. In fact, there is a special disease of fat Dachshunds called 'contact dermatitis'. The rolls of fat on what is left of the legs rub against the rolls of fat on the chest and abdomen. You can imagine what tact is called for in treating these patients when they are accompanied by a lady who needs the same treatment. Spaniels in late middle age may get interested in food to the exclusion of everything else. Chows, Alsatians, Boxers, Bull Terriers, Bulldogs, Elkhounds, English Setters, Labradors, Huskies, Old English Sheepdogs, Pugs, St Bernards, Great Pyreneans, Rottweilers, Samoyeds, Scottish Terriers and Sealyhams are all breeds in which I have seen grossly fat representatives, and in which just plain fat dogs are all too common. Often, and I say this in defence of the helpless dog, the fat dog is accompanied by a fat owner.

Afghans, Airedales, Basenjis, Black and Tans, Border Terriers, Borzois, Chihuahuas, Deerhounds, Dobermans, Great Danes, Irish Setters, Irish Terriers and Irish Water Spaniels, Chin Chins and Pekinese, Salukis, Shetland Sheepdogs, Staffordshire Bull Terriers and Whippets are all breeds that are more likely to remain trim. But – and it's the big but – any dog of any breed can be bloated into early death by overfeeding.

Oxygen

Do veterinarians use oxygen in the treatment of their patients? Yes, we do and every day. It's a necessary aid to general anaesthesia. It's useful in shock and pneumonia, and, of course, in many cases it's life saving. Some people who have an old well-loved pet suffering from asthma or a bad heart keep a canister of oxygen. If city air keeps getting thicker and blacker, I think we should all get in our own private supply.

Pads

If an animal scrapes its pads on gravel or ice you can make a bootee out of a baby's sock. Tie it on with a flat strip of material. If you use cord you'll cut off the circulation.

If it's a deeper scrape, down to the blood-carrying tissue, apply an antiseptic powder and bandage the foot lightly, which should give some relief until you get to the veterinarian.

Don't try to tourniquet the foot unless the blood is just gushing out. A pressure bandage is much safer and will usually control the bleeding.

For sore, hard or cracked pads, olive oil applied two or three times during the day is as good as anything.

Paint

Animals can't read 'wet paint' signs, nor do they know that open tins are likely to spill. Children sometimes paint their pets because they love them, and adults have been known to deliberately spill paint over an animal because, I suppose, they're incapable of loving anything. Whatever the reasons we see it fairly commonly. Usually most harm has been done in trying to get the paint off.

Never use paraffin or kerosene or any of the paint solvents. They cause nasty burns. Try to wipe off as much as you can with dry cloths. Affluent friends tell me that gin will get some paint off. Then use soap and water. If the job is just beyond you, get the animal into the vet. He can anaesthetize and proceed leisurely.

If an appreciable part of the body surface has been covered, or if the eyes or mouth are involved, get it to the vet straight away.

One other word of warning. All paints that contain lead are dangerous, and should not be used in kennels or on dog baskets.

Papilloma

This is a polite word for wart. They may occur anywhere on the body, and depending on their size and location cause more or less trouble. Basically the treatment of warts hasn't changed much for a couple of thousand years. One cuts them off, or burns them off, or ties them off, or uses a combination of all three methods. They don't usually come up again in the same place, but I've seen Cocker Spaniels that grow a crop of warts every six months, as adolescents sprout pimples.

I wish I could give a simple answer to what can be a distressing problem, but unfortunately there just isn't one. Warts are a kind of cancer – granted usually a non-killing cancer - but a cancer all the same. When the researchers come up with the answers to the cancer riddle, we may be able to tackle warts more rationally.

Papillon

Called the Butterfly Spaniel because it's supposed to look like one, but I guess I've seen the wrong Papillons or the wrong butterflies. They say it got its name because of its large upstanding fringed ears. But there is a variety called Phalènes who have drop ears.

They can weigh as little as 1·5kg (3½ lb), but usually those closer to 3kg (7 lb) and standing about 25cm (10 in) have fewer physical problems.

The Papillon is one of the most decorative of dogs and is ideally suited for city life in that it can work off its energy in a small flat. It is also (like the Griffon) among the few toy breeds that can (and does) compete successfully in obedience trials. And I have yet to hear of a stray Papillon. The dedicated British breeders follow their progeny. If they're unwanted at any age or stage they'll have them back. I'm sure to get some angry letters from them. They have deliberately avoided making Papillons popular lest they fall into the wrong hands. Long may they remain unpopular champions.

Paraplegia and posterior paralysis

This is a condition which we see all too often in long-backed breeds like the Dachshund, and occasionally in Pekinese and others. The usual story is a squeal of pain, a bit of shivering and a disinclination to move. On the first day the animal, though reluctant, can usually move about. By the second day he's right off his hind legs, and if he moves at all it's by pulling along with his front legs. It's at this stage that the veterinarian first sees the case. One immediately suspects spinal trouble, and finds out where the trouble is by feeling along the spine and by X-raying. There are, of course, several different possible causes of spinal trouble, and the treatment and outcome depend on the cause.

There are injections which can ease the condition and hasten recovery, but this is one condition where nursing is quite as important as medicine.

The animal must be carried about – and it must be carried so that the spine is not bent. It must be confined to a fairly small area, where it can't injure itself by dragging itself about. Every three or four hours it should be carried to a grassy or papered spot and supported while it defecates or urinates. Your vet will show you how to press its bladder. It must be kept well groomed.

If it can't pass water – and this is one of the common complications – then a catheter must be passed twice daily.

The diet must be fairly sloppy, so that there is no danger of constipation.

Water must be available at all times.

There is one sort of paralysis (the ascending sort) in which despite all effort the animal usually dies.

However, in most types within a week there is some improvement, and at the end of a month the animal is well and happy.

Early diagnosis and treatment are essential, so if you own a Dachshund and he goes off his legs don't hesitate but get on the phone.

Patent drugs

Proprietary remedies and tonics and vitamins and all those highly advertised products said to be recommended by veterinarians everywhere. Every other owner presents his pet to the vet saying, 'I give him his . . . every day', as if that should be enough to placate the gods who make dogs ill. The vet usually carries on with the examination muttering under his breath, 'Oh well, they won't do him any harm'.

The facts are that your pet doesn't need all those over-touted and overpriced tonics and conditioners. I'll admit there are thousands of healthy and happy pets taking them, but there are millions equally happy and healthy that have never seen them. The money is better spent in your butcher's shop.

As for drugs sold across the counter, they can do positive harm in that they often give the owner a false sense of security, and he or she postpones proper professional diagnosis and treatment.

Pekinese

Some of the experts tell us that the Pekinese were originally Tibetan, and most of the experts tell us that they were in fact imported into China from Japan in AD 618. We know for certain that the Peke was adorning Chinese palaces both in the flesh and in art when most of our forefathers were playing cricket with their neighbours' heads. They must have appeared in Europe towards the fifteenth century, because it doesn't take much imagination to see the Peke influence in early portraits of the King Charles Spaniel.

Today there are very few Pekes in China, but they are very popular in both America and Europe. They are a basically very tough breed, difficult to handle and train, prone to skin and eye ailments; they have difficulty in breathing properly, are often oversexed to the point of physical embarrassment, require an inordinate amount of grooming

159

and yet they must be the most decorative and delightful of companions. They are game to the point of folly. They will tackle anything. In illness they are morose and independent, but they won't give up easily.

The Pekinese – and particularly the Sleeve or Miniature Pekinese – must have about as many physical faults as it's possible to have. The protuberant eye is a constant invitation to trouble. The snub nose and bashed in face and foreshortened mouth condemn them to rotten teeth and difficult breathing. That mass of fine hair is a guarantee of skin trouble, and their furry feet require weekly attention if cysts and infection are to be avoided. I've seen Pekes with such crooked little backs that you'd swear they'd never walk, and yet walk they do.

Why does such a breed survive and thrive when other breeds with less faults are losing that basic vigour necessary for survival?

I don't know for certain, but it must be simply that the Chinese always placed temperament (vigour, pluck, or whatever) high on the list of desirable characteristics. They must have culled all the nervous and shy.

In other words, they didn't develop the Peke by breeding runts to runts, but by breeding the toughest of the litters to each other and retaining only those who were both tough and had the physical characteristics they considered decorative. It took a long time, but they did develop one of the few small breeds that one can call a dog.

Pelvis

This, as in the human, is the skeleton of the hips. We are concerned about the size and shape of the pelvis in some breeds of dogs because if it is too small the bitch can't have a normal delivery. The English Bulldog and the Pekinese, for example, have large heads and chests but small rear quarters. Obviously a very small pelvis can't accommodate a puppy with a big front end, and so a caesarian operation is done. Many breeders will have the bitch mated when she is less than a year of age and her bones haven't hardened. They hope to stretch the pelvis so that it can give normal passage to future litters. The real solution is to modify the breed standards so that a more normal body type can win the shows.

The other common problem with the pelvis is fractures as a result of car accidents.

We do not operate on the broken pelvis because we cannot put our patients to bed and immobilize them for long periods. But nature can handle the worse sorts of pelvic fractures. I think it quite astonishing how badly a pelvis can be fractured and still heal. All we can do to help is administer drugs to control the pain, keep a high protein, mineral and vitamin level and, most important, keep the bowels and bladder working.

Within a week most cases are wobbling about. At the end of a fortnight they're well on the road to recovery, and after a month they are almost completely recovered.

Only one word of caution. Do not breed females who have had pelvic fractures. They will almost certainly require a caesarian.

Penis

The penis of the dog is smooth and varies in length from about 5–15cm (2–6 in). It is usually not exposed but is carried in its protective sheath. When erect it is engorged with blood and is easily injured. First aid includes a pain killer (aspirin if nothing else is available) and a soft compress of a saline soaked bandage (one teaspoon of salt to a pint of water), to help control the bleeding, and to help gently return the penis to its protective sheath.

Some precocious dogs, and they are usually found among the toy breeds, may have trouble in that their rather large penis does not return easily to its rather small sheath, and an operation similar to circumcision may have to be done.

Occasionally we are presented with dogs with a nasty discharge at the end of the penis. The owner is very concerned and has to be reassured that it is not gonorrhoea. The assurance is easy to give because animals do not get either syphilis or gonorrhoea. The discharge is usually cleared up with injections and applications of antibiotics. Some cases become chronic and there is little that we can do. However, it doesn't seem to bother the dog, and so you just have to bury your aesthetic sensibilities and put up with it.

Some dogs are almost always in a sexually excited state. It is obvious that they're most undesirable as pets or as working dogs. Tranquillizers can have only a passing effect, and hormone injections aren't a permanent cure. If the condition doesn't pass off with maturity, your veterinary surgeon may recommend castration as the only answer. In the dog – unlike the cat – castration is a major operation and must be done very carefully.

Pneumonia

A common complication of distemper and other infections. Until the advent of penicillin it was fatal more often than not. Today we can

161

cure the bacterial pneumonia rapidly, and we can control the bacterial complications of virus pneumonia, so the condition isn't regarded with the seriousness it deserves. Good nursing is still important to avoid a long drawn convalescence and permanent lung damage. Freedom from draughts, fresh air, a light nutritious diet, daily grooming and warmth are essential. For at least a month after recovery the animal should not be allowed out in the rain.

Pointer

So called because it points to the bird with its nose, body and tail in a straight unwavering line. It originated in Spain, has been exhibited in England for over a hundred years, and was popular long before that.

It is an example of what a real dog should look like – in that you cannot associate any malfunction or proneness to disease with its body shape. The reason is that the breed has always been a working dog and most breeders are not interested in showing a dog that is useless in the field. Any working breed can go to pot if a majority of the people who own it are more interested in show points than in working ability. If, for example, a beautifully marked Pointer who had never worked was considered more valuable than a plainly marked field champion, and if it was mated to another non-working show winner, you would get puppies that would be more likely to win shows and less likely to work well in the field. Keep emphasizing or choosing the beautiful dogs for a few generations and it becomes sheer chance whether or not the offspring will be any good in the field.

Now I am not saying that a non-working dog has more physical problems than a working dog, but I do think it's more likely. Doesn't it stand to reason that a dog who can go out in all weathers and work hard for eight or ten hours is more likely to have the physical characteristics that ensure health and well-being than his distant cousin who has merely looked beautiful in the eyes of a few judges?

Poisons

We used to have a calendar at home. On the front it had a smiling girl holding a dog, the name of the farm implement distributor and the days. On the back in very small print it had helpful information such as how many pounds make a bushel of oats, and the gestation period of the cow, the mare, the sow and the ewe. One section was 'Poisons and Antidotes.' This I memorized, and thought I was ready for any emergency. The only time I used this handy information was quite a few years ago when I regurgitated the chart from memory and put it down (in essay form) to answer an examination question.

In practice a memorized list of antidotes is of little value because one almost never knows what poison is involved. One is presented with a vomiting or a bleeding or a collapsed animal and may suspect poisoning, and later narrow it down to a small group of poisons or even to a specific poison, but what the vet does immediately is to treat the symptoms he sees. Often oxygen or blood or both are given just to keep the animal going while he decides what to do next. Sometimes from the history or from the symptoms he can find the poison, but usually he needs specialized laboratory help.

Today, with the ever-growing list of chemicals with which we are spraying ourselves, our houses and our crops, it takes a determined genius several days to find out which one is doing the killing. Sometimes the only geniuses around are those that are making and selling the stuff, and they are hardly likely to cut off the hand that writes the pay-cheques.

What advice can I offer you? If you actually see an animal bolting some noxious substance then pour some strong salt water or mustard down his throat to make him vomit it back.

If your dog suddenly starts vomiting don't add to its misery by inducing further vomiting. Get it to the vet who will decide what to do.

The best bet is prevention. Dogs on leads do not get into the dump heap and start rummaging.

If you've decided to spray yourself or your house or your garden with some poison, then for goodness sake leave the dog with your mother-in-law for a day or two.

Note: Many poisons are labelled by the manufacturer, 'Not dangerous for domestic animals,' or some similar soothing phrase. I wonder how they imagine that anything that can kill a rat or a snail can be considered safe for other species. *Please* when you take a poisoning case to the clinic take the suspected pack as well. The label may save hours and a life.

Polystyrene granules

It doesn't matter whether your dog sleeps in front of the furnace or out in the barn. It deserves an underblanket filled with this material or something like it. It insulates against rising damp and cold, and is comfortable in the heat. There is no charge for this commercial. But I must declare a vested interest – our animals enjoy the comfort. *Be careful*: the granules must be covered in scratch-proof material. If it isn't, you could easily spend a week cleaning up the mess. It flows like mercury!

Pomeranian

This was once a Spitz, but over a long period has been reduced to the smaller dog – 2kg (5 lb) and less – that we see today. It was very popular in Victorian times, and even after the First World War there were quite a lot about. In the twenties some people thought they looked well with Silver Fox coats and there was a brief flurry of re-popularity. Today one sees few Silver Fox and even fewer Pomeranians. I don't know why the fox has gone out of fashion, but the Pomeranian, bred for looks alone, sometimes became a neurotic, and all too often a snappy, yappy, unsociable sort of beast. Now, with the debs out of the market one's chances of getting a true Spitz type are better.

Poodle

Originally a German water-retriever, but its natural intelligence, its high spirits and its free-flowing movements made it a natural house-hold pet. From the standard size the miniatures and then the toys were developed, and in the last twenty years it has become the most popular breed everywhere.

The Standard Poodle is still a great dog, and some miniatures have retained the stamina and the intelligence of their large forbears. Unfortunately, though, most miniatures and toys that a vet sees are neurotic, spindly, temperamental, nervous and lacking in vigour and spirit. They have badly formed eyes that water, horrible ears, knee joints that wobble and fussy stomachs. The whites and apricots are even worse.

Do you think I'm exaggerating? How many Poodles do you know that live out their lives without bouts of ear trouble? How many little Poodles do you see limping because of a badly formed knee? I could go on for hours.

What has done it or who has done it? Popularity is the culprit. The public wanted smaller and smaller Poodles, so the dealer-breeder, ever ready to satisfy any demand, bred the runts of the litter to each other to produce even runtier offspring. Never mind what faults they have so long as they're small and will produce small dogs.

I can't think of a major fault that we don't see at least once a day in a miniature or toy Poodle. The worst product of runt in-breeding I can recall was a five-month-old white toy Poodle that the owners brought to us because it kept walking in circles. It ate, it whined, it was a cute little powder puff of a dog, but it walked in circles. A cursory examination revealed that the top of the skull had never closed. You could almost feel the poor creature's brains pressing on the skin. Needless to say we advised euthanasia.

Find any excuse you like, but it must be classed as cruelty to continue breeding from animals that are almost certain to produce offspring condemned to a life of coping with malformations.

What should you do if you want a Poodle? Get a Standard. Surely if you can afford a dog at all the extra pound of meat a day isn't going to make that much difference. Space in your flat? They've got brains enough and to spare to cope with that. Exercise? It will do you good as well.

If you insist you want a small dog, and it just has to be a Poodle, then prepare for lots of travelling till you find a breeder that puts health first. I speak from experience.

Portuguese breeds

There are nine native Portuguese breeds, none of which are known outside that country or its colonies. All of them are primarily working dogs, and have the ruggedness that many of their showier cousins lack. The commonest is the Podengo, which is used for rabbit hunting. It is divided into three varieties according to size. The Castro Laboreiro breed is a large mountain herding dog, and is found only in the north. The Perdigueiro is big with a docked tail. It's reputed to be a slow but industrious Pointer. The Portuguese sheep-dog weighs about 45kg (100 lb) and is used for protection of the flocks rather than herding. The most interesting looking breed is the Cao d'Agua, which as you might expect is a water dog. It weighs about 22kg (50 lb) and when clipped looks like a shaggy rugged Poodle.

It's an ancient breed that is still carefully bred by fishermen, who use it to retrieve objects lost overboard. I should have thought it would find a ready reception here, and no doubt some enterprising person will import them, and others will start breeding the runts to each other in order to satisfy the demand for flat-sized dogs. That's not as unlikely as it sounds. It wasn't so many years ago that the Poodle was a working water dog.

Postmen

All too many dogs get in the habit of worrying regular callers like the delivery boy or the paper boy. If you're the kind of idiot that thinks it's cute or clever you won't be able to stop it, because the dog will sense that he's really pleasing you despite your half-hearted commands of, 'No, no, Poopoo. It's only the nice man bringing us our ginny gin and lemon'. If you show and express real disapproval most dogs will desist. A trained dog will, of course, sit on command. Sometimes, though, a dog will take a dislike to a particular caller. One of the remedies that sometimes works is having the person in for a coffee and a chat. He may then join what the dog considers the insiders club of friends to be welcomed.

The psychology is quite straightforward. A visitor like the postman or the milkman appears. The dog barks. The visitor deposits his articles and retreats. The dog says, 'This is terrific! Every time I bark they drop whatever they've got and off they go.' As they say in show business, 'why argue when you win?'

Pot belly

Pot-bellied puppies should be examined for worms. A sample of the motion should be taken to the vet, who will run it through the lab and see what sort of worms are causing the trouble. I suggest a faecal sample rather than taking the puppy along, because there is no point in unnecessary risk, and a visit to a veterinary establishment is a risk until the animal has been inoculated (and for a fortnight afterwards).

Pot-bellied middle-aged animals are often, like their human counterparts, just too fat and lazy. But if the condition appears suddenly or over a period of just a few days it may be rather serious, and you'd better make an early appointment at the vet's.

Professional courtesy

To me this means that when I go to my dentist or doctor he discusses the X-ray plates or laboratory findings with me, gives me a choice of possible treatments, serves me a cup of coffee or a drink if it's late in the afternoon and talks shop. In return for making a nuisance of myself I get a bill (when I do get one) that is marked 'fifty per cent discount – professional courtesy'.

Veterinarians almost always return the favour not only to doctors and dentists but to nurses as well. We find, of course, that doctors and their pets are difficult patients, often for the same reason that veterinarians are. We know just enough to be afraid of the pitfalls, and not enough to be confident of the outcome.

Courtesy between one veterinarian and another has become formalized over the years into professional codes. Basically, one veterinarian may not see a patient that has been treated by another veterinarian without the latter's consent. This is designed as a protection for the dumb animal patient, who cannot protest against being put through the same old procedure for the same old condition. But, of course, many people blithely state that they have not been to another veterinarian, and except in the most obvious cases it's difficult to tell. Inestimable harm may be done by this start and stop treatment which some neurotic people force on their pets by going the rounds from vet to vet. If you want a second opinion for goodness sake say so, and your veterinarian will be only too happy to give you a letter of clearance. The vet who receives the letter will phone your vet and get an outline of the case and the drugs that have been used. It will save time and money and, most important, will advance rather than retard the animal's progress.

Courtesy between the veterinarian and his animal patient really depends on the animal. A well-trained or responsive animal is a pleasure to see and a pleasure to treat. Nervous or vicious animals can only be treated with firm restraint. If they weren't, there would be a lot of one-armed veterinary surgeons.

Prolapse

Eversion of the rectum or vagina may be caused by continual straining during a difficult birth, or because of constipation or diarrhoea. It's a most alarming sight because the delicate membranes are red, raw and sore, and usually bleeding. Give the animal any sedative that is available – even aspirin is better than nothing. Soak some cotton in warmish salt water, cover and protect the delicate tissues, and get on the phone at once. The earlier the treatment the better the chances of recovery.

Prostate

This is a small gland in male animals that lies along the urinary tract just behind the bladder.

Its function is to aid the expulsion of semen during the sexual act.

The prostate gland enlarges during middle age, and it may cause symptoms varying from mild discomfort to pain during defecation or urination. It may even get so large as to cause a blockage.

We see the condition fairly commonly in dogs and we diagnose it by feeling it through the rectum and by X-ray.

The two common treatments for enlarged prostate in the dog are injections of female hormones and castration. Generally the latter is more satisfactory.

Removal of the prostate gland is much more difficult in the dog than in the human, and is not usually done.

Pug

An ancient breed that, like the Pekinese, seems prone to all sorts of ailments but somehow survives them all. I've never yet met one that I didn't like. Their entrance into even a hard-hearted veterinary establishment almost always causes frowns to turn into smiles. If you've got the kind of face that puts people on their guard, why not get a Pug to neutralize the effect?

What do we know about the origins of the Pug? All too little, I'm afraid. We know that short-faced dogs with screwed tails were found in China. References to these dogs can be found in Chinese literature and art as far back as 700 BC. The breed was first introduced to Holland by the Dutch East India Company.

The Pug stands about 25cm (10 in) high, and weighs between 6·8kg (15 lb) and 9kg (20 lb). He looks much smaller because he has such a compact square body that blends into a neckless head. His head and neck are much too short, and as a result most Pugs breathe as fat men snore. When a Pug is excited it almost gasps for breath. The short head also usually means badly placed teeth, and the Pug is no exception.

Despite these drawbacks the Pug is a tough, long-lived breed that usually manages to lead a healthy life and be a delight to himself and his owners. His temperament is best described as equable but aloof. In Victorian times (so Lady Diana Cooper tells us) the Pug was considered the only breed absolutely safe around children.

He has a short tail that curls in a tight roll over his back and a short glossy coat that needs only occasional brushing, and he comes in a wide assortment of attractive colours. Do you want one? I hope so because the breed, although it has a devoted following, has never been as popular as it deserves to be. I think the Chinese knew what they were about. Perhaps they said, 'These are the characteristics we want – but first we want resilience, health, longevity. Any dog – no matter how close it approaches the ideal in appearance – if it is sickly or nervous or short-lived will not be used for breeding and its offspring will be culled.'

I can't tell you if that's the way they did it, and neither can anyone else. But they certainly didn't produce the Pug the way the Europeans produced our modern toys and miniatures, i.e. by selecting for appearance alone.

Pulse

This is felt high up on the inner part of the hind leg. The rate varies considerably according to the size of the animal and its state of excitement, so we usually don't pay much attention to that. We are interested, however, in the character of the pulse, which can be most helpful. It can vary from weak and thready to full and bounding, according to the condition.

Punishment

Dogs by nature wish to please you, so the best punishment is by showing displeasure (and meaning it) and by scolding, not shouting. Don't strike a dog unless he snaps or bites at you. This is a cardinal sin – even in a puppy – and must be immediately and severely curbed. Never strike his face or body where you can do damage that will last much longer than the memory of what caused it. A short, sharp flick at the flanks is usually enough. It's the immediacy and the shock of the blow that punishes, not the force. A punishment that will impress any dog – without hurting it – is being picked up and shaken by the scruff of the neck. Try it on your Great Dane.

The most important part of punishment is timing. The dog can only associate the punishment with his activity at the moment of punishment. If you come home and find the place in a shambles and he's sleeping in the middle of the dust, you've lost your opportunity to vent your feelings. Any punishment he gets he'll associate with sleeping. He might even think he's being punished because he wasn't tearing the joint to pieces. By dog logic, he's quite right. While he was destroying nothing happened. The minute he stopped and had a sleep the heavy hand descended. Similarly if your dog is doing something nasty, like chasing the neighbour's swans, he must be caught and punished while he is still involved in the chase. If you call him and then punish him he'll think he's being punished because he came at your call. The swan episode could have occurred last Christmas as far as he's concerned.

Purgatives

A purgative is like a laxative but it is harsher and stronger, and I say a plague on all purgatives. If something can't be moved with a gentle laxative like olive oil or liquid paraffin, then the purgative can only do harm. If you have any castor oil in your animal first-aid cabinet, give it to your enemies. Why am I so vehement about it? In Italy before the war the fascists used it as a method of punishment, and I have heard some graphic tales of its painful effects. To inflict it on a helpless dog under the guise of kindness is worse than quackery. It's cruelty.

Pyometra

Also called metritis, pyometritis, infected uterus or womb. Literally translated pyometra means pus in the womb, and it is a serious and all too common condition in bitches.

The normal bitch comes on heat twice yearly. The uterus swells and prepares for pregnancy. If the animal is not bred the uterus or womb gradually goes back to normal. At about five or six years of age or older the uterus loses some of its tone and may not shrink back to normal. It may remain swollen and congested. The slightest infection seems to overpower its defences and the whole cavity becomes full of discharge. Drugs may control it, but usually an operation is necessary to remove the womb, else the poisons are absorbed into the system and permanent damage or death is the result.

What symptoms does the bitch show? In over half the cases there is a thick slimy discharge from the vagina. The discharge may be pussy or clear, but it doesn't have the healthy appearance of the discharge one sees in a normal heat. Fastidious animals may lick their vaginas constantly so that you don't in fact see the discharge. In cases where there is no discharge, what we call in rather slangy fashion a 'closed pyo,' the only symptoms may be a vastly increased desire for water and possibly a bout or two of vomiting. The belly may swell and be tense and painful. The temperature is usually about 38°C (103°F).

If you have a middle-aged bitch that has a persistent discharge, or is licking her vagina continually, or has a sudden increased desire for water, get it to your vet at the earliest opportunity.

Some cases are so straightforward he will have the bitch on the operating table straight away. Others may require X-ray or a blood test to confirm the diagnosis. Still others may be borderline cases which will respond to antibiotics. And unfortunately there are always those advanced cases that have been left too long, and where either the uterus has ruptured or so much poison has been absorbed into the system that little can be done .

The operation itself is a major one requiring a great deal of skill

170

and care. Even in the smallest bitches the incision is four inches or longer, along the middle of the abdomen. The uterus and its horns are usually so swollen that it practically forces itself out of the cut. Its blood vessels are huge, and they must be located and carefully tied off. The actual cutting of the uterus must be done in such a fashion that none of the pus leaks into the abdominal cavity.

Most veterinary surgeons do this operation so often that they can finish it in an hour of concentrated work. They like at least one assistant and an anaesthetist. Afterwards whole blood or saline is given to the bitch to help her recover, and this may be repeated the next day. The stitches are taken out in a week or ten days. The animal should be severely restricted for a convalescent period of about three weeks. After that its food intake should be carefully regulated because many bitches will develop voracious appetites after the operation and get as fat as you allow them.

Now for a bit of controversy. In America most bitches are spayed as puppies. It eliminates those messy heat periods twice a year and those false pregnancies and the danger of pyometra. In Britain the only bitches that are spayed routinely are those that are going to be guide or police dogs.

A spayed bitch is every bit as good a house dog as the entire bitch. She'll only get fat if you allow her to. I wonder if the American practice isn't in fact worth adopting in Britain?

Pyrenean Mountain Dog

This is one of the really magnificent breeds. They weigh 45kg (100 lb) and up, but give the impression of being even bigger because of their thick coats. They have been used as guard dogs because they have gained a well-deserved reputation for their reliability with children. If you don't have space and money please don't get one. If you have one, examine it twice weekly for signs of skin trouble, and get it attended to at once. That thick beautiful coat can hide more trouble than enough.

PS: I'm afraid to say this is one of the few breeds of which more recent experience has made me rather wary. I don't think it's the fault of the breed, but rather of the sort of people who get one because as puppies they look like teddy bears. Make no mistake about it. They are big dogs, originally bred as guards. If you raise one as if it were a kind of cuddly toy don't be surprised if it bites when you say 'no'. Children reared without restraint react the same.

Quacks (*empirics*)

A quack is a person without formal training who practises medicine. In human medicine the patient can protest or at least, we can assume, that he deserves what he chooses. Animals, however, are helpless victims of the uneducated purveyors of half truths, so it is up to you the owner to safeguard your animals. Almost anyone can advise treatment, and in ten minutes anyone can be trained to give an injection. It's amazing how many pet-shop proprietors, Poodle parlour attendants and just plain well-meaning fools will make diagnoses and peddle treatments. Not for them the sciences of anatomy, bacteriology and pathology, nor the arts of diagnosis and surgery. They 'know dogs' or 'love cats' and that is sufficient qualification. I have seen cancer treated with liniments by quacks because they thought it was an abscess. I have seen abscesses continually recur because the quack didn't know it was caused by a rotting tooth. I have been presented with an animal that had been treated for arthritis for months. The quack used some sort of heat lamp. The animal had a fractured leg.

Quarantine

The distressing but necessary safeguard used in places like Britain, Eire and Hawaii, that are presently free from rabies. Because the period of incubation (the time lapse between exposure and symptoms) is so long the quarantine period must be six months. Some experts would have it extended to eight months – because one dog did develop rabies symptoms after it had been in quarantine almost seven months. Fortunately the owners were not able to pick the dog up at the end of the quarantine period.

There is no legal way of avoiding the regulations no matter how influential you are. If you're thinking of smuggling, do remember that the penalty magistrates may now impose includes putting you in gaol and killing your dog.

For the most part dogs do quite well in quarantine, but some small toys may succumb to the rather rigid conditions and lack of human warmth, no matter how well run the kennels are. Unless you are terribly attached to your Chihuahua, or it to you, you should seriously consider leaving it with a friend in Spain or Rhodesia or wherever you are.

A final word of advice. Every animal varies in his or her reaction to visits. Some pets are pleased to see their owners but will settle back into kennel routine in an hour or two. Others will pine for days after your visit. Ask the attendants, and if your animal is in the latter category stay away for the full six months. Of course, there are some owners who spend six or eight hours a day outside their pet's cage. This sort of behaviour can hardly be treated by a veterinary surgeon (see also *Rabies*).

Quick

That part of the toe nail or dew-claw which contains blood vessels and nerves. It corresponds to the red part of your finger nail, and in both animals and man a cut or injury to it causes bleeding and pain.

It's easy to see the quick in white nails, if you use a good light. Don't cut too close to it. In black nailed animals you can only guess where the blood vessels and nerves end, so one cuts carefully. The best first aid for a bleeding quick is a soft dressing over the whole foot. Pack between the toes with cotton wool to prevent pressure sores. Elastoplast over the dressing so that the animal can't get it off. Change daily for about a week. Then if it appears to be healing leave it open.

Rabies (*hydrophobia*)

By all odds the most painful malady of man and animals. Just in case the clinical descriptions weren't graphic enough they used to show the veterinary students a movie of a child dying from the disease.

Rabies is caused by a virus which must enter through the broken skin. It's usually a bite that effects its entrance, although it need not be. One can get rabies through a scratch or any sore. The virus is contained in the saliva of the affected animal. Almost any animal can get and transmit rabies. In Central America and in parts of Texas there's a form carried by bats.

If you are unfortunate enough to live in a country that has rabies and you suspect an animal of having the disease do not shoot it. Catch it with a noose on the end of a pole and put it in a cage. If you can't manage it call a veterinarian or a public health official. If it has rabies the symptoms will get worse, and in a few days the animal will be dead.

The reason for this apparent cruelty is as follows. The lab people can only diagnose the disease with certainty in an animal that has died of the condition. The characteristic bodies don't show up in the brain till shortly before death. Diagnosis is terribly important because the animal may have bitten people. As the treatment is both painful and dangerous, one doesn't want to be left in any diagnostic doubt.

Britain is rabies free, and only people who have seen the disease can realize what a blessing this is. There has been a great deal of

173

sentimental cock lately about changing British quarantine regulations. Here are some of the reasons why things should be left as they are:

1 The vaccine isn't always a hundred per cent effective. No vaccine is.
2 As it is man that is injecting the vaccine, the treatment is subject to human error.
3 In some countries a certificate of vaccination can be obtained without the animal being vaccinated. Don't scoff. I worked in Sicily one year and watched the local government veterinarian filling in anthrax vaccination certificates while sipping coffee in the town square.
4 Absolute identification of animals is very difficult. You'd be surprised how many people can't tell their own black Labrador from any other.
5 Several millions of dogs and cats might have to be vaccinated in order to allow hundreds to escape quarantine.
6 If one case developed in Britain or Hawaii and it got loose among a wild animal population, it would be very difficult to eradicate.

Canada, which was free of rabies for years, now has a steadily more difficult problem. Theirs started with one isolated outbreak.

If you have complaints about the present quarantine set-up, that's all right. Doubtless the kennels could be improved. I don't know. But I do know that any shortening of the quarantine period is folly.

A final word about vaccination for those who live in rabies countries. The incidence of rabies varies widely across the continent. In some places it is virtually unknown, and one can forget about it unless a warning appears in the papers. In other states or provinces one only inoculates if there is an outbreak. In some states the problem is ever present, and preventive inoculation is the only sane safeguard. Your veterinarian will outline the local situation at the time of distemper inoculation.

Ravenous appetite

We see many dogs who just can't seem to get enough to eat. A dog who has been working hard for years and is suddenly retired will keep his athletic appetite. As he puts on weight he'll want more to eat. Sometimes, in just a few weeks he will turn into a barrel that wakes only to get refilled. Active animals after a bout of sickness or an operation will often start eating and putting on weight. The process once started is difficult to stop and even more difficult to reverse.

Pampered dogs in middle age develop gross appetites encouraged by their owners' offers of tit bits. It's a difficult habit to break, and most owners don't have the strength or the sense to co-operate fully.

There are, of course, many other causes of ravenous appetite. These include worms, dietary deficiencies and glandular trouble. It may be one of those and habit as well.

If the animal suddenly changes its eating habits your safest course is to take it along for a veterinary examination.

Rectal impaction

This is a condition we see commonly in Pekinese and other long-haired dogs and in older dogs fed on bones. In the older dog it may be due to a lack of bowel tone – sometimes made worse by constant dosing with laxatives. The only remedy that I've found is mechanical. One cleans it out by a combination of enemas and finger probings and massaging. Sometimes an anaesthetic is necessary. Occasionally a general abdominal operation must be done to clean out the mess. It's one of the few conditions veterinarians see that makes them lose their tempers – especially if they are brought the same animal again for the same complaint. Almost invariably the owner is at fault. Long-haired animals are not groomed. Older animals are overfed. They are given bones. The vet wearily repeats his directions. The owner stares. He repeats the same cruel mistakes. The only cure for him is a huge bill.

Restraint

We generally use this term to describe what one does to capture and hold a dog that is either vicious, completely wild, or so excited that it won't respond to ordinary commands and pressures.

Sometimes a loving pet who has been bitten or injured will become unpredictable. Older animals suffering from a painful disease may turn vicious. Even a simple wet eczema may change an animal's temperament.

The larger the animal the more effective the restraint must be. Many of the larger breeds are capable of killing a man.

An ordinary rope with a noose on the end is dangerous because it's difficult to loosen and the animal may choke. A simple, safe and effective device is a rope doubled and passed through a 1·2 or 1·5m (4 or 5 ft) hollow steel rod. One end of the rope is fixed to the rod, the other end lies loose in the hand. You can adjust the size of the noose at the other end of the pole by pulling or slackening the loose end. The pole can be used to keep the animal off if it's actually attacking.

Slip the noose over the animal's head and settle it around its neck. Keep it just tight enough to restrain the animal.

Large or powerful dogs may have to be held with two such rods and ropes while a third person ties a bandage around its mouth.

Use a 7·5 or 10cm (3 or 4 in) bandage. Tie the first knot anyhow so long as it's well back on the mouth. The last knot should be tied under the muzzle and then the bandage should be carried back behind the neck.

Smaller dogs can be captured and held in strong nylon nets. They can then be transferred to metal cages.

Rhodesian Ridgeback

This dark tan breed was developed in Rhodesia and South Africa, mainly from European breeds. It has an infolding of the skin along the spine which causes the hair to point forward. They are inclined to be a one-man dog rather than a family pet and are at their best outdoors. Height 60cm (2 ft), weight about 27kg (60 lb).

Rickets

This is a disease of the bones caused by a deficiency or an imbalance of calcium and vitamin D. It is common in growing animals on all-meat diets. The joints may be enlarged and sore and the bones will be malformed. As the animal gets older it becomes bow-legged as its weight pushes down on the soft bones.

Rickety bones fracture easily and we often diagnose the condition when the puppy is brought in to the clinic because 'it fell off the chair and now it's holding one leg up'.

Treatment in severe cases includes injections and pills. In mild cases cod-liver oil and bonemeal will do the trick.

Rickets is seen most commonly in the larger breeds. If you have a Great Dane or a Pyrenean Mountain Dog or even a Boxer remember that meat alone just won't do. Pick up some calcium and vitamin D pills, or better still lay in a stock of good old-fashioned English feeding bonemeal (famous the world over) and get a bottle of cod-liver oil or halibut-liver oil.

PS: Recent research has shown that too much cod-liver oil can do more harm than none at all. In years gone by doctors would tell mothers and vets would tell clients to ladle the stuff into youngsters by the tablespoonful. Today most agree that a drop or two a day is plenty. Current practice would suggest bones or bonemeal ad lib with say a teaspoonful of halibut- or cod-liver oil a week.

Ringworm

An infectious skin condition that is transferable from man to dog and *vice versa*. It generally starts around the eyes, the gum line or the feet, and it often shows the characteristic rings of denuded skin. Within days it can develop into quite a serious condition. Diagnosis is a bit difficult, as it involves a skin-scraping and a look through the microscope, but treatment is simple and effective. There are pills – rather expensive, unfortunately – which will do the job.

There is usually a dramatic improvement within a few days, and after a week or ten days the owner may think it's cured and stop treatment. The condition then usually comes back. I think that to be on the safe side you had better go back to the vet at weekly intervals for a month or six weeks. He'll tell you the same thing, but you may think he's only trying to scare you.

He'll also tell you that ringworm is particularly unselective. It will happily thrive on your cats, your child's pony and, far more worrying, it can survive long periods in furniture and on fences. He will outline a programme to help you get rid of those resistant organisms. Be prepared for lots of hard work.

Many experienced vets and stockmen don't take ringworm seriously. They calmly watch as it invades a pen of steers and state with the certainty of a successful bookie, 'It's only a matter of time. They'll get over it.' Absolutely true. And it probably doesn't matter in a commercial situation who is scratching what. Those of us who actually live with our animals may be forgiven if we give nature a gentle helping hand.

Oh, one more thing. If your pet has ringworm, better take yourself along to the doctor's. And *vice versa*.

Rottweiller

Originally a cattle dog but it has proved to be an adequate police and guide dog. As it's less highly strung than most Alsatians I would suggest it for those people who aren't really experienced trainers but do want a continental working breed. I wish the standard of the breed didn't specify docking the tail very short. What earthly good does it do? *PS*: May I mention that the best specimen of the breed I've ever seen was presented to me as a puppy for inoculation by a young lady who was so beautiful that it took all my limited powers to concentrate on the dog? She brought it back a month or two later because it seemed to have difficulty going up the stairs and sort of wobbled when it walked. The pup was a mountain of equanimity. Even so it

177

resented any manipulation of its hip joints. X-rays confirmed a tentative diagnosis of hip dysplasia. Despite all our efforts the condition progressed; we had a 45kg (100 lb) dog who couldn't get up without effort and couldn't make the stairs without help. The dog was put out of its misery. The lady bears me no ill will. But incredibly the breeder of that unfortunate creature is still producing puppies from exactly the same stock.

Moral of the story: Try to see the pa and ma and if possible the grandpa and grandma of any puppy you're about to buy. Alternatively go to a show and listen to the gossip.

St Bernard

They say that dogs are like people in that the little ones are snappy and arrogant and always ready to pick a fight, while the big ones are easy going and would rather be left to wag their tails in peace. I can think of some exceptions, notably the Doberman and the Alsatian, but it's certainly true about the St Bernard. This huge dog is a most equable beast who will act as a mattress for any number of bouncy three-year-olds. When he gets bored he'll gently shake them off and seek adult company.

However, if you coop one up in a two-room flat you can expect its disposition to deteriorate. If you chain one for days at a time you'll produce a vicious monster.

Our biggest problem with St Bernards is arthritis, particularly of the hip and stifle joints. Like great fat people, their weight itself accentuates a condition that in a normal size animal would be minor. Again, like the other large breeds they are not long-lived – many being old and crotchety at eight or nine.

If you have the space and the money then do consider getting one. If you don't live in the mountains you're better advised getting one of the smooth-coated sorts. The normal rough-coated type can get the most miserable skin complaints if kept in a hot or damp climate.

Saline (*more properly, normal or physiological saline*)

That concentration of salt in water which approximates the body fluids. A rough guide is a teaspoon of salt in 6dl (1 pt) water. Vets use it a great deal in the form of injections into the vein in all conditions where there is a fluid loss. In shock, kidney disease and blood loss it is a valuable aid. Animals with gastro-enteritis may go dry and start dying in a matter of hours, and often an intravenous of saline will snap them out of it.

178

Saline is equally valuable in the home first-aid kit for bathing abscesses, soothing burns, washing out inflamed eyes or soaking an infected foot. It is similar to the fluid that the body pours out to protect itself, so you can be sure you're not doing any harm – which is more than can be said of most home remedies. Make sure you add the salt to boiling water, boil it for a few minutes, and then cap it in your sterilized bottle.

Salt

Normally one doesn't add salt to the diet of dogs, but if they're on a pure meat diet you should be giving some mineral supplement. The usual dog mineral supplement constitutes less than a half per cent of the dog's diet, and of that a fifth is salt, so you see very little is needed. The other bits of the mineral supplement are calcium, phosphorus and potassium and, in case you're interested, wee traces of magnesium, iron, copper, manganese, zinc and iodine.

Don't get frightened. If you have a normal mooching hound that gets his normal meal plus part of yours, his problem isn't likely to be any sort of deficiency.

Saluki

Looks like an Afghan without the beard or trousers, and is much easier to keep properly groomed. Has been used for thousands of years in the Middle East for hunting, and some of the remaining sheikhs use them to this day for hunting gazelle. In our gazelleless part of the world they are used primarily as personal adornment. They are beautiful indeed, but if you're fat and flabby you'll look silly with a Saluki. They can be highly strung, so don't expect one to be at his best in a household of children.

Samoyed

The breed that typifies the Spitz type. About 22·7kg (50 lb) in weight, they may be snowy white, biscuit and white or cream in colour. As you might expect, being a northern breed they're very much at home in the cold and rather miserable in the city. They are sometimes difficult to handle and I couldn't really recommend them as a family pet. If you're a loner living in the great outdoors it is an ideal dog.

Sanitation

This can be very simple with the household dog if you do a bit of planning. Empty and clean food bowls when the animal has finished so that the bits don't get caked down. Put the dog blanket in a sheet and change the sheet weekly. It's much easier than laundering blankets. Don't pour disinfectant on a dirty surface. Wash it first. Then you'll be disinfecting the surface, not the dirt. Have an ample supply of newspapers for whelping time or puppy time. When grooming put newspapers down first.

Schipperke

A perky breed, 6·8kg (15 lb)–9kg (20 lb), jet black, close-docked tail and fox-like head. Originated in Holland where it was and is used as a boat dog. They make a good healthy, hand-sized family dog.

Schnauzer

A Terrier-like breed that has been popular on the continent for centuries as an all-round guard and companion dog. There's a statue of one in Stuttgart dated 1620. The one we usually see (the dog – not the statue) is about 50cm (20 in) high, but there is a miniature which is 35cm (14 in), or less. The breed is very popular in America, but has never really caught on in Britain.

Scottish Terrier

The jet black chap with all the character. I know they can be nasty little brutes, are prone to all sorts of whelping problems, get eczemas of a severity and duration you wouldn't believe, but I like them all the same. I think one of the reasons I'm almost forced to respect them is the way they, like the wire-haired Fox Terrier, will refuse to admit defeat in illness. They don't want anyone's help. They just want to be left alone to get on with it.

Scratching

This is one of the commonest complaints we attempt to treat. Ninety per cent start with fleas or lice. If you have a scratching beast look carefully to see if your pet has pests. If you don't see them look again because you'll just end up having your vet point them out to you. There are dozens of good powders that will eliminate them (see also *Fleas*).

The only other word I offer is use your own powers of observation. See where the animal is scratching. Head? Is it an ear, an eye, its mouth? Look carefully. If the cause isn't obvious then bring it along to the vet.

You might think this so obvious that I'm wasting my time writing it and you're wasting your time reading it, but I draw on the following examples to prove that people don't look.

I've removed elastic bands from the tails, the penis, the tongues and the ears of animals. The people brought the animal in because it was scratching or biting at the area.

I've removed bits of bone or wood from between the teeth of dogs. Usually they're quite easily seen and easily removed. Isn't it amazing that people are afraid to open their own dog's mouth? *Summary:* Examine carefully. If you can't see and eliminate the cause take the animal along to the vet's.

Note: Bored animals scratch.

Scrotum

This is the sac that contains the testicles. Dogs get sores on their scrotums and scrotal eczemas. I find them most difficult to treat satisfactorily, and indeed have seen some so bad that we ended up castrating the beast. I would suggest that this is an area where you had better seek professional advice within a day of noticing the trouble, because a neglected or a badly treated case will be even more difficult to clear up.

The dog's scrotum bleeds very freely and is difficult to stop. If your dog has been in a fight and blood is pouring out of a rip in its scrotum I'd suggest immediate veterinary help. If it's not available then tape the dog (even the quietest of them resent having their scrotums handled) and try to tie a thread around the bleeding area. Don't for goodness sake take in the whole scrotum, just a wee bit of skin immediately around the opening. If that doesn't work try a tightly held compress. They usually start bleeding again some hours or days later, so please do arrange for expert treatment.

Sealydale

A South African breed produced by crossing Airedales and Sealyhams. It's almost 30cm (1 ft) high, weighs about 9kg (20 lb) and doesn't look like either of its forbears. It now breeds true to type. It's reputed to be a great rat-catcher and an OK family dog.

Sealyham Terrier

Some people say that all Welsh breeds are of an impossible disposition. Anyone who has ever owned a Welsh Collie knows that the Welsh can be wonderful, once you get to know them. The Sealyham, too, takes an extra lot of knowing, but its supporters assure us it's well worth the effort. Personally, I have found my Sealyham patients so difficult that I have a quite ridiculous prejudice against them, but you must consider my opinion as useless as any other prejudice. They do, however, have stacks of guts and character, and if that's what you want in a dog, well, get one. Height up to 30cm (12 in), weight up to 9kg (20 lb); and please don't worry if he doesn't look exactly like those beautiful clipping diagrams.

Sex

Almost all dogs are either male or female but a few hermaphrodites are seen and there have been been cases of 'sex-changes' reported in the scientific literature.

Because we use animals and not they us, we unhesitatingly remove their sex if it's to our advantage. We expect our pets, even those that are whole, to be more interested in their masters than in sexual activity, and by hundreds of years of selection* we have produced dogs that usually prefer their master's company to that of the opposite sex – although we all know that a bitch in heat will tempt even the best trained dog. It is for this reason that guide dogs are usually spayed females and occasionally castrated males.

In America many bitches are spayed as pups, and it eliminates the trouble of heat periods and messes and unwanted litters. Most male dogs are left alone – partly because it's a hazardous operation in the dog, but mostly because they can function very well as males and as pets. Those odd few that can't should be seen by a vet. People are usually embarrassed about how to phrase the complaint, but I can assure you that no veterinary surgeon will crack a smile or a blush if you just say, 'He's too damn sexy. He's always at the sofa or at the children.' Most dogs grow out of the phase but while it's going on it can be most embarrassing. A sudden severe slap across his flanks every time he starts will deter most dogs. Sometimes we try female hormones but more often castration is the answer in those dogs that persist in the habit into adulthood.

Another question that most people find embarrassing to ask is, 'Is sex necessary?' They have been told that their dog should be bred

* It's interesting but possibly confusing that selection has also encouraged sexual promiscuity. The domestic dog's forbear – the wolf – tends to monogamy. Quite obviously man couldn't control a breeding programme if a pair he chose to mate refused to have anything to do with each other. Hence most of our modern dogs ain't too fussy. For a really lucid explanation the reader is advised to read Mr Michael Fox's fascinating book, *Understanding Your Dog*, Blond & Briggs, 1974.

once or twice to 'settle him down', or that the bitch is better for having had one litter. The answer is no. One sexual experience is not going to have any beneficial effect on your dog's or bitch's temperament, and I know of no veterinary reason why it would be beneficial. The dog's mind is not like man's. He doesn't sit around wondering what something would be like. He just enjoys the moments as they occur.

Shaking

Head shaking is almost always a symptom of ear trouble (see *Ears*).

Thin-haired dogs like Greyhounds and Whippets will shake or shiver all over if it's the least bit cold. Most are better blanketed. Nervous dogs – and these can be members of any breed – will shake in the presence of strangers. There is no cure except reassurance.

Involuntary shaking of one part of the body is a symptom of nerve damage commonly seen after distemper. Usually one leg is affected and it will quiver, on and off, all the time but especially when the animal is at rest. The condition is called chorea, and there is no cure although there are some drugs that may control it. Usually the chorea itself doesn't seem to affect the animal's general well-being, but it indicates that the distemper virus has done internal damage as well, and such animals have a reduced life expectancy.

Sheepdogs

Dogs first helped man with his hunting and then with his herding. Wherever there have been sheep, breeds of dogs have been evolved by selection to help them or to protect the flocks from marauders. All the breeds of sheepdog, whether Scots, Italian, Rumanian or whatever, are rugged, well-boned and either long-haired or positively shaggy. Obviously a thin-haired greyhound type wouldn't survive long following the flocks. There are two general sorts of sheepdog. The large types are those that are used primarily for guarding the flocks and the smaller types are used for herding. Although they are intelligent and trainable, most sheepdogs aren't very happy in town dwellings. All that hair doesn't really belong indoors.

PS: A cattle dog is a sheepdog whose owner keeps cattle.

Shetland Sheepdog

Not a miniature Collie but a breed that was evolved on the Shetland Isles. Originally a sheep herder, but most of them today couldn't do a day's work. They have been taken to town with a vengeance, and although they are attractive and affectionate and good family dogs they have lost a lot of the stamina of their forbears. We see a lot of them with nervous tummies and runny eyes. I think the process of 'fining' them down for show purposes has gone far enough. They stand 30cm (12 in) to 37·5cm (15 in) high, weigh 12 to 15 lb and come in the glorious assorted collie colours.

Shih-Tzu

Supposed to have been developed in China by the crossing of Pekinese with a Tibetan breed. I imagine you could travel days through China and Tibet without finding one representative of the breed, but they are adequately represented in Paris, London and New York, so you can spare yourself the trouble. They're a shaggy beast standing 27·5cm (11 in) or less, and they look at the world through a mop of hair which often causes chronic runny eyes. Cut it off or buy a ribbon. They won't look so exotic, but at least they'll be able to see. All that hair that plugs the ears is better out while you're at it.

PS: Standards seem to have altered just lately since the breed has become more widely known. We see puppies (with identical pedigrees) that vary in size and shape from sleeve Pekes to miniature St Bernards. The formula for discriminating purchase is no more magical than for any other breed: take your time; go to shows; buy through or from an established breeder. Unlike other sorts of purchases in the dog world you often pay less for quality.

Shock

The state of collapse which follows some accidents, blood loss or advanced disease. There's a weak pulse, slow respiration and fall in temperature. The theory and practice of treating shock has changed a bit. Originally everyone said use hot water bottles as first aid until oxygen and intravenous medication is available. Then it was pointed out that as the blood pressure was dropping the use of hot water bottles would just bring more blood to the skin and cause a further drop in blood pressure and death. Use ice packs, they said, and drive the blood back in where it was needed. Thank goodness that phase didn't last too long, because it didn't take much common sense to see that a shivering shocked animal or person didn't want to be wrapped in ice. Today most people agree that until the oxygen and intravenous is set up the patient should be wrapped in a blanket and nothing, but nothing, given by mouth. Personally if I were in shock I should appreciate the hot water bottle too.

Shops

In Britain there is legislation empowering local authorities to inspect and licence pet shops. Unfortunately many local authorities licence the pet shops but don't bother to inspect. So Britain in this age of astronauts and moon missiles still has pet shops that for squalor, overcrowding and just plain filth rival the animal markets of the Middle East. Some in the States are little better. They survive because people think they can walk out of a filthy shop with a healthy pup. Even pet shops with a certain standard of sanitation find it impossible to peddle disease-free animals. The mere act of removing a newly-weaned beast from its home, transporting it and putting it in with a bunch of others almost ensures disease. The only safe route is from its breeding kennel to its new home.

PS: The situation hasn't changed at all. I own a share of a pet-shop business in London with kennels in the country. The only inspection either has ever received is the annual request for the licence fee. As we try to maintain standards we would welcome a really rigid inspection. Unhappily most local authorities are so bogged down in paperwork and teabreaks that they couldn't spare anyone a moment from either to discover the difference between a rat and a ratter, a salmon and a salmonella or for that matter, between good and bad.

The pet shop does not sell puppies or kittens (or any pets to children). It acts as an agency to introduce buyers to breeders. The profits come from accessories and food. Terry and Jo who run it spend their share of the profits rescuing other people's mistakes in London's East End.

Skye Terrier

A shaggy little dog that was used 300 years ago for hunting fox and badger. Queen Victoria's interest in the breed popularized it, and today it is an ornamental breed that occasionally gives a half-hearted yap at a passing squirrel. Most of the poor things would trip over their own hair if they ever actually gave chase. When clipped you can see that the Skye Terrier is 30cm (1 ft) high, 90cm (3 ft) or more long, and weighs up to 13·5kg (30 lb). What have I got against the breed? Nothing at all. I'm just pointing out that despite its hunting ancestry today it's in the pampered Poodle class. If that's what you want, get one.

Smells

One of the commonest complaints with which people present their pets is, 'He smells.' Little children are more explicit and say 'He stinks.' Most dogs, though, don't stink all over. Does it come from the front end? The mouth? Look at the teeth. They may be covered with tartar. Is it his breath? That may be diet or kidney trouble. Is the smell from an infected ear? Is it from the rear end? Probably it's his anal glands. Why do I go on? Because most people usually try baths or pills for some weeks before coming along to the vet. They often allow a simple condition to become complicated by their delay.

Animals who have their coats covered by some really noxious substance must, of course, be bathed. If you don't feel up to bathing your Chow Chow, covering the affected parts with tomato juice will often neutralize the odour till you get your willpower wound up. Tomato juice will even mask the odour of a skunk, and that takes some neutralizing.

Snake bite

People who live in snake country usually spend hours discussing snake bite remedies, but very few of them lay in a stock of anti-venom. I knew one agricultural officer who was so terrified that he always wore hip boots in the sweltering heat, but even he didn't have a couple of ampoules of the stuff that saves.

There are two sorts of poisonous bites. The first sort, like that of the Fer de Lance or some of the Rattlers, is almost instantly paralytic and death follows in seconds. The other sort travels slowly and there is time for treatment. The wound should be gashed open and allowed to bleed freely. The anti-venom is injected anywhere in a thick muscle. Most dogs, though, get bitten in the head and the humane thing is to kill them quickly.

Sneezing

This is a much more serious symptom in the dog than it is in the human. It may indicate one of the more serious virus diseases, and if it's continuous the dog should be seen professionally within a day.

Soft-coated Wheaten Terrier

A game Irish Terrier, about 16kg (35 lb) in weight, who is as about as unspoiled as any western European dog can be. If you hanker after the dogs of yesterday place your order with an Irish breeder. I hope I'm not contravening the Race Relations Act if I add that you must make sure you're dealing with someone who actually recognizes the breed as purebred.

Something new or something different

Bichon Frise, Lowchens (Little Lion Dogs), Chinese Crested, Mexican Hairless and lots of big hairy dogs are among the plethora of goodies sent to tempt those of us who aren't happy with the standard menu of Labradors, Poodles and Terriers. I think some of the breeds we are now seeing at shows are really rather weird. That is definitely not a professional opinion. I'm equally amazed by the hairstyles of the young nurses in the practice. No one can really judge unusual breeds. There aren't enough to compare.

I would suggest that one examines the reasons why people breed them and why other people buy them. I know, for example, a perfectly rational racehorse trainer who got a Pharaoh Hound at enormous expense because he reckoned it had more potential than any Whippet he'd ever had. As they say, 'Horses for courses'. As it happened he was wrong – but for the right reasons!

Why do people promote new or unusual breeds?

1 They believe it has some desirable features possessed by none of the established breeds.
2 They believe rarity is in itself a virtue.
3 They want something that no one else has.
4 They want to make money.

Go on. Tell the truth. Why do you want that cord-coated mutt with the fancy name? Do you really think it will make a better pet than an old-fashioned Border Collie?

Spaniel

In many parts of France and America when they talk about a Hunting Spaniel they are referring to the Brittany spaniel. It's absolutely superb in the field, and is far less prone to physical problems than its Spaniel cousins (because it's still essentially a working specimen). This 40–50cm (16–20 in) white worker with red or tan markings should be on the list of priority imports right beside champagne and French bread.

Spay

A term used to describe the operation of removing the ovaries from the female animal. Usually the uterus and its two horns are removed at the same time.

In America bitches are commonly spayed. There's a lot to be said for the practice and more people are having it done in Britain. It's a difficult operation, but not so difficult or hazardous as to make one hesitate. Three or four months is a good time to have it done.

Spaying older or pregnant animals puts the operation into a different category. It takes much longer and your vet is quite right to ask you to pay for his extra time.

Springs and clips

Those things that are used to attach leads to collars should always be of the button and slide sort. About once every two or three months we are presented with a dog that has a spring clip fastened to its nose or its tongue or its ear. The dog is in pain and frightened and the owner is usually in a panic. In order to release the spring you have to increase the pressure and this the dog will not allow, so one often resorts to a general anaesthetic for something that can be removed in a second. We do get the odd ones that have to be cut off. I had one once caught in the dog's Achilles tendon that had almost cut its way through. Anyway, not to panic. Just buy one that can't get caught.

Staffordshire Bull Terrier

Produced by crossing Bulldogs with the old English Terrier, and I think it has the best qualities of both. An absolutely perfect house dog, and a natural guard. The only drawback is their manners with other dogs, which varies from rude to downright dangerous. Keep them on the lead when you're out walking.

Sterility

Although there can be many causes of sterility it is often nature's way of saying she's had enough of that sort of nonsense. When someone presents a 1kg (2 lb) Chihuahua with the request that it be given an injection to make it come on heat we sometimes comply, but more often we mutter something and say it wouldn't work anyway. Nature doesn't want any more runts and we don't want any more caesareans. Similarly with other breeds of dogs we run into sterility problems where man has interfered too much in something about which he knows too little.

Stomatitis

This is an inflammation of the mouth. In growing animals it's often caused by a vitamin deficiency and is soon corrected. It may be a symptom of a more generalized infection, and then antibiotics are usually used. It is commonly found associated with tartared teeth. When the teeth are cleaned up the sore mouth heals. Washing with saline will give some ease, and that old standby borax and honey will soothe a really sore mouth.

Stones

Bladder stones are commonly diagnosed in the dog. Kidney stones are rare. No one knows for sure what causes bladder stones to form and, although it's thought the water has something to do with it, changing the source of water doesn't usually prevent the condition. Dalmatians form their urine in a way unique to that breed, and they seem more subject to the condition.

The important thing for you to know is that bladder stones may cause the most painful sort of obstruction which will lead to death if not treated within hours.

If your dog is straining to pass urine and cannot, or if only a drop or two comes, then get it to the vet straight away. This is one of the conditions where no vet minds being woken up.

He will try to pass a catheter for immediate relief, and will decide (usually with the aid of an X-ray) if an operation is necessary.

The operation involves going into the bladder and flushing out all the stones. If we get them early on it's a simple enough procedure, but it does take a couple of hours.

Unfortunately many cases recur. If it happens a third time within a few months or a year we usually recommend euthanasia rather than subject the poor animal to a whole series of painful episodes.

Stop

The depression between the forehead and the nose. For some unaccountable reason it's a valued feature of some breeds like Chihuahuas. The Mexicans, we are told, used to tie a smooth stone into the frontal depression of the puppies in order to accentuate the stop. Some of the breeders give the impression that they would like to continue the practice.

Stricture

A narrowing of the urethral passage which causes difficulty in urinating. Usually caused by emergency catheterization when the bladder just has to be emptied to prevent toxaemia or death. It doesn't usually cause much trouble.

Strychnine

Dogs are very susceptible to strychnine or its parent *nux vomica*. A dose that wouldn't hurt a baby will cause tetany and death in a large dog. Avoid all medicines that contain it. Use no poison around the place that contains strychnine. The symptoms include a convulsive spasm that can be brought on by a sudden noise. The antidote is nembutal or one of the other anaesthetics. There's little time, so the nembutal must be injected intravenously. If there's no vet around a doctor or a nurse could possibly do it. The nembutal wears off in four or five hours and the spasms will start again, so the treatment must be repeated. If there's no nembutal around any of the tranquillizers or anaesthetics could be tried.

Sulpha drugs

Still widely used despite all the newer antibiotics. The only word of advice which your rushed veterinarian may forget is to encourage the animal to drink lots of water while it's on the drug.

Surgery

What is the difference between operating procedure in the human and animal fields? Very little really. Animal surgery may look a little more rough and ready because conditions aren't always ideal, but standards of sterility must be maintained even when one is doing an emergency caesarian on a cow in a barn. A cow or a dog or a cat is just as susceptible to infection and peritonitis as you are.

Anaesthesia is slightly more complicated in animals because they must be restrained before sleep is induced. One obviously wouldn't have the strength to wrestle every patient to the ground – and a wrestling match wouldn't improve the patient's chances of recovery – so we give injections of tranquillizers before applying the restraint and inducing the anaesthesia.

The only difference in attaining sterility in animal surgery is that animals must be clipped as well as shaved. Otherwise the routine of boiling up instruments and scrubbing hands is the same.

The actual skill among veterinarians varies quite as widely as it does among doctors. Some vets have pioneered techniques and written texts of surgery that are standard works for both professions. Some vets, like some doctors, consider surgery a barbaric form of plumbing and have no interest in it. A man who has specialized in parasites or viruses for twenty years is hardly likely to be adept with the scalpel, although there are some notable exceptions like Sir Alexander Fleming, the discoverer of penicillin, who was reputed to be as clever in the ward as he was in the laboratory.

The majority of practising veterinarians can handle most operations adequately. As a rule vets in dog and cat practice spend three or four hours of their day at the operating table. An average day might include spaying or castrating two or three kittens, removing a diseased womb, correcting a Bulldog's inturned eye-lids or a Poodle's ear, mending a fracture and sewing up an ugly bite wound. After a decade or two they get pretty handy at it.

Naturally some are better at some things than at others, either through practice or inclination. A chap in a hunting district soon gets to know which gunshot wounds can be cleaned up, and which few are best left alone. A vet in a city welfare clinic will see dozens of car accident cases so he's likely to handle them more smoothly than his rural colleague. The end results are usually about the same, but the difference is that some vets will spend much more time on unfamiliar cases.

People are often astonished at how badly a dog can be injured and still survive. It all depends on whether any vital organs have been injured or ruptured and how extensive the injuries are. Even the worst sorts of multiple fractures and lacerated skins have a fair chance of good recovery, but a ruptured liver or extensive brain injuries are almost always hopeless.

In some fields of surgery the veterinarian is unlikely to be as competent as the human surgeon. Ulcers are rarely seen in the dog or cat, and one's experience may, therefore, be too limited. Specialists in human cancer surgery may have spent ten years working in a particular field like tumours of the pancreas or of the prostate. No surgeon outside the field could compare in knowledge or skill. Operations within the eyeball are a specialist's business. There are some notable veterinary surgeons who are as good at it as the top human surgeons, but naturally they are a rare handful.

No veterinarian or doctor is so arrogant that he will hesitate to call in a colleague for his more specialized knowledge or skill.

The mistake that some people make is thinking the specialist is the better man. He is for his speciality. But that's as far as it goes. When he's solved his problem better go back to the man who can define the next problem.

Post-operative care in animals in most cases is simpler than in people. They aren't depressed because of the operation or the condition, as people are through mental association. They can feel the pain just as we do. They may not feel much like eating, but they don't lie and brood about their chances. They'll try their best to be up and about, and they'll consider that aching limb or those nasty sutures as something they just have to live with. Life with its joys and sorrows goes on. Doctor friends have told me they wished their patients reacted as sensibly.

Generally we don't bandage over the incision because most dogs will worry a dressing more than an incision. They accept the incision as part of themselves. Some, though, simply won't leave off licking or biting or scratching at it. Then bandages and tranquillizers become necessary. Some few patients, despite everything, literally destroy themselves by self-mutilation.

Finally a word about pain. No one can assess what an animal feels. There are no measuring sticks. The only people qualified by training, experience and inclination to arrive at a fairly accurate judgement are veterinarians. If you are in any doubt about your animal consult your vet. If you are running a research laboratory that uses animals and you don't have a veterinarian on either a fulltime or a consulting basis you are guilty of gross neglect and cruelty.

Sussex Spaniel

A golden-liver dog weighing 20kg (45 lb). As they say about all slow dogs, he's a conscientious hunter. Unspoiled because unpopular, but no doubt the city folks will get around to the breed.

Swiss Mountain Dog (*Grosse Schweitzer Sennenhurd*)

The huge dog – 45kg (100 lb) – you see pulling the cheese around those villages that you don't dare drive your car to. Don't waste your tears over his plight. The Swiss who regulate everything lay down cart specifications and weights allowed according to the dog's height.

Sydney Silky

Produced by crossing Australian Terriers with Yorkies. Weight about 4·5kg (10 lb). It's got long hair and a short short tail, but then there's no accounting for taste.

Tails

The Manx cat is born without one and he lopes along without trouble. Other cats have tails and man leaves well enough alone. Not so with the dog however. There's a special department of lunacy in man which tells him how much to chop off which dog's tail. Does the dog's tail have a function? I don't know. I do know a greyhound without a tail is a much slower runner. If an adult dog has his tail sheared off or amputated he may lose some of his sense of balance, and some control over his bladder. I'm also of the opinion that breeds that are docked very short, like Schipperkes, seem to have more trouble with anal irritations.

Tails can get sores and fleas and eczema. They can get cut, they can get fractured and they can get tumours. As it's difficult to bandage a tail we prefer to see the patient as early as possible. In the ordinary skin complaints a dressing or two usually puts them on the road to recovery. Bleeding is treated by applying a tight bandage which should be changed daily. Fractures of the tail are best treated by amputation, and tumours, of course, call for amputation of the tail.

Some Great Danes end up losing their tails because they wag them so hard they're always cutting them open. I know it sounds ridiculous, but they just don't seem to associate the pain from the tail with the happiness they're trying to express.

An animal who just feels great may chase its own tail because it happens to be the handiest thing around to chase. If, however, he's chasing it because it's driving him crazy you had better have a good look and see if 1, it has fleas, 2, the anal glands are inflamed, or 3, there are tapeworm segments below the anus.

Powder will get rid of the fleas. If it's anal gland trouble or tapeworms, better get along to the vet and get it seen to properly.

Tape

Taping or tying a dog's mouth is the simplest way of handling him without getting bitten. Use a length of cord, or better still a 2–3cm bandage. Cross it around the muzzle, knot in the middle, leaving equal lengths of cord free. Carry it around the mouth two or three times with your final knot under the jaw. Then take the loose ends back and tie a knot just behind the dog's ears.

Tapeworms

These are flat worms, which means that they are rectangular or oval rather than round in cross section. The common earthworm is round in cross section, and so are most species of intestinal worms.

The tapeworm has a head at one end and then a series of sections or segments. The segments pass out, and it is these that can be swallowed by another animal or by the same animal, finally to hatch again and produce a new tapeworm with its own head, which attaches itself to the intestines and draws nourishment from the host. And so it goes on. The segments look like grains of rice or little maggots, and you can sometimes see them just below the tail of the affected animal.

One more thing about the dog tapeworm. The flea can be a carrier of tapeworms, and if you treat an animal for tapeworms you must get rid of the fleas at the same time.

Dogs don't get cat tapeworms and *vice versa*. People can be infected by neither sort.

Tartar

This is an accumulation of deposits on and around the teeth. Over a period of months or years it can become hard and cement-like. Examine your pet's mouth about once every three months. If there's little tartar you can remove it yourself by gently lifting it off with your fingernail. If there's a great deal of it then veterinary attention is necessary. Don't neglect it, because the teeth will rot under the tartar.

Teeth

Dogs have two sets of teeth – the temporaries and the permanent. Teething problems are usually at their worst around fourteen weeks of age, and the puppy may have bouts of pain and lack of appetite during this period. A child's aspirin will help give a good night's sleep.

Sometimes the temporaries remain in well after the permanents are up. We see it commonly in the toy breeds like Yorkies and Toy Poodles and Pomeranians, and occasionally in miniature Dachshunds and others. Unless you're absolutely certain which are the temporaries and which are permanents you had better leave the job to your veterinarian. More than one dog has lost a permanent tooth or more because the owner has mistaken them for temporaries.

Once the permanents are up it's impossible to tell the age of a dog, although one does hazard a guess from their condition.

Dogs that have recovered from distemper often have mottled or spotty teeth. These generally have to be removed during middle age.

Dogs on soft sloppy diets get badly tartared teeth (see *Tartar*). Opinion is divided about the value of feeding bones, but most vets deprecate the practice because they can cause dangerous obstructions, and more than one dog has chipped his teeth while gnawing bones. A solid rubber bone or one of those rolled rawhide things will keep the teeth clean.

A rotten tooth can cause as much pain to the dog as it does to man and should be looked after just as quickly. Some of the signs of toothache are head-shaking, pawing at the mouth, rubbing the mouth along the ground and dribbling. An animal who approaches food and then refuses to eat it may have tooth trouble.

If one of the small front teeth goes bad one often removes all the adjoining ones because they support each other, and the others would soon go bad.

The big molar teeth at the back are difficult to remove because they have two or three big roots, and if even a bit of root is left in there can be a lot of infection and pain.

Finally, a word about breeding and teeth.

Some breeds have very short jaws because people like them to have short jaws. The Chinese bred the Pekinese and it has a head that, although aesthetically pleasing, is physiologically wrong. I don't know how the Chinese did it, but the Pekinese manages despite his deformities to live to a healthy old age, and many of them retain all their teeth as long as the breeds with normal heads.

In the last twenty or thirty years breeders of other dogs have tried to emulate the Chinese by shortening and broadening the head. The Boxer and the Bullmastiff are examples of breeds that have changed radically within our lifetime.

Many Boxers have seven incisor teeth between the two big fang teeth instead of the normal six. This and a protruding undershot jaw ensures that affected animals can't have a proper 'bite'. We're seeing more and more problem mouths in these two breeds and others.

I don't think I shall incur the wrath of sensible breeders if I say that many veterinarians are concerned about this, and feel that the whole process should be slowed down while everyone has a good look at what is happening. Maybe we can figure out how the Chinese went about it and what we are doing wrong. It may be as simple as putting health and vigour and longevity first in the list of prerequisites and then choosing from among the dogs that pass that test those which are aesthetically pleasing enough to breed from. Admittedly a slower process than ours, but then why are we in such a hurry to destroy our dogs?

Telegony

Your pure-bred Afghan bitch, in an unthinking moment, runs off and gets bred by a handsome incorrigible mutt around the corner. The mutt happens to be half Dachshund and half everything else.

The litter that your Afghan bitch proudly presents looks more like a new species than a new breed. Whatever the puppies are they are certainly not pure-bred Afghans. Eight weeks later they are weaned and you flog them to some dealer, and try to forget the whole episode. But some 'expert' won't let you forget it. 'The bitch is ruined', they tell you. That one misadventure will spoil her and never will she be capable of bearing pure-bred puppies. The mutt's influence will still be inside her and will mongrelize all her litters. This belief, in the influence of a previous sire over a subsequent sire's progeny by the same mother, is called telegony. It has no basis in scientific or practical experience and yet the belief lingers on.

Every new life, whether it be a child, a puppy, a kitten or a pony, is a result of the union of the father's sperm with the mother's egg or ovum. The mother's womb is just the growing ground for that new life. What it's grown before cannot affect the new life. If you grow carrots in a field for ten years and then plant potatoes you can be sure that the potatoes won't look like carrots.

Temperature

The normal temperature of the dog is 38·25–39°C (101–101·5°F). Large breeds may be 38–38·5°C (100–100·5°F). It is recorded by inserting a greased thermometer a couple of inches into the rectum. Have someone hold the animal while you are doing it. A thermometer may break off in the animal if he jerks suddenly.

The temperature may rise a degree due to excitement.

A temperature of 39·5°C (103°F) is regarded as significant, and any higher means that you require veterinary diagnosis fairly soon.

A dropping temperature is even more serious in any animal. A temperature of 38°C (100°F) in small dogs is a warning sign, and 37·5°C (99°F) means get on the phone to the vet. The only home first aid for a dropping temperature is hot water bottles.

Tetanus

This and rabies must be the most horrible ways of dying. The body is locked in ever more pain-racking spasms, but consciousness is retained.

Tetanus is caused by the entry of the tetanus germ through a small prick or puncture wound. The germ can only grow and produce its killing toxins in the absence of air. A large gaping bleeding wound or any open wound is not so dangerous.

The first spasms occur in the head and jaw muscles. There is a characteristic furrowing of the brows. The animal cannot swallow.

Fortunately it is very rare. Only one hundred and some cases in the dog and cat have been reported in the veterinary literature. I have seen only one case. It was in a middle-aged mongrel who had cut his foot a week or so previously. He started with mild symptoms of stiff neck and jaw, inability to swallow and wrinkling of the skin of the head.

Treatment included feeding him intravenously, keeping him anaesthetized for hours at a time and giving him massive doses of penicillin and anti-toxin. Each time he wakened the tetanic spasms were worse and worse. His tail and legs became rigid, but after a few days the spasms lessened and at the end of ten days we felt we were winning. His recovery after that was slow but steady and a month later he was completely normal. The cost of tetanus treatment is very high and after two or three days we didn't tot it up – the owner couldn't possibly have paid. For us it had become a matter of professional obligation.

There's no special danger in handling a tetanus case. The saliva or bites cannot transmit the disease, but a dog suffering from the disease will bite anything so all precautions are taken.

The disease is so rare in dogs that we don't recommend inoculations against it unless the soil is known to be infected with the tetanus spores. I think, though, that one should be aware of the problem and treat small closed wounds with the respect they deserve. Wash them well, soak in hydrogen peroxide and dress with iodine or mercurochrome. If you can't get it properly clean then take the animal to your vet's.

PS: In the fifteen or twenty years since those observations were written I have treated a further half dozen cases: not one survived!

One, an Old English Sheepdog puppy belonged to the gardener of a millionaire client. He sent it down with his chauffeur and a letter from his local vet. The letter said something like, 'In my opinion this is a hopeless case of tetanus.' It also detailed the treatment that had been tried and gave me permission to carry on if I saw fit. After examining the puppy I agreed that the chances were minimal. I told the owner's employer (my client) exactly that. I suggested euthanasia. I was told that if I refused to treat the animal he would find someone who would. I was further reminded that I had stated in print that I had successfully treated a similar case. And obviously expense didn't enter into it.

Despite all the drugs and round-the-clock attention by our devoted nurses (wonderful people – I only managed to marry one of them) the pup died.

To add the mundane, practical end to this account, I sent a bill which only included drugs and extra labour involved. It amounted to about the price of a not bad car. My faith in human nature was slightly restored when the client insisted on paying the proper amount, and followed his cheque with gifts for the girls.

Would I attempt treatment of tetanus today? Certainly! Because, although I've failed so often, other vets have been successful.

Thirst

Animals can get thirsty just as people do on a hot day or after exercise. We have all seen dogs out on a run who stop at every watering place. That's quite normal and nothing to worry about. Dogs like Boxers or English Bulldogs who slobber a lot need a fair bit of water to replace the loss.

An animal who gulps a lot of water and vomits shortly afterwards and then repeats the process is usually suffering from one of the virus infections or from an intestinal obstruction. It should be seen by a veterinarian at the earliest convenient time.

An animal who is always at the water bowl for no apparent reason may be suffering from kidney disease. If it continues beyond a day or two take him along to the vet.

No animal should be without water for more than ten or twelve hours. Even one who is constantly drinking should not be cut off. If kidneys are the cause he needs all that water even more than a normal animal.

Thyroid

We rarely see goitre these days, which is caused by iodine deficiency.

We do see a lot of fat lethargic dogs who do respond to thyroid tablets. As in humans these pills should be given only under supervision and the diet sheet followed. Too rapid a weight loss is just as harmful in dogs as in man.

Dogs with thinning hair may be suffering from a thyroid deficiency. A veterinary laboratory can do a simple blood test to determine thyroid level. If it's down, thyroid pills are prescribed.

I saw one thyroid-deficient hairless Poodle who responded to the pills with such a lush growth that the owner rushed in with a request for some pills to stop the whole process.

Tibetan Spaniel

A sort of taller, less furry version of the Pekinese. They were still being bred in Tibet until the recent take-over by the Chinese, but for some years there have been more of them in India than anywhere else. They're up to 25cm (10 in) high and weigh an average of 10 lb.

Tibetan Terrier

A shaggy little 35cm (14 in) dog with a nice most un-Terrier like disposition. The only two I've seen had eye trouble caused by the mop of hair the breeders encourage over its face. They require daily grooming.

Ticks

A heavy infestation is best removed by bathing the animal in one of the many available solutions. Ticks around the eyes and the mouth and in the ears should be removed by hand. Those that are dug right in should never be pulled out because the mouth part stays in and causes an abscess. They should be loosened by touching them with a bit of cottonwool soaked in ether or turpentine or alcohol. Whisky or gin works quite well if that's all you happen to have.

Remember, though, that the same bit of bush where your dog picked up the ticks is almost certainly still full of the wee beasts waiting for another warm-blooded victim to walk through.

Many ticks are quite indiscriminate in their choice of host, so if you've been out on the same walk you'd better investigate that funny itch.

Tomato

Both in the soup and in the juice form is a good source of vitamins. Tomato juice is a valuable deodorant for animals that get covered in unspeakable stuff. It can even be used to 'deskunk' dogs, and that takes a lot of doing.

Tongue

Tongues can get ulcers and cuts and they can become inflamed and nasty. I think it's a tricky enough organ to be left strictly out of the field of home medication.

Tonsilitis

Yes, the poor dears do get it, and it causes a rather painful swelling and difficulty in swallowing and gagging, and occasionally vomiting.

Most cases respond to antibiotic injections but some keep popping up again and again and then a tonsilectomy is done. White Poodles are common sufferers.

Home nursing includes a soft diet and rest. The animal should not be allowed to get cold or wet as the infection may spread.

PS: The incidence of tonsilectomies (operations to remove the tonsils) in humans has been studied by statisticians. There are decades during which the operation is popular. Also it would appear that children of affluent parents are more likely to have their tonsils removed than children from poorer families. I wouldn't like to carry the conclusions too far, but for what it's worth, my experience is that many puppies may have bouts of tonsilitis which are easily controlled by medicines. As they mature the bouts become less frequent and less frightening. Unless the indications for the operation are absolutely clear I'd be inclined to let our dogs and our children retain their natural organs.

Conclusion: Operations that are easily done are popular.

Training

Dogs vary widely in temperament and intelligence, but usually all are trainable and can become sane members of the family.

No breed is more intelligent than all others but some breeds are more likely to have intelligent representatives, and some strains that have been selected for intelligence are of course quite superior. Mongrels are no more intelligent than pure-breds. The shape of the skull is important. You may have noted that practically all working breeds have the same shape of skull – neither over elongated nor too scrunched up.

Size of dog has little to do with trainability. One is more likely to notice untrained large dogs because they can be dangerous. An untrained Pomeranian or Yorkie is a nuisance, but no one is likely to complain to the police.

Age is no deterrent to training. In fact you can teach an old dog new tricks. Guide and guard dogs are usually not selected until they are a year or a year and a half of age. However, if an adult dog is being sold because it has bitten someone, then you had better beware of your chances of successful retraining.

Training is really a matter of patience, regularity and simplicity. Professional trainers and theorists have a lot to say about the instinct of dogs which they describe as the hunting instinct, the working or herding instinct, the retriever instinct and the pack instinct. Actually most dogs, whatever the theory, are terribly pleased to do anything that pleases a master they respect. If they get into a pack they will forget any master and go rampaging as of old. It is for that reason that no dog, however well trained, should be allowed to roam loose.

If you are the kind of moron who thinks a dog should be let out on the streets and roads you deserve any prosecution that results from its damage.

A final word about theory. The characteristics that kept dogs going as a species are nervousness, aggressiveness, viciousness and bad temper. The docile trainable house dog wouldn't survive long in the wild. Man has attempted to control all those undesirable characteristics without destroying the dog's initiative.

Now for the actual training. Calm and quiet are the marks of a good dog handler. He doesn't lose his own temper. He never nags or yells. He indicates what he wants and speaks his approval or disapproval in measured tones. He knows what he wants and lets the dog know it. In short, he is the master and in firm control.

Regularity, simplicity and patience are all that are required to teach your dog to come when you call, to sit or stay on command, and walk beside you without pulling or hanging back. Don't start training when he's still a full-blown puppy unless you're extra patient. Don't let Pa train him one day and Ma the next. One person in the family should be designated trainer.

You should train at regular times each day, preferably not first thing in the morning when he's just bounding with energy, and not too close to feeding times.

The first series of lessons should be given in the same place. Lessons should be five or ten minutes and gradually lengthened. Use only one word, and that word only for each command. The common command words are SIT, STAY, COME, HEEL, SHAKE (a paw), BRING, DROP, etc.

The first lesson after puppyhood house training is getting the beast used to collar and lead. Most pups will scratch at a collar for a few minutes, but if they are distracted or soothed will soon accept it. They will almost always fight the lead much as a colt will, but if you hold on firmly they'll soon learn that it's a useless struggle.

The next lesson is 'Sit'. Fold the lead in your left hand and hold the collar with your left hand. With your right hand press firmly but gently on the small of the back and say 'Sit' in a firm normal voice. Hold him in the sitting position for a few moments, gently stroking or soothing at the same time. Then move off and say 'Come', holding him now by the end of the lead. He will usually move before you've got the command out, but will gradually associate the word with the movement.

Then, again holding by the collar, say 'Sit', and again press him down as before. After three or four repeats (congratulating him each time) try it with just the command 'Sit', but still holding his collar. If he sits congratulate him, but if he doesn't don't scold. Just repeat 'Sit' and press his back. That is usually enough for a first lesson. At the lesson the next day repeat the command 'Sit' and press him down at the same time. Then try without the press. At the end of five minutes he should be sitting with just the command, but you will still be holding him by the collar.

The third lesson you can start with the command 'Sit' without the back press. By the end of the third lesson you should be able to command 'Sit' and just control him by the end of the lead.

One gradually progresses to the point (usually seven or eight five-minute lessons) where the dog will respond to the word 'Sit' without collar or lead.

I know this sounds like an awful bore, but remember that dogs don't reason. They associate, and that is why one must repeat things time after time. If you can do nothing else than spare those seven or eight five-minute sessions, then at least you will have a dog who can be controlled if he's within sound of your voice. Too, the dog who knows what his master wants is a happier dog, and he can only know that if he knows what actions to associate with which words.

'Come' is taught by pulling him towards you with the lead. At the end of a lesson or two he will come without the pressure of the lead, but you still retain the lead until you think he's advanced enough to come without its restraining influence.

Whatever you do never use the command 'Come', and when he responds punish him for some previous mistake. He will associate the punishment with his coming to you.

'Stay' is the graduate division of 'Sit'. Some trainers, however, prefer 'Sit', 'Lie' and then 'Stay'. For the family pet it doesn't really matter whether he lies or sits when told.

The first time you say 'Stay' and move off he will follow you, but you must return immediately saying 'No' and return him to the 'Sit' position. Gradually you can increase the distance you move off. You can try rounding a corner. If he comes after you firmly return him to the sitting position. During training never say 'Come' if he's in the 'Stay' position. Always go to him to release him and then say 'Come'.

Some lazy trainers will teach 'Stay' while they themselves sit reading or talking. They simply hold the lead down with one foot. If the dog moves they repeat the command 'Stay' and tighten up on the lead.

'Bring' or 'Fetch' is usually taught initially with the aid of a 4·5m (15ft) lead or line – using a small rubber ball or rubber bone (not so small that he can swallow it, please), which you roll along and say 'Fetch'. If he's a natural chaser and picker-upper then you have no trouble in gently hauling him back with the encouraging 'Come' and some pressure on the lead. If he's not interested then go on to another lesson until one day he comes to school with the idea. 'Drop' is taught by gently removing the object, saying 'Drop' and stroking him approvingly. Don't punish. He will know when you are disappointed with his performance. Never, never pull the object from him or grab for it. He'll think it's a new kind of tugging game. If he won't give it up remove him from the ball, not the ball from him. You do this by holding the ball and pulling him back.

'Heel' is best taught with the choke collar and lead. Put it on so it falls slack if you're not actually applying pressure. If the dog pulls or hangs back you apply pressure. If he walks at your side then the collar is quite comfortable. He'll soon associate comfort with the proper heel position.

Never, never go into traffic without the collar and lead. Every veterinary clinic spends hours patching up dogs who 'never ran into the streets before'. Don't go into traffic even with the collar and lead until the dog has got quite used to walking at heel in the house and garden. He's got quite enough to cope with in the way of new (and sometimes frightening) sights and smells and sounds when he's first taken out without having to learn about collars and leads at the same time.

A few words about puppyhood. The puppy newly separated from its litter mates and mother is bound to feel frightened. Don't let his first introduction to the house be a general mauling by the kiddies. Only a Labrador or a Bull Terrier temperament could survive that. Set up a playpen for the puppy with a warm bed in a corner. After he's explored it all and settled down a bit he may be fed.

If he whimpers he should be given a well-insulated hot water bottle and left alone. Don't cater to those cries in the night else you'll have a permanent problem.

House-training is best taught by putting the puppy out after every meal. Don't punish him if he crawls over to the corner of the rug and does his stuff. Pick him up and put him outside. Then clean up the mess and use a bit of deodorant so that he won't associate that spot with his toilet area. A dog rarely wets his own bed. You just have to teach him that his bed includes the whole house.

Chewing or gnawing is a natural thing to all growing dogs. It strengthens the jaws and teeth. When puppies are teething they must gnaw to help loosen the temporary teeth. Obviously you must not punish a natural habit. What you can do is give them one object to chew on. A rubber bone or a rawhide bone are both suitable. Allow him or even encourage him to chew on that, but on nothing else. Whatever else you are, be consistent. Don't laugh when he chews your old slippers and get into a fury when he chews your Christmas cigars. He doesn't know the difference. Punish him if he chews anything other than his own rubber bone. Don't nag at him. Just scold him briefly and give him his own rubber bone.

Puppies who snap at one should be punished. People think it's cute when they're wee puppies and the same morons wonder why they bite as adults. The time to curb it is at the outset.

Puppies who jump up at people should be discouraged by gently treading on their hind feet at the moment they jump. Small dogs who actually leap at people (usually at children) should be met with a sharp thrust of the hand. Both these habits, though cute and endearing in the young, can be a nuisance in the adult.

Puppies who start barking the moment they're left alone should be punished because it's a very difficult habit to break in the adult. The adult can sometimes be broken of the habit of incessant barking by a sharp tug on the choke collar every time he starts. Give praises if they remain quiet.

Puppies at the age of six or seven weeks should be taken out for short car rides. They'll be excited by the new sounds and sights and are less likely to get car sick as adults, because travel sickness is often just a fear of new sensations.

The pup should be carried to the car and on no account taken on the streets until two weeks after his permanent distemper inoculations. As explained before, it's really wiser that the young dog shouldn't be taken into traffic until he knows how to walk at heel.

And now for a few common-sense explanations that every vet usually makes half a dozen times a day. I wonder if anyone listens?

People come with the complaint that a dog barks incessantly or chews the rug or snaps at their mother-in-law. The vet explains about training and about punishment. The invariable reply is 'Oh no, I couldn't strike a dog', 'I couldn't be cruel to an animal'.

Inevitably the same people return a few weeks later with the request that the animal be put to sleep. I'm sure every veterinary practice has dozens of such experiences every year.

Is it really less cruel to condemn a dog to death through lack of training than it is to train him properly, even if that includes some punishment?

Another cruelty that many so-called animal lovers commit is leaving a dog alone for hours on end. They wonder why the poor animal develops vices and neuroses. If you must have a dog and you must leave him alone for hours at a time then get two, and preferably not of the large working breeds. How can you expect a huge healthy bouncy Boxer to sleep in his little corner all night and all day as well?

Some dogs have an overdeveloped sexual drive. If they are allowed to they will roam all over looking for an accommodating female. The roaming will become an incurable habit. The only cure that I know is injection of hormones. If that doesn't work castration is usually suggested.

Punishment for any misdemeanour should rarely be necessary, but when it is it should be a short, sudden rap on the flank or, better still, picking the animal up at the shoulders and shaking it. This latter is the way bitches punish their young or the way pack leaders punish.

Reward should really be your approval, which is all your dog really wants. A kind word or occasional tit bit can be an expression of that approval.

Both punishment and reward are only valuable if used at the appropriate times. For example, if an animal has been told to 'Stay' and then he comes to you and you praise him, you are really praising him for coming. You should praise while he's still in the down position. Then give him the command to 'Come'.

Never, I repeat, say 'Sit' and then punish. You are then punishing because he obeyed you by sitting down when told.

Never shout his name at him when he is doing wrong. Shout 'No'. If you use his name he will associate it with disapproval.

Don't threaten him. Punish and get it over with. Nagging is as destructive in animal as in human relationships. Either reward or punish, but don't go on and on at the poor creature.

Finally, training is much simpler than reading about it. All dogs are individuals and respond in their own particular way, but none of them are immune to that emotion, sloppy as it may sound, called love. They will return it a hundredfold.

Tranquillizers

Those little pills that are supposed to make modern life bearable. Personally, I prefer my happiness in liquid form. My psychologically oriented friends tell me that my assorted neuroses are so deeply embedded that they are hidden even from myself; but whatever the reasons, I can do without the pills and so can most dogs. Some, however – and I'm afraid the toy breeds again top the list – can't get through the day without a pill. An unexpected visitor, a noisy lorry or a thunderstorm is enough to set them shaking with fright. It may sound funny, I know, and it leaves one open for all sorts of sophisticated remarks, but really what is one to do if not prescribe a pill that will allow the poor animal a semblance of quietude?

It's not the dog's fault that it was born a quaking bundle of nerves or that it was purchased by someone who has turned it into a neurotic.

Even normally stable dogs will hide under the bed on Guy Fawkes or Hallowe'en night. A few days before, we vets always get a string of dog owners who want a few pills to tide them over the event.

Periodically a very nervous person comes in with an animal that is quite normal and tries to persuade us that the dog is a nervous wreck and needs some pills. Usually these people are phenobarb addicts. We offer to prescribe some pill other than the one they want, and they assure us that it's been tried but it just doesn't work on their dog. We then usually suggest that they leave the animal for a few days so that we can look into its condition, whereupon they leave.

Incidentally, all dogs vary considerably in their response to tranquillizers. Some dogs who have never dared to bite a human will lose their inhibitions and turn into rather dangerous beasts while under the influence of the dope. Others will just wag their tails in the canine equivalent of a smile and go to sleep. If the one your vet has prescribed doesn't seem to do the job, tell him about it and he'll try another.

Travel sickness

Dogs are not always happy travellers. They reflect their owner's nervousness and unless taught early on that travelling is fun will always have a tendency to vomit as you round the first fast corner. Many dogs associate the car or bus with a trip to the nasty veterinarian who pokes at them with fingers and needles. Little wonder they react to the car like children to the dentist. Sometimes a couple of talks in the stationary automobile and a couple of short drives around the neighbourhood will change the association of ideas.

Before long trips food and water should be withheld for three or four hours. Saucerfuls of water can be given *en route* when you stop for those essential exercise breaks. Glucose added to the water will postpone hunger pangs. Don't feed for about an hour after arrival.

Pills which your vet will dispense can be most helpful, but please don't give them to an unaccompanied dog. They may wake up in strange surroundings and panic.

Greyhounds should always be accompanied on a trip. Although they may not vomit, they may get epileptic seizures if shipped like so much baggage with just a label around their necks.

Tuberculosis

With the almost universal adoption of pasteurization of milk, tuberculosis in dogs has almost disappeared.

The very rare dog who belongs to a tuberculosis sufferer may contract the disease. I've never seen a case reported of a human who contracted the disease from a dog. We advise euthanasia for all animals suffering from the disease.

Turpentine, paraffin, kerosene

Should never be used to remove paint from dogs. It can cause nastier burns than the paint.

Tying, tied

A term used to describe the coupling of the dog and bitch. It is an actual physical coupling caused by the expansion of the end of the dog's penis which can swell to an almost alarming size. One should never attempt to separate a tied couple. They may remain tied for from twenty minutes to a couple of hours. The enlarged bulbar end of the penis will gradually reduce and the animals will separate. Meanwhile you can best help them by leaving them alone. If you have a nervous bitch she may be prevented from harming the dog by some gentle soothing talk during the boring unwinding period.

Undershot

The lower jaw protrudes beyond the upper jaw. It is seen in some Pekinese and Pugs, in too many Boxers and Bullmastiffs and in the majority of English Bulldogs. The English Bulldog is such a mess that I assume no one is really interested in producing pups that can live a normal life. Pugs and Pekinese seem to weather all their abnormalities, and most average buyers of those breeds end up with a satisfactory pet. If you are interested in either a Boxer or a Bull-mastiff please don't let me put you off by telling you to be careful. They are magnificent breeds and there are lots of good healthy pups around. One recent survey has shown that about two-thirds of them do have normal heads so the odds aren't too bad. However, if you'd rather not gamble on your chances of getting a healthy pup spend an extra guinea and insist on a veterinary examination before completion of purchase.

What is wrong with a lower jaw that juts out belligerently? It prevents the animal from having a normal bite. Often it means tooth trouble. It is usually accompanied by a soft palate that partially blocks the breathing passages so that the animal dribbles and slobbers and breathes with difficulty. Sometimes the tongue protrudes beyond the abnormally short upper jaw and gives the animal an idiotic look. The upper jaw can't grasp the food so the hapless beast must eat by using its lower jaw as a sort of shovel. Should I go on?

Urination

In the dog, passing water is a social as well as a physiological act. The first time a male raises a leg is akin to an adolescent's first shave. They are surprised and pleased, and they go off with a new swaggering interest in life. At least once a day we are asked how he can visit so many posts and trees, and give every one the benefit of his visit. The dog (unlike man) usually starts with a half-full bladder. The reflex that starts it off is the smell of another dog. The reflex that starts man off is the full bladder. The dog's penis has a bone in it, and its constricting effect means that positive pressure must be exerted. The moment the pressure is relaxed the flow stops. And then, too, I suppose practice makes perfect.

If a dog strains to pass urine and cannot, or if he passes it in painful drops, or if there is blood in it, you must see a veterinarian as soon as possible (see also *Bladder* and *Kidneys*).

Vaccination

Call it inoculation or what you like, but get it done. Keep the pup away from other dogs till it is seven or eight weeks of age. Phone your vet and make an appointment. Keep the pup away from other dogs for a further fortnight to allow the immunity to build up. If you are living in an isolated spot, or if you have a large garden and the dog is never in contact with others, you had better get a booster dose every year or so. Most dogs, however, meet others in the park or on the streets so we assume they get reinoculated naturally. Are there any dogs that shouldn't be done? No! Some people with toys like Yorkies or Chihuahuas think they are too small and 'can't take the vaccine'. Nonsense. They can't be without it. The same goes for mongrels. They are just as susceptible as pure-breds. What diseases do you wish to prevent? Distemper, hepatitis and leptospirosis. Usually two or three separate shots are required.

PS: More recent experience suggests that wherever you live, the first shot should be given at seven or eight weeks of age, the second shot two or three weeks later, and after that a booster every year.

Vaginal discharge

The bitch has a clear to bloody discharge when she comes on heat. It is a healthy looking non-sticky kind of discharge, and it doesn't irritate her delicate membranes.

If a bitch has a thick, pussy or smelly discharge it may indicate the very serious condition called pyometra. This is an infection of the womb, and requires immediate veterinary attention.

A bitch about to give birth will have a 'lubricating' discharge which prepares the way for the puppies. After whelping there may be a discharge for a few hours or days. If it's a greenish discharge or a thick, bad smelling discharge the bitch should be seen by a vet. Antibiotic injections and/or hormone injections will usually clear it up.

Vallhund

A stump-tailed distant cousin of the Corgi, this Swedish breed is half way between the Cardiganshire and Pembrokeshire types in both appearance and size. Like the Welsh Corgi it is a superb drover and working dog, but it has been taken to Stockholm where all sorts of country folk go to pot. I'm not saying that the Vallhund has become morose or a drunkard, but the three specimens I met in Stockholm were well on the way. None of them actually bit me, but it was not through lack of effort. I know that the Swedes are very sensitive because all sorts of people take pleasure in criticizing them, but let me hasten to assure them that this book is only about dogs.

Vegetables

Many clients are worried because their dogs won't eat vegetables. Don't worry about it. If he likes them let him have them. What kind? Any vegetable at all except potato peelings will do. Quantity? Oh, just use your head. A tablespoon or two of your leftovers will add a bit of variety and nourishment to his meat and biscuits, but a bowlful of left-over broccoli or mashed potatoes might just cause a bout of diarrhoea. Raw or cooked? If he likes raw, of course they're better.

Vice

One of the very distressing vices of dogs is masturbation against objects or against the children. We see it most commonly in dogs going through what you might term adolescence – from about six months to eighteen months of age. Now it's a fact that many couples get their first dog about the same time as they are having their first baby. There may be some subtle psychological reason, but I think it's more likely that the average couple just don't wish to be tied to the home by a dog, but if they are 'settling down' anyway a dog is little additional nuisance. Some people think it's beneficial to a child to be raised with animals. Whatever the reasons it often happens that the dog is going through its first sexual awareness at the same time as the baby is just toddling. Some awkward and even dangerous scenes can occur. They happen in a small minority of cases, but it's a real problem nonetheless. I'm afraid there is no real cure except time. Most dogs grow out of it. Sometimes tranquillizers help a bit. If you simply can't part from the dog then I'm afraid the baby must be kept in its playpen. Older children can cope quite nicely. Teach them to tread on the dog's hind paw each time it jumps. Cruel? Of course it is, but less cruel than having the dog put to sleep because of too many awkward incidents.

Another common vice for which many dogs are destroyed is sheep-worrying. Even a Pekinese can panic a flock into suffocating corners. It's a vice that must be curbed severely by punishment at the first sign.

Once a dog gets the idea that chasing sheep is fun, it's very difficult to break the habit. Either you keep him under control at all times, or you'll end up in court and the dog will end up in kennels or worse.

Another vice – fortunately a rare one – is that in which a dog will attack any menstruating woman. I mean attack with fangs bared and ready to kill. This vice is as incurable as it is inexplicable, and such a dog should be put down.

I don't know if viciousness should be classified as a vice. Most vicious dogs get that way because they have been allowed to by doting but ignorant owners. You'd be surprised how many small lap dogs will bite for little or no reason. Often a puppy who is encouraged to snarl will grow into a dog that bites.

The only cure is restraining. Pills won't help a bit, although they can make a vicious dog tractable for a few hours. Some dogs are just plain brutes, and they require a master trainer with stacks of patience. I usually advise that if there are children or elderly people in the home it's best to get rid of a dog who has turned vicious.

There are hundreds of other vices, varying from the harmless to the dangerous. A dog who has learnt to open a milk bottle and spill its contents for the lap or two he can get before it drains away isn't much of a menace, but if the same dog goes down the road knocking down all the milk bottles just for the fun of it, you'd better do something about it before the neighbours do.

A dog who bristles at another dog may just be going through the motions. If he has an insatiable desire to kill all other dogs you'd better consider it a vice and keep him under severe control.

Many dogs will chase cats. My own cat rather enjoys being chased. He leads the neighbouring Pekes up and down the Mews whenever he can manage to wake them up. I have watched my cat trying to interest Bella, the Mastiff who lives around the corner, in a foot race. It's all cute and interesting. But let me assure you that if a Greyhound were to move into the neighbourhood I would scream blue murder and protest that it had a vice and should be kept on the lead. Why? Simply because it could outrun my cat and I don't want my cat killed.

In other words, the seriousness of any vice depends on the circumstances.

Virus

The whole family of germs that are distinguishable from bacteria because 1, they are so small they can't be seen under the ordinary microscope but must be photographed by the very powerful electron microscope, and 2, they will not grow and multiply on artificial foods like meat or soup as do the bacteria. They must be grown on living material, and that is why their study and their manufacture into vaccines is so expensive.

Viruses are responsible for a wide range of diseases which are becoming increasingly important. The reason is that the 'miracle' drugs like penicillin and streptomycin will attack bacteria but have no effect on the viruses. As the bacterial diseases come under control the virus diseases for which we have no effective treatment become the killers.

Poliomyelitis in man, distemper in dogs, foot-and-mouth in cattle are examples of virus diseases. Fortunately there are vaccines that can build up the body's protection against most of the virus diseases. The polio vaccine is only a few years old. Distemper vaccines have been tested and proved for over thirty years.

Summary: There is no effective treatment for distemper. There is a safe effective vaccine to prevent it.

Vitamins

If you are reading this book your dog is probably getting too many vitamins. True. Many people force far too many vitamins into their animals. If your adult dog is getting a bit of meat, a few biscuits and scraps off your table, it's quite unlikely he's suffering from any more deficiencies than you are. There are five periods when a dog needs vitamin supplements: when he's a growing puppy he'll need additional vitamin D; if he's recovering from an illness your vet will supply supplementary vitamins; ageing dogs may need supplementary vitamins; pregnant bitches need help in feeding those new lives; after a worming pill, vitamin pills are indicated. At all other times you can forget the blandishments of the advertisers.

Vizsla

The Hungarian Pointer, about 60cm (2 ft) high, weighing up to 36kg (80 lb) with a short, dense, yellow coat. An absolutely superb sporting dog, he can point and retrieve as well as any other breed. The Hungarians are now looking for dollars. If you have any dollars and want to impress the boys with something really different and really good import a pair. It'll be a drawn-out process but it will be worth it, because the Hungarians are paying particular attention to maintaining export standards.

Vomiting

One of the body's defences against material it cannot handle. Dogs may vomit from time to time quite naturally. A greedy dog that bolts a huge dinner may bring it all up and then leisurely savour it a second time. Disgusting, possibly, but the dog doesn't know that, and it's apparently without ill-effects. Try not to make a fuss about it. Cut down the quantity and make meal time a non-nervous affair. Feed him in a quiet room without children or competing animals about.

A young animal who vomits may be infested with worms. If it is pot-bellied and vomiting I would certainly suspect worms and advise you to take a sample of its motion along to the vet.

An animal who vomits and also has a cough, or runny eyes, or red inflamed eyes may be coming down with one of the serious virus diseases like distemper or hepatitis, and should be seen by your vet.

An animal may vomit because it has an obstruction in its bowel caused by some object that just won't pass through. Hairballs, tennis balls, bone splinters, pins, bits of carpet, may all cause a stoppage. Sometimes in a thin dog it's possible for a trained and experienced hand to feel the object; more often an X-ray or a series of X-rays are necessary to find the object. If the vet is suspicious that there is an object but the X-rays don't show it he will feed the dog an opaque substance like barium meal. Its progress down the gut can be followed by a series of X-rays. It will stop at the obstruction or slowly filter by the obstruction and outline it. We are using more barium these days because many of the new plastics don't show on X-ray, and dogs just will swallow plastic toys and plastic dish mops and plastic anything.

An abdominal operation is usually necessary to remove the object. If all goes well Fido will be back on solids in a week.

Remember that he won't have learnt a thing from the experience. His mind is just incapable of associating the nasty vet and his X-rays and stitches with the tennis ball he swallowed. He might go back home and swallow another.

Middle-aged and older dogs who vomit several times a day for two or three days may be suffering from kidney disease, tumours, or uterus infection. Needless to say, any home treatment can only do positive harm.

Summary: An isolated act of vomiting is not important. If it is repeated two or three times in one day or occurs after each feeding get the animal to a vet. Don't force anything into a vomiting animal. The only safe home aid is starvation for twenty-four hours.

Vulva

The external sexual organ of the bitch. It may become very sore and inflamed and enlarged. Usually it's because the bitch has been licking at it either because she has a vaginal discharge or because it's been cut or injured. The only safe home aid is bathing with warm salt water every two or three hours and keeping the bitch away from it. An Elizabethan collar helps. If it's still painful after two or three applications you'd better get professional help. The vet will determine the cause. If it's a vaginal discharge it may be very serious (see *Pyometra*). It may be a bladder infection (they are usually cleared up in days) or it may be a local injury that has become infected and requires proper cleaning and internal medicines.

Water

Good clean water in a clean bowl is necessary for all animals at all times. There are simply no exceptions, but for a couple of conditions when your vet will ask you to cut out or limit water for two or three days.

Weaning

The separation of the young from the mother. Nature thinks it should be a gradual process, and I have no argument with nature. The following calendar might show how simple and gradual it is.

1st week: Cull weak or deformed or surplus puppies. Dock tails and cut dew-claws (a veterinarian's job if you don't want trouble). Daily look at navels and a touch of iodine or Dettol if inflamed or sore. Bathe gummed eyes with saline (teaspoon of salt to a pint of water, boil and store in a closed container).

2nd week: Puppies may need extra food so give them a try. Some will start stealing from the bitch's bowl. If puppies' nails are scratching the mother, trim them.

3rd week: Most puppies will start lapping.

4th or 5th week: Worming if necessary. Worm before weaning or after weaning, never at weaning time.

5th and 6th weeks: Most puppies are getting as much from their own bowls as from their mother, or even more.

7th week: The mother may be getting more and more impatient with the puppies. She is spending more time away. They are constantly looking for the feeding bowl, and occasionally looking to the mother.

8th week: The puppies should have found their new homes; the bitch will have been 'dried off', after the puppies were removed, by the simple method of taking away her food and water for twenty-four hours.

The weaned puppies will be getting four meals a day. Two are meat and two are milk and cereal. At ten to twelve weeks the puppies get their first distemper shot. At fourteen weeks teething pains are at their worst, and meals are cut to three daily.

The ideal weaning age is seven or eight weeks. There are 'breeding farms' in the States and in Britain that produce puppies for the pet-shop market and ship them ten or twelve in a crate like so many cabbages. These puppies are usually weaned at four or five weeks and they never get over that initial set-back.

Summary: Introduce the puppies to cereal and meat at three or four weeks. Leave them with the mother for seven or eight weeks.

Weight

How do you estimate it? Smaller ones can be placed in baskets and weighed; subtract the weight of the basket. Larger ones can be carried in your arms while you step on the scales; subtract your own weight. Bigger ones can be weighed on those large flat baggage scales that the railways so conveniently provide. Any porter will weigh your animal for a small fee, and give you a free diagnosis at the same time.

Weimaraner

A most dramatic looking breed, its body shape is like a taller, slighter Labrador (and there's nothing wrong with that) with a short upright tail. The colour of most Weimaraners is a unique steel grey, and they have grey ghost eyes. Impossible to describe, once seen they are never forgotten. One hears all sorts of stories about the aristocrats who kept them in Germany for some hundred-odd years, without releasing a single specimen for outside use until the American army 'liberated' them at the end of the war. In fact, the breed has been known outside Weimar for many years, but it was enthusiasts in the American army who popularized the breed in America.

The Weimaraner is a superb pointer and a good retriever. He can be trained to hunt feather or fur, and have equal enthusiasm for both. I once drove with two friends and a pair of Weimaraners from New Jersey to Wyoming. It's a fair trip to coop up a couple of big dogs for, and I must say that much of my enthusiasm for the breed originates in the perfect manners that that pair showed. They were no trouble in the car, they behaved beautifully in the motels and camping grounds, and they were impressive in the field.

There is an obscure spinal ailment found only in Weimaraners, but as it's rare and no one seems to know if it's hereditary or not, it's unlikely that we'll come up with a solution for some years. I can't tell you any way of avoiding dogs that are likely to be affected.

Where should you buy one? Not in Britain I'm afraid; there are too few to choose from. America and Germany have the best selection.

Welsh breeds

Cardiganshire and Pembrokeshire Corgis are known all over the world. They can be top cattle and working dogs, or they can be misery itself. The strain and the breeder are what matters. Some places in Wales have standing orders from the London dealers for all they can produce. They come to London crated, and you can buy a crate full of a dozen puppies for £120 or a couple of hundred dollars.

They retail for up to double that sum. You can imagine how little selection or culling or care has gone into them. Find a breeder of working Corgis, pay a little more, and your chances of getting a good dog will be much greater (see also under *Corgi*).

The Welsh Terrier too is known everywhere and cherished for its smart appearance, its vigour and its plucky temperament.

I have known some that were quite impossible, but by and large it's a good unspoiled breed that can live a long healthy life even in a city apartment. They look like smaller Airedales at first glance, and to my untutored eye at second glance too, but I can assure you that the Welsh Terrier has been known for over a hundred years and may in fact be older than the Airedale.

They are a handy-sized 20 lb, and about 15 in high. They have close, wiry, black and tan coats.

The Welsh Hound is a 2 ft 70-pounder, and most of them have rough coats of black mixed with red or fawn. There are still some famous packs bred in Wales. Although it's been bred there for 200 years it's virtually unknown elsewhere.

The Welsh Collie or Welsh Sheepdog is a smooth-coated collie type, weighing 30 to 40 lb, that has been exhibited for a hundred years and was known long before that. It must rank as one of the greatest and certainly the most sensitive of all working breeds. I think it's a crime to coop them up in over-heated rooms and allow them to scratch themselves to death out of sheer boredom. If you want a lap dog get one. If you want a dog that can learn as much as you're able to teach that can work day and night in all weathers and that is absolutely reliable, then get a Welsh Sheepdog.

The Welsh Springer Spaniel is a red and white 40-pounder that works as well in water as on land. If you know anything against the breed I'd be pleased to hear from you. I'd also be surprised.

West Highland White Terrier

A small dog – 6·8kg (15 lb) – that is all fight and go. The only all-white Scots breed, it was developed from the Cairn about a hundred years ago. He's become popular because of his size and his clean, sharp appearance. He's a hunting dog, not a flat dweller, and confinement doesn't agree with his temperament. As a result we see dozens of them so nervous that they're a misery to themselves and their owners. Tranquillizers can only relieve the poor creatures. What they really want is a working holiday in Argyll.

Wheatgerm oil

Sometimes it's in fashion to feed it to breeding animals and sometimes it ain't. Some people (particularly the manufacturers) say it's helpful for greater fertility and better litters, but most animal nutritionists don't think it's necessary to add wheat germ oil to the normal well-balanced diet.

Whelping

Giving birth, or parturition, occurs two months after breeding, with a leeway of a day or two either way. The bitch swells up, her udder gets full and her external sexual organs enlarge. As actual whelping approaches she will get restless, may seek out a corner or make a nest. All you can do to help her at this stage is encourage her to go in the area you have chosen and provide blankets and newspapers. If her udder is very swollen and painful you can gently apply olive oil. Most bitches are best left alone. Check every hour to see that all is going well. After labour starts the first puppy should appear within minutes or up to half an hour. You may help only if the water bag has broken, or if the feet or head of the puppy have actually appeared. Sometimes a gentle pull is all that's needed.

As the puppies appear, the enveloping sac should be removed, the mouth wiped clean, and the puppy vigorously slapped or massaged to start breathing.

Complicated? Of course it is. It's as complicated as life itself, or as simple, if that's the way you prefer to see it.

Do I really think you can do it on your own if you've never seen it done before? No I don't, but hundreds of people have had to do it for the first time without previous experience, and somehow they've muddled through.

What is the best practical approach to the whole business? If it's a first time for you or for the bitch ask your veterinarian to attend. Arrange it all when you bring the bitch in for her five or six week check-up. Once you've seen one you should be able to handle a normal one on your own.

If the bitch, 1, is old, 2, has had difficulty in previous whelpings, 3, has had a pelvic injury, 4, is small and has been bred to a larger dog, 5, is a Scottie, or an English Bulldog or one of the other breeds noted for difficult whelpings, 6, is not in good condition, you'd better rarange to have her stay and whelp at the veterinary kennel or have the veterinarian attend at your home.

If a normal bitch goes into labour and strains for a half-hour without results, get on the phone to the vet. If she produces one or two pups and stops, you'd better do the same.

Don't let any of this put you off having your bitch bred. The vast majority of puppies are born without trouble and without any human help.

Which *biscuit*?

In Britain it's difficult to choose because most are unlabelled. In America some wonderful complete diets (except for fat which can be added) are put up in biscuit or meal form. If you get a good one it's the most economical way of feeding a dog, and quite sufficient for all its requirements.

Which *breed*?

The largest you can afford and have space for up to Labrador or Alsatian size. If you're lazy or house proud, avoid long-haired dogs. Avoid the very small breeds and the very large breeds and the eccentric looking breeds, i.e. if you don't want trouble be a square.

My personal recommendations include: Airedales, Beagles, Border Terriers, Boxers, Bull Terriers, Chows, Collies, Dachshunds, Foxhounds, Elkhounds, Setters, Great Danes, Retrievers, Irish Terriers and Kerry Blues, Pekinese, Pointers and Standard Poodles, Pugs, Rottweilers, Schnauzers, Staffordshires, Weimaraners and Yorkshire Terriers. I warn you to be careful in choosing any of the other breeds, but pay particular attention if you want an Afghan, Alsatian, Bedlington, Boston Terrier, Borzoi, Chihuahua, Wire-Haired Fox Terrier, Lakeland Terrier, Maltese, Pomeranian, Scottish Terrier, Saluki or Sealyham. I am terribly sorry, but I think that your chances of getting a trouble-free dog of the following four breeds are slim: Miniature Poodle, Corgi, English Bulldog and Cocker Spaniel.

Which *inoculations*?

See *Distemper* and *Rabies*.

Which *sex*?

Males are stronger, more self-reliant and less subject to seasonal change. Females are cheaper to buy, easier to train, and when not on heat much more attached to their owners. Males are more inclined to fight other dogs. Females, if unspayed, are a proper bother twice a year. Best buy for first-time dog owners – a spayed bitch.

Which *species*?

If you don't have the time and inclination for walks, don't inflict your sophistication on a dog. If your home is just a place where you change clothes between engagements, don't expect even the self-sufficient cat to be happy. In other words, a dog is almost a full-time occupation, a cat somewhat less so. A dog shouldn't be left day after day while its owners go off to work. A cat can live happily with a family or person that is only home part time – but that time should be regular and dependable.

If you're a night owl, consider a pair of gerbils. If you want little responsibility and lots of pleasure consider a pair of budgies. I suggest a pair because it's not right to inflict a lonely existence on any individual being.

Which *tinned food*?

The one with the most protein (meat), least water and other fillers for the least money. The watered down stuff might look OK in those television advertisements, but remember that most dogs used on TV are professional models and they're paid to eat the stuff.

Which *tonic*?

None of them is necessary.

Which *veterinarian*?

The one closest to you who is interested in small animals. Many veterinarians will treat only the large domestic animals like cattle and horses. Some do so because they simply can't bear that minority of neurotic people whom one must meet occasionally in dog and cat practice. Others feel that they aren't properly equipped to deal with dogs. They'll send you along to a colleague who is. In an emergency any veterinarian will treat any animal.

Whippet

Looks like a scaled down version of a Greyhound and it is still used for racing. Very popular in some districts, where every second dog seems to be a Whippet or Whippet cross. They don't much like the cold and should be kept blanketed on rainy and cold days. They have little actual protection against the weather. We're always hearing about the problems people have getting them to eat. Unless they're exercised a lot they don't need to great deal. They are used in animal acts because they can be easily taught to walk on their front feet.

Height about 45cm (18 in); weight about 9·5kg (21 lb). Temperament usually gentle in the home and nervous in strange surroundings.

White

The Samoyed and all its cousins of the Spitz family are white by natural genetic dominance. In most other breeds white is a colour that man has selected for, and it is usually a recessive characteristic and may be associated with other recessive characteristics. There is scientific evidence available, if you have the time and energy to look for it, to support my contention that dogs that are white all over are more prone to illness and skin trouble than are their coloured and spotted cousins.

Boxer breeders have recognized this for years, and white Boxers are culled at birth by conscientious breeders.

Worms

My Professor of Parasitology served in the Royal Canadian Mounted Police before he went back to school and college to become a scientist. He brought the outdoors into the laboratory, and the scientific approach to practical problems. Twenty years ago he was on his guard against the indiscriminate poisoning with which some chemical manufacturers would have us wipe out the lower creatures of this earth. He taught us to view with scepticism the claims of anyone who had anything to sell.

Time and time again he reiterated that more animals are injured or killed by worming pills than by worms. It is only reasonable to assume that any chemical capable of killing a worm must be capable of doing injury to the host of that worm. Yet every pet shop and every chemist will blithely hand out packages of worming powders or pills which people force down their pets' throats. Usually they don't know if the animal has worms, and even if they have seen the worms they don't know what sort of worms they are. Even the most widely selfish drug pedlar doesn't claim that his brand of poison is effective against all sorts of worms.

Right? Right. We know there are different sorts of worms and different drugs to deal with them.

What do you do if you see that wriggly mass in your pet's stool? Pick it up with a matchstick and put it in a jar or a matchbox. Take it along to the vet and ask him for the appropriate drug. Best to take the animal along, too, so that the vet can judge the size of the dose. If that's inconvenient be prepared to tell him the weight of your pet within 1kg (2 or 3 lb).

If you merely suspect that an animal has worms, your vet can check by testing a sample of its motion. He'll tell you when he wants the sample (not Christmas Day, for example) and he'll ask you to bring him a fresh sample in a clean container.

This sample or jar of faeces may not contain any adult worms, but if the animal has worms in its gut the chances are that those worms are laying eggs, and those little eggs will be passing out with the animal's motions. The sample is mixed with salt water and spun in a centrifuge. The eggs being lighter will float to the top. A bit of the fluid at the top is transferred to a glass slide and examined under the microscope.

The eggs for each type of worm are as different as a hen's egg is from a robin's. One can also get an idea of how severe a worm infestation the animal has from the number of eggs seen on the slide.

But like all laboratory tests its greatest value is as an aid to the clinician who is examining the animal. He must decide what value to place on the lab results.

After the diagnosis the appropriate pills are dispensed. Most are to be repeated in ten days time. A week after the second dose you may be asked to bring another sample as a check to see that the pills have done their job.

A few common sense precautions should be taken after the worming. If you turn the animal out in the same old infested patch of garden it will probably be reinfested. Puppies during those important growing months when worms can do permanent damage should not have the opportunity of poking their inquisitive noses into piles of faeces, whether it's their own or not.

How you can prevent this is really up to you. If you have only one litter of puppies to raise and you don't mind bending down every four hours you simply follow them around and scoop the stuff up.

If you are one of the unfortunates that has been led to believe you can make money breeding dogs, found out you can't, but can't bear to stop, well then you had better resign yourself to concrete or better yet sand in the runs. If the problem just seems beyond cure you may have to get wire-bottomed or slat-bottomed cages.

I seem to have got ahead of myself. Where do the puppies get the worms in the first place? From the mother. They can actually be born with them or they can get them during suckling, because the worm eggs can pass out from the mother and get attached to the fine hair around the nipples.

Prevention, we have heard it so often that we have stopped understanding what it means, is better than cure. If you intend to breed a bitch or a cat have her checked for worms *before* she comes on heat. Treat her then. Have her checked once two or three weeks after breeding. A week before whelping clip the hair under the belly and wash around her nipples with soap and water.

If despite everything the puppies have worms (or if, as usually happens, you have bought a little pot-bellied puppy in a pet shop because you felt sorry for him) then find out what sort of worms it has and get the appropriate dose of the right drug. Then by sanitation – which means cleaning up – prevent the animal from getting reinfested.

Most people think that an animal with worms rubs its bottom or bites at its tail. In fact this is rarely a symptom of worms, and in the adult animal is almost always a symptom of either anal gland trouble or some obscure referred pain.

The usual symptoms of worms in a young animal are thinness, pot-belly, dry scruffy skin and bouts of diarrhoea. In the adult, worms may cause little more trouble than an occasional bout of diarrhoea.

Summary: If you see or suspect worms don't use any old powder you are sold across the counter. Get your vet to find out what sort of worms they are (see also *Tapeworms*).

X-ray

Of course we X-ray and quite routinely. As you might expect X-rays are of most value where the thing you are looking for has a great contrast with the surrounding tissues. For example, bones show up beautifully on X-ray, and before one sets most fractures a picture is taken to see exactly how the bone is shattered. Stones in the kidney or bladder show very clearly on X-ray. Tennis balls, sewing needles and many other objects that a dog may swallow show very dramatically. Some things, like the new plastic dish mops, may not show at all, and then one must outline the object by feeding the dog an opaque substance. Ulcers and strictures are outlined in the same way. Air, whether in the bowel or in the lung, shows up well.

Many conditions, though, can't be diagnosed with the same degree of accuracy by X-ray. A diseased kidney may look the same as a healthy one. A liver riddled with cancer areas may look quite OK. Some people are disturbed when we X-ray their dog and come back and tell them we still don't know what's wrong. The unfortunate thing is that we don't have an instrument that lights up like one of those gambling machines and names the disease. All the X-rays and lab tests are still just aids to help the clinician arrive at a diagnosis.

One other thing. Dogs won't sit still for the picture. Someone has to hold them. If the vet or his assistants did it they would soon get an overdose of roentgen rays. In the early days of X-rays many doctors got nasty burns. If you are not prepared to hold your animal, then it must be anaesthetized while the picture is taken. Some animals simply will not be held and these, despite the owner's co-operation, must be sedated or anaesthetized.

Yorkshire Terrier

The larger they are the less trouble you can expect, but all of them are amongst the toughest toys there are. Few of them get beyond middle age with all their teeth intact because of that narrow little muzzle that crowds the teeth together. But the loss of their teeth doesn't affect their pugnaciousness, and every vet knows a toothless old Yorkie that will nip and hurt. I suppose the commonest complaint we hear from Yorkie owners is, 'He hasn't eaten in two days.' Usually it's nothing to worry about so long as they're still having their lap of tea or milk. If you're buying one avoid the showy little long silky ones, and try to get one as close to the old rugged hunting type as possible. Height up to about 20cm (8 in), weight 3kg (7 lb) down to as little as 1kg (2 lb). A hundred years ago it weighed 6·8kg (15 lb), and was the gamest rat-catcher in the business. Thank goodness they've lost none of their spirit in the process of reducing them to fit into the pockets of mink coats.

Frank Manolson
C is for Cat £1.00

The comprehensive guide to every aspect of cats and their care. Written by a vet, this invaluable handbook covers everything that cat owners need to know about the habits, personality and problems of their pets.

'An encyclopaedia worth its weight in gold' DAILY TELEGRAPH

Tony Soper
The New Bird Table Book 70p

'If you are among those thousands of bird lovers who put out food for your feathered visitors in winter, erect bird boxes in summer and try to maintain a bird table all the year round – and then find that somehow the birds don't come; here is the book for you . . .'
THE DALESMAN

'Most comprehensive, containing everything that anyone could possibly want to know on the subject' CAGE AND AVIARY BIRDS

'One of the best introductions to ornithology in a long time' TEACHER'S WORLD